# NEIL HARVEY

## THE LAST INVINCIBLE

AUSTRALIAN CHAMPION TEST BATSMAN, SELECTOR,
RECORD BREAKER AND LAST OF BRADMAN'S INVINCIBLES

ASHLEY MALLETT

Hardie Grant
BOOKS

Published in 2021 by Hardie Grant Books, an imprint of Hardie Grant Publishing

Hardie Grant Books (Melbourne)
Wurundjeri Country
Building 1, 658 Church Street
Richmond, Victoria 3121

Hardie Grant Books (London)
5th & 6th Floors
52–54 Southwark Street
London SE1 1UN

hardiegrantbooks.com



NATIONAL LIBRARY OF AUSTRALIA
A catalogue record for this book is available from the National Library of Australia

Neil Harvey
ISBN 978 1 74379 740 2

10 9 8 7 6 5 4 3 2 1

Cover design by Luke Causby
Cover image: Steven Siewert/Fairfax
Typeset in 11.75/17 pt Adobe Caslon Pro by Cannon Typesetting

Printed in Australia by Griffin Press, part of Ovato, an Accredited ISO AS/NZS 14001 Environmental Management System printer.

FSC www.fsc.org MIX Paper from responsible sources FSC® C009448

The paper this book is printed on is certified against the Forest Stewardship Council® Standards. Griffin Press holds chain of custody certification SGSHK-COC-005088. FSC® promotes environmentally responsible, socially beneficial and economically viable management of the world's forests.

Hardie Grant acknowledges the Traditional Owners of the country on which we work, the Wurundjeri people of the Kulin nation and the Gadigal people of the Eora nation. We recognise their continuing connection to the land, waters and culture, and pay our respects to their Elders past, present and emerging.

# CONTENTS

# FOREWORD

NEIL HARVEY IS Australia's greatest batsman after Don Bradman. I have played with and against many of the great players since World War II, and I rate Neil as the best batsman of my time and right up to the modern era.

Neil Harvey was the complete cricketer. He was confident, never brash and he exuded a warmth and humility that made him a very popular and inspirational teammate. Apart from his brilliant batting against the pace bowlers, whom he took on with nimble footwork, the traditional way, back and across, head over the ball, Neil was a sensational player of slow bowling. He had sparkling footwork and was often yards down the track to hit the ball either on the full or half volley. When he got to the pitch of the ball, there was no hesitation: he belted the ball all the way along the ground, forever finding an inviting gap to hit another exquisite boundary.

Harvey had all the shots: he drove, cut, hooked and swept with confidence. I'll never forget three Harvey Test knocks: his 92 not out on the last day of the Second Test match against England at the SCG in December 1954, when he stood tall hooking and cutting Frank Tyson, whose pace and fire went through the rest of the Australians.

Then there was his 96 on the coir matting in 1959/60 against Pakistan in Dacca (which is now Dhaka, in Bangladesh), when it was over a hundred degrees in the water bag and poor Harv was suffering from dysentery. He was ever rushing from the field to the toilet. This was an innings of rare skill and courage, a batting masterclass against the odds.

Perhaps the most remarkable Harvey innings was the time in Durban (1949/50) when Australia, all out for 75 in the first innings, had to score 336 to win the match on a rain-affected, turning pitch with variable bounce. Springbok off-spinner Hugh Tayfield took an incredible 7/23 in Australia's first dig and Lindsay Hassett's men were in dire trouble at 4/95. Tayfield was pitching the ball around leg stump and spinning across the left-handed Harvey. Harvey used his feet, the swiftest of balanced movement, to get to the pitch of Tayfield's deliveries, and he began hitting the ball sweetly against the prodigious spin over mid-wicket and mid-on. Sam Loxton scored 54 and then Colin McCool stayed with Harv until he hit the winning runs, finishing with 151 not out. Australia won the match by five wickets. Apart from his skill as a Test batsman, Neil was quite the most brilliant fieldsman. He was always fast to the ball and he was perfectly balanced when he had a shot at the stumps.

Neil had an astute cricket brain. I lost count of the number of times he would advise Richie Benaud. Harvey should have been made captain when Ian Craig got the job in 1957 and he must have been bitterly disappointed, but in South Africa in the summer of 1957/58 Craig, badly out of form, wanted to drop himself. Third selector Peter Burge was happy to see Craig drop himself and Harvey made captain, but Neil, who was both vice-captain and the other selector, would have none of it. He called Burge aside. He made it clear: no Australian captain had ever been dropped on tour, and none would be now. Burge didn't argue.

That show of total loyalty alone demonstrated why Neil Harvey was such an inspiration to us players. He was to my mind the complete cricketer. He would have made a fabulous Test captain given the chance to lead Australia for an extended period.

At the time of writing my dear old mate Neil Harvey is 92 years of age and I, a mere 91. We try to catch up regularly, but with the pandemic and lockdowns it has been difficult for everyone.

I am proud to have played with and against Neil Harvey, proud to call him a close friend and am delighted that Ashley Mallett is writing Neil's story.

It is my great honour to be asked to write the foreword.

*Alan Davidson, AM MBE*
*Strathfield, Sydney, 2021*

# INTRODUCTION

WEDNESDAY 22 DECEMBER 1954 dawned clear and bright, and was about to flood Sydney's North Shore in sunshine. I jumped out of bed, woke my brother Nick and – armed with bat and ball – we headed to our Chatswood family backyard, where there was a roughly flattened area of turf, the pitch, and an old fruit box standing on end, the stumps. By the time I had turned nine years of age I was hooked on cricket. The 1954 copy of *Wisden*, which my grandfather had given me for my birthday, covered the previous season's first-class cricket throughout the world. It included the 1953 Ashes series in which Australia were pipped at the post, losing the final Test at The Oval, due to some excellent spin bowling by Jim Laker and Tony Lock. I read and re-read the descriptions of the Tests and county matches until the pages became a little brittle. The words resonated and stuck in my memory. I formed a great affection for those players, such as Neil Harvey, Keith Miller, Richie Benaud, Alan Davidson, Ron Archer and Ian Craig. Amazingly, Craig was just seventeen when picked to go on that tour. He hadn't even reached the age where he could go into a pub with the rest of the team. When the likes of Lindsay Hassett, Miller and company alighted from the team bus – or the coach, as the English preferred – to quench their thirst at the odd welcoming inn, Craig was left on the bus, no doubt learning about English life from the bus driver, who was sworn to remain on duty as sober as a judge. Craig fascinated the schoolboys of Sydney for he was only a few years older than us. Fancy a boy of seventeen playing Test cricket.

On 2 June 1953 Craig had stood among thousands of Londoners, lining the streets, to watch the newly crowned monarch, Queen Elizabeth II, being taken back to Buckingham Palace from Westminster Abbey in an altogether different coach, the magnificent Gold State Coach. A perfect complement to this grand occasion, the coach, built by Samuel Butler in 1762, had been used at the coronation of every British monarch since King George IV in 1821. Drawn by eight horses, the coach, with its precious cargo within, rumbled along the streets of London with the new Queen waving graciously throughout the journey.

After bowling for an hour to my brother in the backyard it was off to breakfast, shower and to dress up in my Sunday best: shorts, shirt, tie, jacket and long socks. Granddad, whom we always called 'Pop', was dressed in a grey suit, shirt and tie. He always wore a grey felt hat, which complemented his outfit perfectly. Pop was taking me to the Sydney Cricket Ground to watch the last day's play of the Second Test match against England. This was the first time I had seen a big match.

I had however, like Craig, seen the Queen. The clothes I was wearing to the cricket were the ones Mum had bought especially for me to wear in February 1954, also to the SCG, when my school, Chatswood Primary, went to stand about with thousands of other children from dozens of Sydney schools holding Australian flags to wave frantically as Queen Elizabeth and the Duke of Edinburgh drove past in an open-topped black limousine, one of the first events of the Sydney leg of their royal tour that year. I remember the smell of freshly mown grass – the sheer lushness of the turf upon which we stood. To me this was sacred ground, for the likes of WG Grace, Victor Trumper, Don Bradman, Keith Miller, Ray Lindwall and indeed Neil Harvey had performed so heroically on it. In those days you could not simply wander on to the ground before a big game of cricket began, during any breaks or, indeed, after stumps were drawn.

The day we saw the Queen was different. We walked onto the SCG in our droves, lined up in precision file and waited in the blazing sun for a couple of hours before the royal couple's limousine appeared. I remember seeing the little flag fluttering at the front of the vehicle looking like a miniature Royal Standard, flown only when the Queen is present. As hundreds of schoolchildren frantically waved our Australian flags, the royal limousine sped past and it was over. I managed a fleeting glimpse of the royal couple, but to be honest, it was something of an anticlimax.

I was hoping to see a little more of the cricketers on my second day at the SCG than I did the royal couple on my first. I was so excited I gulped my food, giving rise to a quiet reprimand from my mother. 'Now, Ash. Don't scoff your food. Won't do when you are dining at Buckingham Palace with the Queen.' I caught Pop's eye.

He had the hint of a smile on his face and he gave a little chuckle. In those days Chatswood was a sprawling suburb, ever growing, eventually into the seeming metropolis it has become today. Our family home was in Hawthorn Avenue, near the Lane Cove River, which ran alongside the Chatswood Golf Links, at the time a terrific playground for the adventurous young. Dad drove us to Chatswood railway station and the train took us over Luna Park, across the Sydney Harbour Bridge and into Central (or might it have been Wynyard station?). Pop hailed a taxi and we were driven to the SCG in style. Well, I had suspected that this day's outing was a double-edged affair – a pre-Christmas present and Pop taking me to the Test match to see a famous Australian victory. We chatted all the way. Pop had a great sense of fun. 'You are in for a treat today, Ash. The Australians should win. Why, Harvey could just about score the runs himself.' By the time we walked through the Members' Entrance – Pop had been a spectator at big matches at the SCG since Trumper first played there in the 1890s – fans were scurrying to grab the best vantage point, but Pop and I stopped at the nets, which in those days were part of Sydney No 2 Ground. There the players from both sides were going through last-minute preparations. 'Look at Harvey,' Pop said with a smile. 'He's in for a great day.' I managed to identify a few luminaries: Australia's acting captain, Arthur Morris, stood speaking with Alan Davidson and Graeme Hole. Sir Donald Bradman was in earnest conversation with Richie Benaud, all enjoying Harvey blazing away in the background SCG nets.

'Ash, I've never seen footwork as nimble and swift as Harvey's. Well, perhaps not since the glory days of Bradman … and Trumper before him,' Pop enthused. On the England side, Frank Tyson and Brian Statham were limbering up. Neither bowler was flat out, but to a nine-year-old boy, they were mighty fast.

Peter May, who had scored a brilliant 104 the previous day, with elegant ease, was batting against Tyson, Statham and Alec Bedser, who was dropped from the first Test, and he presented all comers with the straightest of straight bats. England captain Len Hutton and the wicketkeeper Godfrey Evans stood chatting. I could not keep my eyes off the scene. It was somehow magical: a touch of cricketing heaven. To me these Test players were veritable gods from Olympus. As the players gradually filed from the nets, Pop and I settled down on a bench seat right on the pickets in front of the MA Noble

Stand. Mum had packed us a meal, including her specialty and my favourite: lemon sandwiches. For those unfamiliar with my mother's sandwiches, they were thinly sliced lemon on a thinly spread bed of butter. I didn't have to share them at cricket afternoon teas, for no-one came near them, but they were my favourite.

The food, a bottle of lemonade and a longneck of stout (Pop loved a shandy on a hot day) were safely stashed away in his Gladstone bag. Pop's Gladstone bag was his pride and joy. He had had it for years and he kept the ox-hide skin of this little portmanteau suitcase highly polished. His gold initials, AGW – Alexander Garnaut West – were faded but still visible on the side of the bag. I was more interested in the contents.

I didn't ask Pop whether Mum had included the funny little peaked cap that went with my grey suit. Harvey, who Pop said rarely batted in a cap, was his favourite and he was soon to become mine. His rich dark hair seemed to enjoy a life of its own when he played a drive or a cut, and it was all as plain as day to an impressionable youngster when you saw him at close quarters flaying the bowling in the nets.

'They won't get it so easy in the middle,' Pop warned.

Harvey was the man of the moment. He was in the peak of form, having belted the Englishmen to the tune of 162 in the previous game, the First Test at the Gabba. Australia hit 601 for the loss of eight wickets and Ian Johnson's men won handsomely by an innings. On this last day of the Second Test, Australia had got itself into a winning position. Only 151 runs were required on this final day, with eight wickets in hand, and a win was expected by the Australian team and almost everybody at the ground that morning. Surely a formality, I thought. But neither the Australian team nor the fans could expect the brilliant pace bowling of Frank Tyson and Brian Statham.

They called Tyson 'Typhoon' and indeed, he bowled like the wind. Jim Burke lost his castle early, then in walked Graeme Hole. He took guard, looked about the field, but there was nothing confident about him. Hole was like a baby bird frozen to a fencing wire in the middle of a hailstorm. Tyson moved in with huge strides. There was menace in every step. His first ball to Hole was a yorker. Hole, with his high back-lift, was too late and the ball took out the middle stump, causing it to cartwheel dangerously towards the England 'keeper Godfrey Evans, standing 40 metres back from the stumps.

The batting side tumbled against this relentless attack. Only Harvey stood apart. He hooked, cut and drove with ease. Tyson was easily the quickest bowler I had seen, and would remain so until Australia's Jeff Thomson happened upon the scene two decades later.

Tyson had blistering pace; remember too, there were no helmets in those days. If you were a hooker, you had to get your head inside the line of the ball. Harvey's innings was simply magnificent; breathtaking, in fact. Pop reckoned Harvey's red-blooded batting that day was as good as any of Trumper's epic innings on the SCG, which he had seen at the turn of the century. We had a marvellous view from our seats on the pickets, especially of a ruddy-faced Englishman in the outfield, Colin Cowdrey, standing just a yard or two away. Quite incredibly almost fourteen years to the day later, Cowdrey would become my first Test wicket – and Harvey would be one of the selectors who had included me in the team.

Pop and I were so enjoying Harvey's knock, but the main concern was that he was running out of partners. Richie Benaud scrapped for fifty-three minutes for just 12 runs, then played an inglorious slog at England's medium-paced off-spinner, Bob Appleyard. The ball soared high into the afternoon sunlight; Tyson took the ball comfortably, running in from mid-wicket to accept it mid-pitch. Ron Archer and Alan Davidson both departed early.

I'll never forget the last man in – Bill Johnston. In particular, his bat. He wandered to the middle to meet with Harvey with the score standing at a sorry 9/145. Australia needed 78 runs to win. Johnston had a bat so heavily bandaged, so tattered and torn, it looked as though it had somehow survived – just – the spinning blades of a chaffcutter. With clever manipulation of the strike, Harvey continued his assault on the England attack and the last pair had taken their partnership to 40 before Johnston tickled one down the leg side and Evans took a fine tumbling catch. England had won the match by 38 runs. Harvey remained undefeated on 92. Pop and I sat at the pickets in disbelief. We felt cheated: Harvey had been thoroughly let down by his teammates, none of whom had made more than 16.

Another boy who would go on to play for Australia was also there that day. John Inverarity and his father had travelled across the country from Perth to be in attendance for the whole five days. They were having quite the trip: next was the Davis Cup finals at White City, after Christmas, where the Americans, led by Tony Trabert and Vic Seixas, beat the Australians, who included Lew Hoad and Ken Rosewall, before journeying to Melbourne for the Third Test in the new year. 'I have some vivid memories,' Inverarity recalled, one of which we share. 'I shall never forget Bill Johnston coming in to bat last with a big part of the inside edge of his bat missing. Probably a centimetre deep and five inches long.' Some eighteen months later the Malletts moved from Sydney to Perth. Two years after that I first bowled to Inverarity, when he was playing for Scotch College and I was a member of the WA State Schoolboys side. Ten years later, in 1968, Inver and I were selected in the Australian touring side in England. Remarkably, the first

Ashes Test at Old Trafford that year was the next time either of us attended a Test match.

But back to the summer of 1954/55. Neil Harvey had become my hero. I yearned to have wavy black hair and bat left-handed like this dynamic stroke-maker (and to bowl fast like Typhoon Tyson). A day at the cricket where players on opposite sides put on a masterclass of the highest order can so inspire a boy.

When the match ended Pop and I sat for a while and contemplated what might have been. Pop poured himself a shandy; I sipped lemonade.

Rather than being despondent about Australia losing, I felt a very different mix of emotions – privilege and excitement among them. Mainly I thought of how one day I might play on this famous ground in a Test match. There was something special about the place. It was almost as if the ghosts of the great past players were welcoming you to watch a Test match for the first time on the hallowed turf. They were friendly ghosts.

Pop then packed up his Gladstone bag and we left the pickets.

Already the sprinklers had the centre square awash. I distinctly heard the occasional pop of a champagne cork emanate from the England dressing-room as Pop led me through the crowd, down the back of the members' stand in the walkway between its back wall and the SCG nets, through the little members' gate, onto Driver Avenue and beyond, until we found a taxi opposite Kippax Lake. People walked slowly.

All the talk was about Australia's lamentable batting – apart from Harvey's unconquered 92. Most people meandered, as if without purpose, their heads bowed.

Pop held his head high and strode along the pavement proudly.

Me?

My heart soared, for I had wings on my feet.

CHAPTER ONE

# THE BABY OF THE INVINCIBLES

*'Sam, tell your little mate if he doesn't hit the ball in the air he won't get out.'* – Don Bradman

WITH A GLINT in his eye, Neil Harvey danced down the track and pounced on the ball like a cat nailing a mouse.

When the nineteen-year-old Victorian joined Keith Miller in the middle, Australia's score stood at a lowly 3/68. Arthur Morris (6), Lindsay Hassett (13) and Don Bradman (33) had fallen and Australia was in big trouble. England had amassed 496 in its first innings at Headingley, Leeds, in the Fourth Test match of the 1948 Ashes, and looked very much in the box seat to defeat Don Bradman's team.

Harvey clearly remembers that July day, and well he might: he was on his first tour for Australia and playing his first Test overseas. 'When the third wicket fell, I knew it instinctively by the thunderous roar of the crowd. I was inside the dressing-room and had one pad on and was about to strap on the other when Sam Loxton rushed into the room from the outside balcony. "Hurry up, Ninna. Braddles is out! Good luck."' Harvey thought it a good thing that he did not have to hang about for hours on end padded up, waiting to bat next. 'Always best to go straight in as soon as possible after you are padded up.'

Harvey was always confident in his ability to take the attack to any foe, but he was concerned about the way in which England off-spinner Jim Laker was getting the ball to spin like a top. The Englishmen were cock-a-hoop in making early inroads, especially getting Bradman so cheaply. They sensed that Laker would soon account for the young Ashes debutant, Neil Harvey. The youngster walked briskly to the wicket. Many a Yorkshire lass at the ground that day would have swooned a little at the sight of Harvey making his way out to battle, his shock of black hair shining in the mid-morning north England sunlight.

Mind you Keith Miller, who was right up there in the good looks department, was already in the middle trying to work out how he might fare in the wake of Bradman's departure and what advice he could give a young man making his Ashes debut.

The moment Harvey arrived in the middle to join Miller, the great all-rounder threw back his head like a frisky colt, laughed and said, 'Hmmm, well now Ninna. I think, ahem, I should take Laker for a while. Let you settle in.' The 'ahem' and the 'hmmm' were Miller's characteristic non-verbal tics, while 'Ninna' is how everyone addressed Harvey, a nickname whose origins are lost in the fog of time.

Miller knew all too well that Laker's ripping off-breaks would worry the youngster, for the wicket, already taking lots of turn, was a bit up and down. The state of play in a game of cricket never worried Miller, well, not at least until after his war service. Years after this Leeds Test match Miller was asked on *Parkinson*, by interviewer and cricket fan Michael Parkinson, about the pressures of performing on the big stage in Test cricket. 'Pressure?' asked Miller. 'There is no pressure in cricket. I will tell what pressure is … flying a Mosquito at 20,000 feet with a Messerschmitt up your arse!'

Miller took the first ball from Laker. The England off-spinner gave the ball lots of air and Miller charged down the track and hit the ball clean out of the ground over mid-on. Soon enough another Miller big hit cleared the boundary.

Harvey cottoned on straight away. 'If my nerves needed a tonic this was it. There's no doubt that standing at the other end watching somebody smack the bowling over the fence can do wonders for your own confidence.'

Soon the sheer enthusiasm of youth took over and Harvey began to advance so far down the track Laker may well have thought the youngster wanted to shake his hand.

What Laker could never have known was that Neil Harvey was always eager to charge down the wicket to any spin bowler. He had been doing it since junior cricket, and it would come to be recognised as a hallmark of his batting.

Respected radio broadcaster and cricket writer AG 'Johnnie' Moyes of summers past, exuded sheer delight in watching the emergence of young Neil Harvey, who he predicted would become Australia's best since Don Bradman. It was Harvey's youthful exuberance with the bat in tandem with Keith Miller and Sam Loxton at Leeds in 1948 that won him over.

Suddenly the youngster was transformed into the metaphorical cat pouncing on anything overpitched, killing the spin and sending the ball to the mid-off or cover boundary. Helped by Miller's example, Harvey's innings suddenly came to life. Any trepidation about Laker had been dispatched.

In a shade over ninety minutes Miller and Harvey hit 121 runs before Miller fell to the bowling of England's captain and occasional right-arm medium-pacer Norman Yardley.

Miller's batting had a profound effect on the young Harvey. The former air force fighter pilot exuded confidence. He was strong and carefree and always performed better for Australia when the chips were down. He was a free spirit – an attitude that didn't always sit well with cricket administrators, or with his captain, Donald Bradman, who was anything but a free spirit.

As a case in point, during the final stages of World War II, Flight Officer Keith Ross Miller, Mosquito night-fighter pilot, broke formation on a bombing raid returning from Germany. He wanted to fly over Bonn, the birthplace of German composer Ludwig von Beethoven – for Miller had a great love of classical music. He found a musical soulmate in Neville Cardus, the great England cricket writer, and equally good rapport with the maestro of conductors, Sir John Barbirolli, who conducted the grandest orchestras all over the world. Miller was a man who lived life to the full, and it was another great English cricket writer, John Arlott, who wrote of Miller that he 'seemed to be busy living life in case he ran out of it'. And that was how he and Neil Harvey batted this July day, making the England attack dance to their tune.

Their partnership had given Australia an outside chance of getting back into the game. As Miller departed for 58, in came Neil's great friend, fellow Victorian and roommate, Sam Loxton. Aged twenty-seven to Harvey's nineteen, Sam was like a big brother to Neil. He was the bloke Neil turned to for advice, as he had early in the tour when struggling for runs while playing the counties. Neil wanted Bradman's advice about his batting. He was getting out too easily and hardly making a run. He was frustrated and felt he needed help. Neil did not feel confident about approaching Bradman, who was, of course, cricket's living legend, a distant and imposing figure. Besides, there was almost a generation gap between their respective ages: Bradman was twenty years older than Neil.

'I approached Sam and told him that I wanted him to speak to Bradman about my form, but I was a little hesitant,' Harvey told me. 'Don't worry Nin I'll fix it with George,' Sam said confidently. Loxton had a rapport with Bradman, which not everyone did. He revered Bradman, as many did, but it was special for Loxton, who had done so since he was an eleven-year-old, when he saw The Don make an undefeated century against England at the MCG in the Bodyline Series and was 'sold on Bradman'. Loxton always called Bradman 'George', The Don's middle name, and he was the only player in the 1948 team game enough to address him as anything but 'Don' or 'Braddles'. Sam approached Bradman, then relayed Bradman's message back to Harvey.

'Ninna, George didn't say much about your method or your technique. In fact, nothing. What he did say was "Tell your little mate if he doesn't hit the ball in the air, he won't get out."' Practical, commonsense advice; nothing too complicated – that was the Bradman way. He reckoned that if a player was good enough to be picked in an Australian cricket team he would find a way to bat or bowl himself back into form. There was no semblance of a bedside manner with Don Bradman.

When Loxton arrived at the crease Australia were 4/189, still 307 runs short of England's imposing first innings. Loxton was a man who revelled in the challenge, as he did here, smashing five sixes and nine fours as the two put on a stirring fifth-wicket partnership of 105 in just ninety-five minutes.

Up the other end Harvey belted seventeen fours on his way to 112.

'Getting that first Ashes century was great. I felt as though I had won the State Lottery.'

Upon reaching his century Harvey took on the right-handed off-spin of Laker, belting him for three consecutive fours – before hitting across the line of one and being clean bowled.

All the players in the dressing-room saw Bradman throw his head back in dismay, but the captain did not say a word then nor did he mention Harvey 'throwing' his wicket away in such a crude manner at any time after the incident. Bradman was never one to engage in histrionics. Loxton fell for a brilliant 93.

'Sam really deserved a century,' Neil recalled. 'But he lost patience and he tried to hit Norman Yardley into the Rugby Ground, missed the ball and was bowled. What a pity he couldn't get those extra seven runs.'

The runs kept coming, with opening bowler Ray Lindwall making 77, helped out by the injured Ernie Toshack, who batted with a runner. Australia managed to get to a total of 458 – just 38 runs behind.

England, batting a second time, began brilliantly with Len Hutton (57) and Cyril Washbrook (65) putting together a 129-run opening stand. Bill Edrich followed the opening pair with 54, Denis Compton hit 66 and Godfrey Evans was unconquered on 47 when England declared – after only five minutes' play on the last day. The decision to bat on puzzled many but the England captain Norman Yardley reasoned that the pitch, which had already shown signs of turning big on the last few days, would break up even more with the use of the heavy roller, which as the batting captain he called for before the start of play.

Australia was set an imposing victory target of 404 in just 345 minutes. It seemed impossible – no team had even made 400 to win a Test. The pitch took spin. It turned square at times and the bounce was irregular. If England were ever going to beat this Bradman-led team, it was on this last day at Leeds. Yardley did not figure that Laker would bowl so badly on a wicket perfect for him. He was strangely erratic, almost as if the pressure of all of England expecting a home-team victory played on his mind and did his head in. Compton, the specialist batsman, was the only other spinner in the team.

A part-timer, Compton bowled left-arm wrist spin. He could turn the ball either way; the left-hander's leg break, known as a Chinaman, and the wrong-un or googly, bowled from the back of the hand, which spun away from the right-hander. Compton got the first wicket, Lindsay Hassett caught and bowled for 17. Compton should have had the second wicket when he got one past Arthur Morris when he was on 32, but Evans missed an easy stumping. And he should have had the third as well, Bradman, but Jack Crapp at first slip spilled the chance with the score on 121.

After lunch the England spinners bowled too many long hops and full tosses. It was fruit for the sideboard for Morris and Bradman. Then when Bradman had scored 59 he was again dropped at slip off Compton. In desperation Yardley called for the new ball, but there was not one genuine pace bowler in the England squad and the runs continued to flow.

Back in the attack Compton had Morris dropped by Laker at square leg when the Australian opener was 126. Then Evans missed stumping Bradman on 108. Missing a chance given by Don Bradman is akin to a writer penning an immortal line on his computer only for the brilliant passage to disappear from the screen, flying unseen into cyberspace as if whisked away forever by the fairies at the bottom of the garden. Now they had missed him twice. The 'what ifs' on that last day at Leeds in 1948 were destined to lie at the bottom of the empty glasses of many an England supporter. Meanwhile the batting exploits of Morris and Bradman were lauded across the empire. Morris was eventually dismissed for 182, bringing Miller to the wicket, who made 12, departing when Australia were just 7 runs off victory.

That brought Harvey to the wicket. He made one scoring stroke – a four to bring up victory. The impossible had been done, and the Australians had done it with seven wickets and fifteen minutes to spare, on a treacherous, turning wicket. In his first Ashes Test, his first Test overseas, teenager Neil Harvey hit the winning runs in one of the most-storied Test matches of all time, the stuff of legend even seventy years on.

The crowd swarmed onto the ground. Harvey later recalled: 'I was totally unprepared when the crowd invaded the pitch. As Bradman hared past me to avoid their clutches I cried out, "What do I do now?" He replied, "Son, we get out of here."'

Bradman had finished 173 not out. It pushed his average at the ground to a scarcely believable 192, and it is worth a moment to recall his scores there: 334 in 1930, 304 in 1934, 103 and 16 in 1938, 33 and 173 not out in 1948. And as it turned out, he would not score another run in Test cricket.

Decades later, the 1985 Australian team complained about the sideways movement of the Leeds wicket. I wrote to Sir Donald, and received a reply, which included this gem: 'The television viewing of the First Test was disappointing. Far too many people seem to think that batting becomes impossible when the ball is swinging or seaming off the pitch. It has always done that at Leeds – I found it playable!'

A strange moment was to follow when Bradman and Harvey made their way through the crowd and got to the dressing-room.

The spin bowlers on the tour, especially the leg-tweakers Colin McCool and Doug Ring, had become almost forgotten players of the team, disadvantaged by the new-ball rule of 1948, allowing a new ball after 200 runs were scored. Consequently they were destined to bowl endless overs in the nets and to get the odd county match. These men felt left out, veritable discards. Bradman arrived to find the non-participating players among the group singing a song to the tune of 'Champagne Charlie':

*Ground staff bowlers is our name*
*Ground staff bowling is our game*
*At the nets we bowl all day*
*In a match we're never asked to play*
*Ground staff bowlers is our game*
*We're the idlers of the dressing-room*
*Ground staff bowlers is our game*
(*From the Boundary*, Ray Robinson, Collins, London-Sydney, 1950, p. 26)

Bradman was dumbstruck. He failed to see the humour in the little ditty. He simply stared at the singers in disbelief. It could have been a scene out of *Mutiny on the Bounty* when Captain Bligh was confronted by that take-over of his ship. Thankfully, no-one was keel-hauled or even hauled over the coals for this little sing-along. Unlike Bligh's deputy, Fletcher Christian, the Australian vice-captain Lindsay Hassett was loyal to the core. Hassett felt it was his duty to make light of the awkward moment. Hassett burst out laughing. And everyone else laughed along with him. Except Bradman.

The 1948 tour was a wonderful adventure for the young Neil Harvey, from the moment the RMS *Strathaird* left Fremantle on 19 March, for most of the others in the team were his heroes. After the ship docked at Tilbury, the side was feted beyond all their imaginations. Upon arrival Bradman announced that on behalf of the people of Victoria he was giving the people of England 17,000 food parcels. Even now, three years after the war, the people were still on food rations. Britons were largely undernourished and many were on the bread line. England had suffered so much during the war, enduring a fight for their very existence, first in The Battle of

Britain, then The Blitz and the endless carnage on the Atlantic, with wolfpacks of U-boats destroying food supplies and even hospital ships, to try and cripple Britain. But life went on. Sport was part of it – cricket and soccer too, the Australians attending the FA Cup final at Wembley in their first week, sitting next to the royal box, watching Manchester United defeat Blackpool 4-2. The stoic English lived as best they could. And they continued to go to the theatre.

*A La Carte* was playing at the Savoy and *Bob's Your Uncle* at the Saville. The West End put on a variety of musicals and the early part of the tour for Bradman's men was training at Lord's by day and dressing up to attend an official function or a stage show by night. The players attended a reception at Australia House, where Bradman is said to have pressed the flesh of adoring fans with some 200 handshakes. With Bradman, I suppose the number had to reach at least 200.

The Invincibles attended the Coliseum Theatre to watch *Annie Get Your Gun*, and St Paul's Cathedral to watch the commemoration of King George VI and Queen Elizabeth's silver wedding anniversary service. A highlight at the end of the tour was having afternoon tea with the royals at Balmoral Castle in Scotland.

Coinciding with their tour were London's 1948 Olympics, the first since those in Nazi Germany in 1936. London was called upon, at short notice, to host the Games. There were, of course, still shortages of essential products. Despite the difficulties in presenting enough decent food and facilities for the athletes and spectators, London put on the show. Starting blocks for sprinters were introduced for the first time and the Empire Pool was the first covered Olympic pool. A young American, Bob Mathias, became at age seventeen the youngest athlete in Olympic history to win a men's athletics event. Perhaps even more remarkable was that Mathias won the decathlon only four months after taking up the sport. The Netherlands sprinter Fanny Blankers-Koen was the dominant woman athlete of the Games, winning all four sprint events she entered. Karoly Takacs, formerly a member of the Hungarian world champion pistol shooting team, had had his pistol hand shattered by an exploding hand grenade in the war – so he taught himself to shoot with his left hand. In 1948 Takacs won the gold medal in the rapid fire pistol shootout.

It was a heady time for Neil, who loved rubbing shoulders with the Australian cricketers he most admired. He was just nineteen, the baby Invincible. Next youngest was Sam Loxton, aged, as we know, twenty-seven. Neil said the tour was a terrific experience and batting with Bradman was 'a dream come true'.

Neil was teetotal. He did not touch any form of alcohol until he had reached the age of twenty-nine. The tour was a 'dream', as Neil says, but the long sea voyage presented its own challenges to the members of the side. The majority of the team had served their country in the theatres of war: Britain, Europe and the Pacific. The likes of Miller, Morris, Ring, McCool, Hassett, Toshack, Bill Johnston and Sid Barnes loved a drink and the freedom that had come with the defeat of Germany and Japan. Harvey got to know them better on the long sea voyage – twenty-eight days at sea on the RMS *Strathaird.* During the war the *Strathaird* completed two convoy voyages from Australasia to the Middle East, then sailed to Liverpool for a re-fit. In June 1940 she took part in Operation Ariel, the evacuation of 6000 civilians and troops from British Honduras to Trinidad before transporting 114 Foresters to Greenock in Scotland. She remained a troopship until 1946, when she was returned to P&O.

On her way to Tilbury there was a stopover in Colombo, in what was Ceylon and is now Sri Lanka. There was no pier at the wharf;

the team had to be rowed ashore in a flotilla of small craft. The Australians played a match against a Ceylon XI in which Loxton had a lot of trouble in avoiding bowling full tosses. 'Sam, I hope by the time we get to England you have adjusted your length,' Bradman said.

Loxton was unimpressed. 'George, the pitch is short. I am certain of it.'

In his book *Farewell to Cricket,* Bradman later wrote that during the lunch adjournment he had the pitch measured. It turned out to be short by two yards – twenty yards instead of the regulation twenty-two. Loxton was none too happy with Bradman not giving him due credit for picking the shortness of the pitch.

The players had various tasks during the voyage. One was signing autographs – thousands of them. They were to be distributed to fans about England upon their arrival. Bradman signed at the top, then vice-captain Lindsay Hassett. Third on the list – in alphabetical order from thereon – was Barnes.

A ten-year-old Frank Keating, who was to become a good cricket writer in England, sent his autograph book off to Don Bradman with a request to sign it and mail it back to him. To his unbridled joy, not only was the autograph book returned to the boy, but enclosed was a sheet upon which the entire Australian team had signed. Years later Keating took a closer look at the autograph sheet. Sid Barnes's signature is not exactly on the ruled line it is supposed to be confined to – and seems almost printed on the paper.

Before the team left Australia Barnes ensured that he had packed a stamp pad – and a copy of his signature on a specially made rubber stamp. The story goes that Barnes paid a pocket-money pittance to a 'youthful shipmate' to stamp his 5000 sheets. Keating wrote that Neil Harvey may have been that 'youthful shipmate' – but Harvey denies having had anything to do with Barnes's little plan.

Barnes's ploy was more successful than that of swarthy fast bowler Ernie Toshack, who had befriended a young lady during the voyage – well, his nickname was The Black Prince – and he talked her into signing his signature on his behalf. The ruse should have worked, for the girl had a good hand – but she could not spell Toshack's surname. All the sheets, and there were hundreds of them, had to be redone by all the players who had already signed. Bradman, it seems, wasn't the only one failing to see the funny side to the ploy.

Fitness on board ship may not have been a problem for the teetotal Harvey and Bradman, who always knew how to look after himself, but there might have been less enthusiasm for daily physical exercise among the others.

Years later, Neil 'Harpo' Marks, former NSW cricketer, raconteur and brilliant wordsmith blessed with a delightful mix of the Henry Lawsons and Banjo Patersons, told the story about their fitness regime. Ray Lindwall and Arthur Morris were at a cricket function when an interviewer sidled up to them and asked: 'Tell me, gentlemen, do you believe the 1948 side was as physically fit as the present-day teams?'

'Of course we were,' Ray answered.

The interviewer was not convinced. He asked for a run-down of a typical day for Bradman's players aboard ship. This was Lindwall's answer, as recorded by Marks in *Tales for All Seasons:*

*Lindwall, with tongue slightly in cheek, nodded and began. 'Well,' he said, 'we slept late and got up just in time for a hearty breakfast. Then after breakfast some of us would head for the bar for a heart-starter, to get us going for the day. After that we'd wander outside for a game of deck quoits, to raise a bit of sweat and then, when we got a bit dry from being in the sun, we'd move back to the bar to quench our thirsts. We'd have a drink before lunch and after freshening up, go to the dining room for a four-course meal washed down by a good bottle of wine and then move off to the cabin for a bit of a nap. On awakening we'd have a shower get dressed and meet in the bar for pre-dinner drinks. After a few "snorts" we'd enter the dining room have a sumptuous meal with a few drinks and then go to the dance in the evening. At the end of the dance we'd go for a walk round the deck with some nice ladies to keep us company and then we'd go back to the bar for a nightcap. After that, off to bed for a peaceful night's sleep.'*

*The interviewer was slightly taken aback by Ray's description, so he turned to Arthur Morris and said, 'Arthur is that a good description of a day aboard ship?'*

*Arthur grinned and replied, 'Yes, that's pretty accurate, except I don't remember the deck quoits.'*

Once the Tests began, Neil found it difficult to break into the side, and was twelfth man for the first three Tests. The side was settled and only someone breaking down with injury or illness might offer him a chance to make his Ashes debut. And that is precisely what happened.

Sid Barnes fielded in close at short leg, even to the slow off-spin of Ian Johnson, whom everyone knew would get clobbered at some stage. Barnes fielded ridiculously close to the batsman, a clear strategy to annoy the batsman and at the same time get in so close he could catch any ball that rebounded off the pad or boot. In the Third Test, at Manchester, Sid's luck ran out. Dick Pollard pulled a short one from Johnson straight into his body. Umpire Frank Chester later described the ball that hit Barnes's left ribs as travelling 'like a bullet'. Barnes was carried from the field by four bobbies and taken straight to the Manchester Royal Infirmary, his left side temporarily paralysed. 'I had some Minties in my pocket when I got hit but I haven't seen them since those policemen carried me off,' he later joked to his mate, fellow Test player Ken Mackay. The injury ruled Barnes out of the Leeds Fourth Test. Harvey didn't rate his chances of replacing Barnes in the Test XI, because he thought Bill Brown, the third opening batsman on tour, was certain to replace Barnes.

Harvey was having breakfast – a kipper; it was either that or toast and marmalade – when Bradman came up to the table at which he was dining. As Harvey was about to tuck into yet another kipper, Bradman gave him the news: he was playing.

One little problem.

'There I was in England in 1948 and I didn't have a bat of my own,' Neil said.

'And I certainly didn't have batting gloves. When we got over there was this guy Frank Bryan who used to make cricket pads and we all got a pair each. Slazenger used to make the Don Bradman–autographed Sykes bat then and we each were given two of the bats.

'I used one of those bats after a few early failures on tour,' Neil recalled. 'I promised myself that if I ever got another Test, I would use the new one. I got my chance and took the spanking new bat out to the middle and made 112 and 4 not out with it.' The extraordinary thing about the bat was that that was the only time it was used in any match.

'Surrey stalwart and leading bat manufacturer Stuart Surridge was at the Leeds Test and he said he would like me to use his gear in future. The Sykes bat was stored away in the Harvey household for years. It must have been in the 1970s when I was a fellow Test selector with Bradman and my old mate Sammy Loxton, who was home with us having a meal. Sammy was on his way to Adelaide to watch a Test. He asked "Where's that bat of yours that you used at Leeds?" I told Sammy it was in a cupboard.

"I am going to take it to Adelaide with me."

"Why, Sammy?"

"Mind your own business. I'll bring it back."'

In Adelaide, Loxton caught up with Bradman: 'This is the kid's from Leeds. Would you like to put something on it?' Bradman wrote on the bat: 'This is a symbol of a great innings by my friend Neil Harvey during Australia's greatest ever Test victory, Leeds, 1948 – Don Bradman.'

Neil was rapt.

'The inscription on the back of the bat is written in fountain-pen ink. It won't come off. It's a treasure. My daughter has kept it safe, along with my 1948 blazer and baggy green cap of that year.'

Using the Stuart Surridge bats turned out to be a nice sideline for Neil, who got three shillings for each such bat sold, which in a good year would yield him three hundred pounds.

The Invincibles were of course so named for not losing a match on the entire tour, and there is a long-held view that Bradman was hell-bent from the outset of the 1948 tour on doing just that. Indeed Bradman, who was not a fan of too many team meetings, held only one such meeting, and that took place at sea, somewhere between Colombo and England, during which the question was broached, as the captain raised with his team the possibility of the side going through the entire England tour undefeated. 'You have the ability to do it,' he said.

But the following little story might just test that line of thinking. Australia played Surrey twice, the second time from 30 June to 2 July. Thanks to big runs from Lindsay Hassett (139) and Bradman (128), the tourists raced to 389. Kennington Oval – or simply The Oval – was the venue, not far at all from Wimbledon, where the men's singles final was due to be played on the last day of said match.

Australia needed 122 runs in its second innings to win. Normally Harvey and Loxton would bat five and six, respectively. But this day Bradman sidled up to the pair and said, 'Pad up boys, you're opening. Just knock off the runs as fast as you can.' As our intrepid pair walked to the crease there was a flurry of activity in the dressing-room. The rest of the team showered, dressed in their civvies and slipped out a side door and into the waiting hire cars that were all revving in expectation of a fast getaway. Harvey (73 not out) and Loxton (47 not out) smashed the attack and it was all over in just under an hour. 'When we got back to the dressing-room, there was not a bloody soul there,' Neil recalled. 'They'd all gone to the tennis and had taken every car. Sammy and I had to catch a tube to Wimbledon. We ended up watching the game with the rest of the boys, except Bradman. He was in the royal box. I sat next to Doug Ring, our leg-spinner, and all he said was ... "Did we win?"'

The extraordinary aspect of the day was that if either Harvey or Loxton had been dismissed before the 122-run target, the match would have been awarded to Surrey by way of a forfeit. There would have been no 'Invincibles' then. For the record, American Bob Falkenburg beat the Australian John Bromwich in five absorbing sets, 7-5, 0-6, 6-2, 3-6, 7-5.

Heavy rain throughout the week leading up to the Fifth Test at The Oval caused a lot of tension among the ground staff. As it turned out the start was delayed until noon. People around the ground could not believe that the England captain won the toss and decided to bat on a sodden pitch under leaden skies and with more rain threatening. Lindwall (6/20), Miller (2/5) and Johnston (2/20) went through England in just 42.1 overs. England all out 52 – Hutton 30; the rest, bugger all.

England had made many changes; the most significant was the selection of leg-spinner Eric Hollies and the left-armer, Jack Young.

Australia put on an opening stand of 117. When Sid Barnes (61) was dismissed, caught behind off a Hollies leg break, in came the legendary Don Bradman. He was greeted by thunderous applause by an appreciative and adoring crowd. When The Don got to the middle, captain Norman Yardley shook hands with The Don, gathered his team about where Bradman stood and, taking off their caps, the England team gave the Australian captain a rousing three cheers and the crowd joined in.

Bradman then faced the bowling.

The first ball, leg break, he played to the off. Then he went half forward hesitantly to the second – a perfectly pitched wrong'un, and the ball fizzed between Bradman's pad and flailing bat and crashed into the middle and off stumps.

Bradman, bowled Hollies, 0.

The silence around the ground was deafening. Bradman turned on his heel, put his bat under his arm and marched off the ground, his head held high. As the crowd stood as one, cheering and clapping the departing legend, Eric Hollies turned to Jack Crapp and lamented: 'Best fucking ball I've bowled all season and they're clapping him (Bradman).'

When he reached the dressing-room, Bradman sat near his locker and said, 'Well, fancy doing that ...'

Sid Barnes sat down next to Bradman and, breaking into a mischievous grin, said, 'You know Braddles, with my little cine camera here I managed to capture your entire last Test innings.'

For years after that match, when Bradman got the most famous duck in Test cricket history, people would ask Arthur Morris: 'Did you play in Bradman's last game at The Oval?'

'Yes, I certainly did. I was at the other end when Hollies bowled Don for a duck.'

'Oh. Did you get any runs?'

'Yes, I scored 196.'

At the end of the tour Bradman was knighted for his services to the game. He was feted throughout the land. In the 1949 edition of *Wisden*, the eminent English cricket writer RC Robertson-Glasgow's opening lines to a glowing tribute to Sir Donald went thus: 'Don Bradman will bat no more against England, and two contrary feelings dispute within us: relief that our bowlers will no longer be oppressed by this phenomenon; regret that a miracle has been removed from among us. So must ancient Italy have felt when she heard of the death of Hannibal.'

Bradman's duck denied him a Test average of 100, settling instead on 99.94. Four more runs would have done it. Harvey said later, 'If I hadn't hit the winning boundary at Leeds and allowed The Don to do so he would have averaged 100. Blame me!'

The nineteen-year-old Neil Harvey grew on the 1948 tour in a number of ways – certainly as a batsman and surely as a much hardened, much improved and more worldly young man.

He scored 1129 runs at 53.76 with four centuries in the twenty-two first-class matches he played, with the three other centuries being 126 v Somerset at Taunton, 110 v South of England at Hastings and 100 not out v Sussex at Hove. His fielding delighted the English fans. Harvey possessed good hands and a bullet-like throw you would expect of a brilliant baseball infielder.

By the end of the historic 1948 tour Neil Harvey was well on his way towards a stellar Test cricket career. But that is in the future; it is time now to explore where it all began, in the back lanes of inner-suburban, industrial Fitzroy, Melbourne.

*Don Bradman*

Neil Harvey was certainly the best left-hander Victoria has had.

The best word you could use to describe his batting style is 'fluent'. His cricket used to flow. He had a wide range of shots – all the shots in the book – and he was never an inhibited player. He was very confident and of course he had every reason to be confident because he was a very good player. In addition, he was probably the best cover field we had – a magnificent thrower. Neil had all the shots – the drive, cut, pull and hook. It was always a joy to watch him cut loose against the opposition on the Test stage.

*Sir Donald Bradman – the game's greatest batsman*

CHAPTER TWO

# THE HARVEYS OF FITZROY

*'You can't play a piano without using both the black and white keys.'*
– Pastor Doug Nicholls (Fitzroy, c1943)

THE CLOCK STRUCK one. In unison the neighbours slammed shut their dining room windows. The year was 1941 and that December day was only days after the Japanese attack on Pearl Harbor.

In a narrow cobblestoned laneway another battle was taking place. The Harvey boys and other urchins of the downtrodden suburb of Fitzroy were engaged in a game of cricket. The cobblestones were slightly sloped at the sides and they ran into a small flat gutter area. The ball skipped off at different angles. Eleven-year-old Neil Harvey was batting. His keen eye and flowing strokes even brought some fathers away from their Sunday roast. They watched in admiration and applauded Harvey's display.

The Harvey boys were destined to grow up strong-minded, honest and hard-working. Horace Harvey was head of the clan. Born in the little Cornish settlement of Kapunda, South Australia, he moved to Broken Hill, NSW, as a young man, where he worked for the Big Australian, BHP, driving horse-drawn trailers.

In 1914 he married Elsie May Bitmead and their first two children, Rita and Mervyn, were born in the mining town dubbed the Silver City. Later the family moved to Newcastle where they had two more sons, Clarence, who was born on St Patrick's Day and was always known as Mick, and Harold. Both Harold and Ray were born in Sydney, before the family moved to Fitzroy, in Melbourne. Horace got a job with confectioners Life Savers, which was located next door to the building that housed the company's workers at 198 Argyle Street. The family was as poor as church mice. Horace Harvey paid £1 a week to rent their home and while it was a humble, spartan existence there was an unbreakable bond of love and joy within the tight-knit Fitzroy household. Horace's brother Stan also worked at the confectioners; a keen athletics enthusiast and gymnast, Stan rode a pushbike to work and liked to perform handstands on Horry's verandah during his lunch break. The nineteenth century two-storey house has long been demolished, to make way for a textile factory, but the cobblestoned laneway which ran alongside the house is still there.

The two youngest boys, Neil and Brian, were born in Fitzroy; Robert Neil Harvey on 8 October 1928.

Perhaps due to his Cornish descent, Horry was raised a strict Methodist. He disallowed gambling, alcohol, tobacco and profanity in his household. Horry was a good cricketer and once scored an epic 196 in a match for the Walter Sully Cricket Club in Broken Hill in 1908. He challenged his six sons: 'See if one of you boys can beat my 196 for Broken Hill.'

But in the back streets of Fitzroy, batting conditions had always been tough. The Harvey clan – all six boys – Mervyn, Mick, Ray, Neil, Brian and Harold played the inevitable 'Test' matches on the cobblestoned lane using a wet tennis ball, which fairly shot from the surface and presented lots of problems for the batsman, as the ball either spat at the throat or scurried across the cobblestones like a Jack Russell on the hunt. Neil was the only left-hander among Elsie and Horace Harvey's six boys, their 'mollydooker in the middle'.

In his first year at Fitzroy's Falconer Street Central School, Neil was chosen to represent the school. He was then aged nine and in fifth grade. 'In those school matches the games were played over the one afternoon, when the sides shared the number of overs to ensure victory for one of the teams,' Neil recalled. 'Batsmen had to hit the ball hard and often. If a youngster gets the idea early in his cricket that the ball is there to be hit, it will probably stick with him throughout his career. I know I always liked to play that way.'

The Harvey boys were avid readers of all things cricket. They read of the champion players of the period from just before the outbreak of war in 1939 and throughout the world conflict. They read of Don Bradman practising alone in the backyard of his Shepherd Street, Bowral, home and the way he learnt to watch the ball, a rebounding golf ball off a tank stand, which he would hit with a cricket stump.

'Fortunately, with such a gang of us at home, we would organise our own games without having to rely on some individual effort, such as the exercise Don Bradman had devised. We did something quite out of the ordinary to help us.'

The cobblestoned laneway was the venue for the Harveys and their mates – some ten lads in all – to make up two teams for the much-awaited regular Sunday cricket match. 'Our method of scoring was to run where we could, with two runs being allotted for hitting the kerbstone at the end of the lane; four for reaching the fence on the opposite side of the road and six for banging the tennis ball over the fence.'

The neighbour on the opposite side of the lane from the Harveys' home was to cop it sweet whenever the gang was playing cricket of a Sunday, for his living room window was right in line with the lane and the boys broke more than the odd window of a summer's night.

A broken window inevitably led to an immediate announcement: 'And so ends today's entertainment.'

They decided it was imperative to keep the ball down. Hit the ball as hard as you like, but nothing in the air. A batsman was automatically given out if he was caught on the rebound by a ball he hit onto a nearby roof. Neil can still hear his mother's plaintive cry during the boys' highly competitive games: 'Keep that ball away from my washing!' As the only left-hander among the group, Neil was more likely to whip the ball away over the fence and near Mum's washing than he would loft the ball over cover, across the laneway and through the neighbour's window. All the Harvey boys liked batting most of all, although Ray developed a good leg break. And he could bowl the wrong'un. Neil usually found himself behind the fruit box, which served as the stumps. He was a wicketkeeper-batsman when he began his school cricket.

'I remember coming home from school one day and Ray and Harold were playing in the backyard – it was all concrete – with a marble and a bat they had made from a piece of wood. They shoved this thing in my hand and said, "See how you go with this." The first marble I faced skidded off the concrete like lightning and before I could get the bat down it hit me in the knuckles and broke my fingers. It hurt; my word it hurt, but it taught me to be more aware of what was going on.'

Pain and speed – two of cricket's eternals. They come together in Bodyline, the 1932/33 Ashes series, which continued to have a huge impact on the games the youngsters played on the streets and in the laneways of Fitzroy right up until the early stages of WWII.

The term 'Bodyline' entered the language care of an article by Hugh Buggy, one of the nation's great journalists. When he filed his story about the day's play he used two separate words – 'body' and 'line' – at the end of a few paragraphs to set the scene of England captain Dr Jardine's seeming unsporting tactics of bowling short, lifting deliveries at the batsman's body to a packed leg-side field. Buggy filed his report and ended with something rather tame: 'and bowled on the line of the body'. But a sub-editor, no doubt just back from the pub, his head swimming in a sea of clever headlines, ran the words together to coin a word – BODYLINE.

Hugh Buggy was no ordinary journalist. He poked and delved into a story and when he got a sniff, be it controversial tale or a good colour yarn, Hugh was like a dog with a bone. He wrote for many publications in and about Melbourne and at some stage of every day he was there in the pressroom of *The Argus* banging away on an ancient typewriter, perpetually enveloped in a thick cloud of smoke from his pipe: Buggy's eternal flame. He thrived in the atmosphere of hot metal, with newspapers being somehow put together by a big team of journalists who had ink in their veins and compositors who cut the letterpress metal to put words on the page. There was no room for error. No computers, not a skerrick of political correctness to be found within the confines of these news houses. Hugh was among a blessed group of journalists who always got the story. They drank like fishes and swore like troopers, but there was an unwritten code of honour: they never printed anything on hearsay.

Buggy covered the Melbourne police strike of 1923, the fatal shoot-out between 'Squizzy' Taylor and Snowy Cutmore in 1927. He was there in Brisbane when Kingsford Smith's aircraft landed after his trans-Pacific flight in 1928. And he covered the opening of the Sydney Harbour Bridge in 1932. NSW Premier Jack Lang was just about to cut the ceremonial ribbon and declare the bridge open when suddenly a man riding a horse, brandishing a cutlass, broke from the small crowd of officialdom to slash the ribbon with his sword. Hugh was the first man to grab some words with the galloping swordsman, Captain Francis de Groot, whose name conjured up visions of some character leaping straight from the pages of Alexandre Dumas' immortal work, *The Three Musketeers*. But, no, in reality Buggy soon found Groot to be a rather confused Irishman.

In November 1950 Hugh Buggy arrived at Neil Harvey's home in Fitzroy, where he lived with his younger brother, Brian. It was a few months since Neil returned from his record-breaking tour of South Africa. Buggy had seen Bodyline first-hand and how a barrage of relentless pace bowling could demoralise even the toughest of teams. Buggy was intrigued by a trend in Australia which put a great emphasis on pace bowling in the minds of the nation's budding cricketers. There was more than an air of physical danger and psychological damage to those batsmen on the front line.

And the boys who bowled their little hearts out in the back streets and slums of Fitzroy throughout the thirties and the latter stages of the Great Depression cottoned on quickly to the obvious advantages of bowling as fast as they could with the idea of scaring the living daylights out of every emerging batting talent in the district. Hugh Buggy wanted to know, how did the Harvey boys – and more especially Neil Harvey – cope with the bully boy fast bowlers?

It was around the year 1937 when Neil Harvey graduated from the Argyle Street lane cricket to state school matches. By that time Neil's brothers Mervyn, Mick, Ray and Harold were all pretty much ensconced at Fitzroy North State School in Falconer Street and they had all copped it sweet from the youngsters wishing to give them 'old Harry' trying their darndest to 'knock their blocks off' at every opportunity. But they found that the young Neil Harvey was no easy prey with a bat in his hand.

Most of the budding bowlers at the school saw themselves as fast and clever. They rocked the ball down in school matches and the park with the attitude, 'if we bowl so fast the batsman can't see them, they will fall as easy as pie'. Their ploy worked on some of the newcomers, but never did they intimidate one of the Harvey brothers.

Perhaps they saw Neil as their chance to get one back on the Harvey boys, all of whom stood up to them.

When Neil arrived at Falconer Street, he was quite small and the bully fast bowlers eyed their target with schoolboy relish. When they first came up against Neil Harvey they tended to scoff when they saw him: he was only a little fellow, and when the older boys first set eyes on him, they put on their fiercest scowls and decided to scare the new bloke by rocking them in. To their great surprise Neil took them on and the fast bowlers got the shock of their young sporting lives. Neil refused to be intimidated. He displayed his mettle on the concrete pitch and in the schoolyard. Neil neither pulled away nor ducked. He did none of the things a frightened new boy was supposed to do.

On the contrary, Neil recalled some of the most enjoyable talks round the dinner table with his father, Horace, and his older brothers saying that there is nothing 'easier to paste than loose or erratic fast bowling'. Instead of pushing a tentative and trembling bat towards these tearaway merchants of speed, Neil straight-drove them and off-drove them with nonchalant ease. He loved this non-descript stuff, but the youngster said little, letting his bat and his sparkling footwork and total lack of fear do the talking. Neil's fame at Falconer Street soared and at the age of nine he was selected in the school team, where most of his teammates were aged twelve or thirteen. Neil had learnt his lesson, though, from that marble incident, and kept his wits about him as the quicks tried to knock him over. Aged eleven, he became the team's wicketkeeper.

Within a few years, in 1940, Neil was delighted to be selected for Victoria to play in an interschools match against Queensland. The visitors were led by Ken 'Slasher' Mackay who, by 1946, was in the Queensland state team and, of course, Slasher went on to play with distinction for both his state and Australia.

At the age of thirteen Neil was proud to see his name among a list of players pinned to the dressing-room door at Fitzroy Cricket Club. He had become a member of the Fitzroy CC Fifth XI. Before long he was promoted to the thirds, who went all the way to that year's grand final, in which they would face Melbourne at Old Scotch Oval.

'Although I made the final round and scored a good 77, I never expected to be selected to play in the grand final,' Neil said.

On the first day of that final there was near pandemonium in the Harvey household. Most of his brothers were also playing, but in higher-grade teams. Horace and Elsie Harvey dashed from one ground to another, to ensure they did not favour any one son.

Neil recalled fondly: 'I borrowed Mick's bike and after a good luck farewell from my parents, I set off for the ground with my bat across the handlebars and cricket bag perched on top.'

The bat was not Neil's. He borrowed it from the school cricket kit just for the occasion. It was a junior-size bat, a Harrow (Edgar Mayne autograph). Neil was too small to use a full-sized bat. He might not have owned a bat, but Neil was well acquainted with them, for at school he was given the task of oiling the school's cricket equipment, including bats. 'Mum ironed my shirt and shorts and I cleaned my sandshoes with Kiwi white.'

So Neil jumped on Mick's bike and rode off to the Old Scotch ground. The Harrow bat proved to be a beauty in the hands of the young star. Neil scored 101 and 141 not out. His efforts even brought two cash rewards of 10 shillings from his father, who had pledged long before to give Neil ten bob every time he scored a century.

After his brilliant batting, Neil returned his borrowed bat to the school's sportsmaster, who was suitably delighted: 'Neil Harvey, you can borrow the bat any time you like and borrow any of the other gear as well.' The youngster's twin centuries were also recognised by the Fitzroy Cricket Club and during the winter he was given an inscribed piece of crystal in recognition of his marvellous batting double. Fitzroy won that grand final.

Harold Shillinglaw, who later played three Sheffield Shield matches for Victoria and 63 games of football for Fitzroy in the VFL, became a good mate of Harvey's when they were students together at Collingwood Technical School. He batted with Neil during the epic 1941 grand final.

'Neil ... I reckon he used to count up to eight in his sleep because I batted with him one day, we put on 50 and I never touched a ball. He'd get to seven (balls) and go bang and he'd get one run ... or three!' Shillinglaw laughed. 'In the final we put on 130 in one innings and I got about 25 of them and Neil scored more than 100.'

After Neil had notched his second hundred for the match and victory was achieved, he overheard a little conversation between the rival captains.

'I can still hear my skipper Bill Vautin saying to Melbourne's captain, Arthur Dickens, "Would you like to meet him, Arthur?" "Meet him? Don't you think I saw enough of the little so and so out in the middle?"'

Shillinglaw and Harvey had a mutual mate at school, Len Fitzgerald, and the three played sport together. Fitzgerald vividly recalled the 1943 Collingwood Technical School football team: 'Neil Harvey was full-forward and kicked about 120 goals.

Harold Shillinglaw used to play centre-half-forward and I played centre-half-back.'

Shillinglaw said of Neil Harvey, the footballer: 'He could do almost anything. He could mark; for his size he was a tremendous mark. He could run all day. And he was equally adept in kicking either foot.' Those attributes were passed down the family line to his grand-nephew Robert Harvey, who played 383 games in the VFL/AFL for St Kilda, twice winning the game's highest individual award, the Brownlow Medal.

'As for Neil's cricket,' Shillinglaw continued, 'he was unreal. When we were kids we used to play cricket against a picket fence or in the street and they could never get him out. We were playing against kids who were sixteen, while we were only ten or twelve, and when he got a bat in his hands the older kids used to try anything, including chucking the ball at him, but they couldn't get him out.'

Fitzgerald too was to make himself a name in sport. He became one of the youngest VFL/AFL footballers of all time, debuting with Collingwood aged 15 years, 349 days in 1945. He later moved to South Australia where he played with distinction for Sturt, winning three coveted Magarey Medals. He played basketball alongside Harvey and Shillinglaw for St Marks age teams, part of the Church of England Boys' Society in the VBA basketball. They later played basketball together on a much bigger stage: in 1950 Fitzgerald, Shillinglaw and Harvey teamed with other prominent Victorian sportsmen to play against the famous Harlem Globetrotters at Kooyong Tennis Centre before 17,000 fans.

Harvey's 120 goals in a season had caught the eye of the Fitzroy Football Club, who in 1944 signed him up and promised him games with the seconds. Neil trained two nights a week, but it did not last. After due consideration he quit football and decided to concentrate on baseball as his winter sport.

Len Fitzgerald, who should know, remembered: 'Neil could have been a league footballer at the time. He was going to play Fitzroy seconds with me and they used to play baseball as a curtain raiser to the big football matches. We were playing Melbourne seconds and he was supposed to play and his brothers sort of stood over him and he played the curtain-raiser in baseball instead. He went on to become an All-Australian baseballer.'

So cricket and baseball it would be – and the Fitzroy Cricket Club was where he learnt the game.

It began with the presentation of a medallion. Each local school was to choose a worthy recipient and the chosen one was presented with a medallion and invited to enjoy the facilities of the Fitzroy CC facilities for a season. This meant rubbing shoulders with young and seasoned cricketers, some of whom had represented Victoria, even Australia in Test cricket.

'The honour entitled the medallion winner to practise in the senior net and bat against all the leading players,' Neil said. 'I believe all six Harvey boys won the medal at some stage. I won my medal at the age of twelve, and wandered up regularly to practise on the club's magnificent turf strips.'

On Neil's first practice afternoon, he met Morris Sievers, who had toured South Africa with Australia under the captaincy of Victor Richardson in the summer of 1935/36.

'I vividly remember how I had to reach up to shake his hand, with the top of my head just in line with his waistband.' Within three years the young Harvey would be playing alongside Sievers in the Fitzroy CC First XI.

Two Fitzroy men – Joe Plant and Arthur Liddicut – had a huge impact on Neil's cricket. They were wonderful mentors. Both men played for Fitzroy and Victoria. They were also the main coaches at Fitzroy during Neil's formative years. Both men were all-rounders, Plant an off-spinner, Liddicut a medium-pacer who could occasionally turn his hand to off-breaks. Neil's penchant for getting yards down the track to drive the spinners had its beginning with Plant's coaching – an unusual routine that did not involve a cricket ball.

'Joe spent hours getting me to dart down the pitch as fast as I could to get to a spot he had marked. It was probably a most unorthodox way of coaching, but it worked for me and proved thoroughly effective. After we had a long work-out with me charging down the wicket to get to the mark, Joe would introduce a ball and get me to play similarly – me getting to the pitch of the ball and thumping his flighted off-spinners. They wanted me to attack. Joe (Plant) was the man who got me moving down the wicket to attack slow bowling. It worked a treat for me,' Neil said.

That sparkling footwork that entertained cricket fans across the globe looked natural, but behind it lay hours and hours of practice at the Fitzroy nets. It was at this time that Plant and Liddicut convinced Neil to give up wicketkeeping. 'Arthur (Liddicut) told me to quit wicketkeeping and concentrate on my batting,' Neil recalled.

Fitzroy was also home to Bill Jacobs, a leading wicketkeeper in grade circles for years who went on to be a legendary administrator with the Victorian Cricket Association (now Cricket Victoria). Jacobs played 266 consecutive matches for the club between the summers of 1937/38 and 1955/56. He took 279 catches and completed 169 stumpings in his stellar district career. He played in six VCA finals and helped the club win three premierships in 1938/39, 1939/40 and 1953/54.

He was there when Harvey walked through the doors.

'Neil Harvey was something special from the moment he arrived at Fitzroy. He was outstanding at the age of thirteen. He had no formal coaching, just tips from playing cricket with his brothers in the cobbled laneway which ran alongside their home at 198 Argyle Street. Neil had everything: timing, an eagle eye, fleet footwork and a superb array of shots. He was also a brilliant fieldsman.'

A year after that arrival, Neil debuted with Fitzroy CC First XI. Jacobs became a state selector for Victoria and managed the Australian team's tour of South Africa in 1966/67 under the captaincy of Bob Simpson, then the Australian tour of West Indies under the leadership of Ian Chappell in 1972/73. Bill also managed the Rest of the World team, under the leadership of Garry Sobers, in Australia in the summer of 1971/72. Bill Jacobs died aged 93 in July 2011.

'District cricket was a terrific learning ground for me,' Neil recalled. 'All my brothers played at Fitzroy and we had a good side. The social scene consisted of a few beers in the rooms after the game. At Fitzroy we were lucky because we had the licensed bowling club adjacent to the ground, so those who had a drink could go there. Of course the opposition was invited.'

These were the war years, but they are still fondly remembered as an innocent time, when people would leave their front door unlocked, their car keys in the ignition, and sleep on a mattress in the front yard on the hot, balmy summer nights, in the days before air conditioning.

'These were days of genuine sportsmanship,' Neil recalled. 'There was no bad behaviour on the cricket field and you made life-long friends.'

It was also all very local – club cricket was very much a suburban competition and the players got to the games the best way they could. Neil used to walk to the Brunswick Street Oval.

'Otherwise I would catch a bus or a tram to other grounds. You pretty much went to the game dressed to play. I took a Gladstone bag along with me to carry my boots. You did not have any kit to worry about. I did not own a bat, nor any gloves or pads.'

The district wickets were uncovered, ever open to the elements. Matches could be played out over two Saturdays on lightning fast tracks or, especially at the start of the summer months, sluggish wet tracks. Neil reckons the vast difference in conditions helped him cope with slow wickets with variable bounce and faster pitches that encouraged fluent stroke-play – drives, cuts and hooks.

Fitzroy in those days was highly industrial, a suburb of factories and modest workers' cottages in the shadows of the gasholders. Only a decade later large swathes of the suburb would be condemned as a slum, demolished, and rebuilt with multi-storey housing commission flats. There was a common thread among the people. They were all working class and they were as poor as church mice.

One of Neil's early heroes was Doug Nicholls, the champion Fitzroy winger in the VFL. Nicholls became a pastor, was awarded a knighthood and in December 1976 Pastor Sir Douglas Nicholls became the first Indigenous Australian to become a state governor, when he was appointed the vice-regal head of South Australia.

During Neil Harvey's formative years he grew up following Doug Nicholls' sporting progress and he greatly admired the manner in which Doug brought people together. One of Doug's favourite sayings stuck in Neil's memory. In opening a public meeting one night in Portland, he said: 'You can't play a piano without using both the black and white keys.'

'He was a great advocate, a man of the people and a terrific example of a wonderful sportsman. I was conscious of Doug's heritage but that didn't matter a bit. He did a fantastic job of bringing people together and I was just so proud to be part of it.'

During his short period as Governor of South Australia, I had occasion to ask Sir Doug why it was rare to see an Aboriginal cricketer play the game at the highest level. Was it because cricket was the 'Invader's game?' I asked.

Sir Doug roared laughing. The average Indigenous household could not afford the clobber needed to play cricket: shirts, creams, socks and all the rest was beyond the financial reach of his people.

Sir Doug was a Fitzroy legend. In more ways than one. A great sportsman, a great advocate for his people and a natural facilitator for reconciliation and peace, and a great example to a young and impressionable Neil Harvey.

For most of their young lives the Harvey boys dutifully followed their parents' sage guidance in life: work hard, be honest. The 1940s was a time of family togetherness, everyone eating together at the one table. The Harvey parents guided their children without being overbearing. Horace Harvey was justly proud of holding the family batting record, but he kept away from suggesting anything to his boys about technique or how to bat. He did offer encouragement, though. If one of the boys got runs, he said 'well done'; if not, 'better luck next time'.

The results are clear. Eldest brother Merv went on to play a Test for Australia, while two other brothers, Mick and Ray, played for Victoria. Later Mick played for Queensland in the Sheffield Shield and became a leading first-class and Test umpire. Brian, the youngest, was a Victorian state baseballer and useful all-rounder cricketer for the Fitzroy First XI up until the summer of 1961/62. Tragedy struck the Harvey family in 1969. Brian was working for the State Electricity Commission (SEC) in South Morang on a large pylon. A message came from down the line ensuring Brian that the power had been switched off. It hadn't been. Brian was struck down in the prime of his life. He was just 37.

'I always considered Merv to be the best player of the Harvey boys,' Neil said. 'An opening batsman with a good defence and a quick eye, he could tear an attack to pieces, I shall never forget one innings he played for Victoria versus NSW at the MCG. Ray Lindwall was at the peak of his powers and bowling at his fastest. He bowled Merv a bouncer and Merv, a good hooker, promptly hit it into the crowd at fine leg. There was much to like about Merv's batting. Michael Slater reminded me of Merv in the way he showed no fear in hooking the short-pitched deliveries from the fast bowlers. That time when Merv was appointed Victorian captain, he told the selectors: "Don't worry about me, there's a lot better one at home."

'Mick was a solid batsman. He had a good defence, but he struggled against top-class spin bowling. He opened for Victoria and then Queensland. Mick hit three Sheffield Shield hundreds for Queensland. He opened against Len Hutton's 1954/55 England side and made 49 with Ken Archer. He helped give Queensland many worthwhile opening stands.

'Ray was the most brilliant of the clan – a real dasher. He looked very good when in full flow. Unfortunately, the better bowlers in Sheffield Shield cricket detected a weakness in his footwork, something which kept his scores to a moderate proportion. I often thought if this flaw in his footwork had been worked upon and rectified, Ray could easily have become a Test player.'

Between them the Harvey brothers made a total of 25,532 runs in 773 games for Fitzroy CC. In 125 games for Victoria, Merv, Ray, Mick and Neil scored 7964 runs, and in a collective 405 first-class matches a total of 26,532 runs. There was no women's cricket for sister Rita to play, but she happily scored for Horace's team, Felix Socials in the North Suburban Cricket Association. Altogether, they did Horace and Elsie proud.

*AG 'Johnnie' Moyes*

Neil Harvey was the darling of the Australian crowds, just as were Joe Darling and Clem Hill, left-handers of a previous generation. They were sturdy, thickset; Neil seems almost frail by comparison. He has followed the Australian tradition by being a century-maker in his youth and he seems likely to fill the gap caused by the retirement of Don Bradman. In the field he is magnificent, fast and certain, completely unspoilt by success; a credit to the game he adorns.

*Johnnie Moyes was a journalist, an ABC radio cricket commentator and a shrewd, insightful cricket author. These words were first published in* A Century of Cricketers *(Angus & Robertson, Sydney, 1950), written when Harvey was at his exciting, youthful best.*

*Gideon Haigh*

I first met Neil Harvey when I was writing *The Summer Game* and visited him in St Ives. It was magic to see him pick up the old Sykes bat with which he scored his 112 at Leeds in 1948, and which he told me he never used again, on account of his being recruited to Stuart Surridge soon after. He was generous and thoughtful but pithy, practical, no nonsense. Whenever he was quoted in subsequent years about this or that in the modern era, that was the voice I heard: he didn't have a beer with future generations, so much as talk the same way about them all. And unlike most ex-players, who cultivate emollient, media-friendly exteriors while often keeping most astringent sentiments to themselves, Harvey just said what he felt. We used to value that as a society; we've grown a little ... brittle.

*Gideon Haigh, journalist, newspaper columnist, author, also calls it as it is. There is a touch of Neville Cardus, the great English cricket writer and music critic, in Gideon's writings.*

CHAPTER THREE

# THE NATURAL

*'Well played, son, we'll be seeing you in England next year.'*
– England 'keeper Godfrey Evans

NEIL HARVEY THE young Fitzroy batting whizz-kid was steadily making his mark. He was making consistent runs for Fitzroy and the Victorian selectors thought picking the young man to play against Tasmania, which was not yet in the Sheffield Shield season, might be just what he needed to build his confidence.

Neil wasn't overly impressed with the Tasmanian team. He believed Victoria had picked a virtual Second XI and the opposition was 'moderate'. The eighteen-year-old Neil Harvey gave the Tasmanians a right royal pasting, smashing a whirlwind 154. 'I didn't think much of it and promptly returned to club cricket over the new year of 1947,' Neil recalled.

'While I got a decent score it was against a side that were not then playing in the Sheffield Shield. They played against the odd state side but only occasionally. Yet, to my delight, the match in which I scored 154 was deemed first-class – so that was the first of my sixty-four centuries at that level.'

The New Year – 1947 – was soon to smile on Neil Harvey. Neil didn't give much thought to playing for Victoria again that year. He got stuck into playing for his Fitzroy. Then came the big break. The Victorian team for the northern tour – games versus NSW and Queensland – had been selected. No Neil Harvey. Then fate took a hand.

At the last moment, Gordon Tamblyn became unavailable – his replacement was one Neil Harvey, who was 'surprised and delighted that I had been selected to replace him'. Harvey didn't expect to get a game in any of the matches, fully prepared to be Victoria's twelfth man in both games. He was spot on in the game against Queensland. Harvey carried the drinks. But in Sydney Neil was included in the Victorian XI, with Bill Johnston named twelfth man.

Harvey batted at the fall of the fourth wicket. He confessed to being 'as nervous as a kitten' and 'I'm afraid … I batted like one'.

When he reached the batting crease, he was facing the wily NSW leg-spinner Fred Johnston. Things happened so quickly that it all became a blur in Neil's mind.

'I played a couple of balls from Fred, then I pushed forward to a wrong'un. The ball beat my outside edge and in pushing forward I slid over the batting crease.'

To his dismay, Neil heard a triumphant yelp from Ron Saggers, the NSW wicketkeeper, as he whipped off the bails with Harvey stranded out of his ground.

Harvey, stumped Saggers bowled Johnston, 0.

Oh, what must Joe Plant have thought … 'get down the track and nail the half volley'.

Harvey was dreadfully disappointed. 'I felt like crawling into a hole and staying there forever, but my teammates rallied about me and they eased the pain, a bit, with their sympathy and assured me, "there's always a second innings".'

He was still a bundle of nerves as his second innings approached. He was facing a pretty good NSW attack, including Ray Lindwall, Australia's best and most lethal fast bowler.

Harvey's imagination ran wild. 'Knowing Ray, and I got to know him, I can just visualise what he was thinking. "A new batsman – first game – on a pair of ducks – what more can I give him than a really fast yorker?" That's exactly what happened but I think Ray fooled himself with that first ball. He bowled it too quickly and the ball hit my bat before I had time to get it off the ground. The ball shot wide of gully and I was off the dreaded pair. My reflexes were a lot quicker next over and I managed to carry on and hit 49.'

Harvey retained his spot when Victoria took on England, which was touring Australia, the first Test cricket it played after the war overseas. He went into bat during a batting collapse and helped resurrect the Victorian innings. When he reached 50, the England 'keeper Godfrey Evans said cheerily, 'Well played, son, we'll be seeing you in England next year.'

Harvey was flattered, but he knew he had a long way to go to give himself a chance of making that tour in 1948. He scored a terrific fighting 69 before the very same Evans caught him off Doug Wright.

England was led on that tour by Wally Hammond, who was looking forward to a series of good sportsmanship and goodwill to his fellow cricketers, friend and foe. He was to be disappointed. Don Bradman, whose batting prior to the First Test seemed to suggest he was a mere ghost of his former self, was all about reasserting his supremacy and leading Australia to a crushing victory over Hammond's men. Bradman did find form and he also led his team with the same old determination and inflexible steel the Englishmen knew so well.

In Brisbane in the First Test Bradman was controversially given not out when on 28 in Australia's first innings. All at the ground, except for umpire George Borthwick, thought Bradman to have been caught in the gully by Jack Ikin off the bowling of Bill Voce. Bradman stood his ground and he went on to hit 187. Most of the Englishmen and some of the Australians, including Keith Miller, thought the ball caught the edge of Bradman's bat and he was clearly out. It was the defining moment of his summer's so-called 'Goodwill' tour.

That doyen of cricket writers Sir Neville Cardus wrote: 'In the first half hour of Bradman's innings he committed more miscalculations and streakiness than memory holds for all one's experience of him ... Soon after lunch the miracle happened; Bradman's innings rose from the dead, a Lazarus innings.' In the Second SCG Test Bradman hit 234, so too did Sid Barnes, and the Australians again won convincingly. Australia won the first two Tests by an innings, with a draw in Melbourne.

The Harvey family received great news during the summer when Merv was selected to play in the Fourth Test at Adelaide. He opened the batting with Arthur Morris in the Fourth Ashes Test at Adelaide Oval. Amazingly, he was in the team, opening the batting, because of an injury to Sid Barnes – exactly the way that younger brother Neil would first be selected in an Ashes team.

Merv scored just 12 in the first innings. This was the match in which Alec Bedser pitched his famous leg-cutter on the line of leg stump and, having moved appreciably, it hit Bradman's off stump, bowling him for a duck. Bradman maintained that 'that ball was the best ever to get my wicket'.

In the second innings Merv fared better, scoring 32 in a 116-run opening stand with Morris – who made centuries in both innings.

When Barnes recovered, Merv's Test career was over. He never got another chance to play for his country.

War service had curtailed the cricketing career of both Merv and Mick. They probably spent their best cricket years in the trenches. Merv was twenty when Australia last played a Test, twenty-one when war broke out – and made his Test debut aged twenty-nine.

This 1946/47 season had been a big leap forward in Neil Harvey's cricket career, and when the winter of 1947 arrived the baseball gloves were out for the Harvey clan. Neil was selected in the Victorian team to contest the Claxton Shield in Adelaide.

He excelled and Victoria won the Shield, the first of three in a row. He missed those 1948 and 1949 Claxton Shield victories, otherwise engaged: the 1948 Invincibles tour of England and the 1949/50 Australian tour of South Africa would occupy all his energy and time.

All the Harvey boys played for Fitzroy Baseball Club, revelling in the contest and rapt that on many a Saturday the baseball club took on an opponent as a prelude to the VFL match at Brunswick Street Oval, Fitzroy's home ground. 'I stuck to playing second base; Merv was on third and Ray was our shortstop,' Neil said.

Baseball training was a breeze, for all the Harvey boys owned their own glove and in the winter months just before nightfall the smack of leather gloves would be heard. All could catch well and throw the ball at lightning speed. Their baseball could not help but improve their fielding in cricket. At second base Neil developed his throwing arm to a great degree. His arm wasn't very high, at about three-quarters, neither round arm or over the top – perfectly in between. Any ball hit along the ground in the infield which went within cooee of Harvey was pounced upon – and the runner was thrown out with his bullet throw to first base. Harvey covered a lot of ground as if he were patrolling a large area of cover on the cricket field rather than staying within the confines of first and second base.

When future Australian Test captain Ian Chappell was growing up, he heard a good deal about the excellence of Harvey's baseball through his father, Martin Chappell, who played in the Claxton Shield competition for South Australia against Victoria in Adelaide in that very 1947 competition.

'Martin talked about Harvey's smooth fielding and his solid hitting. As that tournament (1947) was played in Adelaide I probably saw some of the games, but I have no recall. That season Victoria won the Claxton Shield. Martin played in two Claxton Shield carnivals (1947 and 1948).'

Recently a friend loaned me an old autograph book, which included signatures from the Australian cricket team in the summer of 1946/47 and the England team of the same summer. On closer inspection, the old autograph books also contained the signatures of the 1947 Claxton Shield opponents – and there are the names Neil Harvey and Martin Chappell.

Ian Chappell was to forge a strong association himself with baseball in this country. He too played Claxton Shield baseball for SA and was – on at least two separate occasions – selected in the All Australian Baseball team. For cricketers of these generations baseball loomed large as the best winter sport – until the late 1960s when baseball became a summer sport.

*Mark Nicholas*

I've seen Harv on film. Like Compton, he stood with his feet together and played back a lot, using the pace of the ball. He was handsy and quick on his feet, as they had to be, given the bats and pitches. But you know all that. With Greg Chappell and Ricky Ponting, he makes up the Australian middle order post-war. I've got all three ahead of Smith, which makes today's generation laugh.

I was always amazed by the warmth and respect he and Davo appeared to show to me. Two men I think an enormous amount of. I know Davo better and just love that man. Please send them my good wishes and huge admiration should you speak to them. Harv may not even remember me but, no worries, he's a proper hero. Neither ever treated me as an outsider; in fact, exactly the opposite.

*Mark Nicholas, cricket commentator, captained England A and played for Hampshire for nineteen years, captaining them for ten.*

*Tim Rice*

To be honest I don't really have a Neil story, beyond the fact that I used to fix him theatre tickets when he was over here (in London). He loved musicals but always seemed keen to attend ones I hadn't written! I didn't mind at all – he showed great taste. I was of course a massive fan of my fellow left-hander and am honoured to have been a friend. I remember so well his great innings in 1954 when he and Bill Johnston nearly won the Second Test (at the SCG) with an amazing last-wicket stand. Neil made 92 not out (I am writing all this from memory so I hope I have my facts right). I wasn't there of course – I was only ten and in England – but it was so exciting hearing the crackly commentary on the radio and reading about it in the paper the next day. A great series – not just because England won!

*Tim Rice is a globally renowned lyricist, author and brilliant after-dinner speaker. He is famous for his world-acclaimed stage hit collaborations with Andrew Lloyd Webber and Elton John. Among his credits are* Evita *and* Aladdin. *Sir Tim is an avid cricket fan, and he has something very special in common with Neil Harvey and his biographer, for Tim, like Harvey and Mallett, has also claimed the wicket of England's Colin Cowdrey.*

CHAPTER FOUR

# INDIAN SUMMER

*'Had Michelangelo been a cricketer he would have batted like Harvey, with the touch that made chips of marble fly everywhere as he pressed on with the creation of a great piece of sculpture.'*
– Ray Robinson

THE SUMMER OF 1947/48 marked the first time a team from India toured Australia. The team was led by Lala Amarnath – and it turned out to be the perfect Indian summer.

The Test selectors made their intentions clear when they included Neil Harvey in an early season Australian XI to play the Indians in a tour match at the SCG in November 1947.

Harvey had already shown excellent form scoring 87 for Victoria against Amarnath's men at the MCG, sharing a 151-run partnership with his mate Sam Loxton, after his brother Merv had opened the batting. Neil's lightning reflexes against the quicker bowlers and swift, sure footwork against the slow men won him an array of admirers; his skill and red-blooded stroke-play won the hearts of the young and tickled the memories of the old. His fan base soon extended nation-wide.

The 1947/48 summer was enriched by the all-round performance of Amarnath, who hit a brilliant unconquered 228 against a strong Victorian attack on the MCG. 'His cover driving that day was wonderful,' Neil recalled. 'I know only too well how Lala was striking the ball for I was at cover trying to stop them. It was truly a great innings with his runs coming at a very brisk rate.' Amarnath did not take his terrific form against the state teams into the Test matches.

India batted first in the tour match against the Australian XI and was bowled out for 326. Australia replied with 380 – Bradman notching 172, Keith Miller 86 and Neil Harvey a handy 32. Bradman's hundred was a significant milestone. 'I had the honour of being right there in the dressing-room when Bradman completed his one hundredth first-class century,' Harvey recalled.

It was also a big occasion for Harvey. 'This was the first time I saw Bradman bat. Amazingly I had no experience of first-class cricket before the war and I mean watching the great players such as Bradman, (Stan) McCabe and (Bill) Ponsford on the MCG. The big matches seemed to coincide with my being either at work or playing grade cricket.'

Batting again, India scored 304, leaving the Australians with 250 runs to win the game – a comfortable enough victory target, or so it seemed. A strange thing happened with the score on 60. Bill Brown, who was batting for a spot in the Test team, had contributed half the runs. He had also been backing up too far at the non-striker's end. Vinoo Mankad, the Indian opening bat and left-arm orthodox spinner, had already warned him once, but when Brown did it again, Mankad took off the bails in his delivery stride, and Brown was run out.

The controversy perhaps overshadowed the rest of the match – Mankad bowled India to victory with 8/84. He failed to dismiss Harvey, who remained undefeated on 56, top scoring for the home team.

'I was delighted with my first taste of the big stuff,' Harvey said after the match.

The week after that game Harvey was again batting at the SCG. Three of the Harvey boys were named in the same Victorian Sheffield Shield side to play NSW. Brother Ray joined Neil and Merv. Neil top-scored with 62; Merv scored 45 and Ray 43. Victoria won easily, by nine wickets. When Merv first played for Victoria in 1940/41 he had boldly predicted: 'There's another Harvey coming along nicely and he's going to be the best of us all.' His prediction was looking good. The stalwarts at Fitzroy Cricket Club knew only too well what Merv Harvey was saying. Messrs Liddicut, Plant, Sievers and Jacobs knew where their young protégé was heading.

Harvey was keen to continue his good form. The next match for Victoria was against Western Australia in Perth, all three brothers playing again, in the second game the westerners played in their inaugural year in the domestic competition. Merv captained Victoria in the absence of regular skipper Lindsay Hassett. Neil kept his form up at the WACA Ground, sharing a partnership of 173 with Merv (141) that day. Neil was out for a brilliant 94, backed up with 41 in the second innings.

'On the last day of the game a telegram arrived for me at our hotel asking me to report immediately to Sydney for the Test match. Ernie Toshack had pulled out because of a bad knee and I was to replace him in the twelve.'

Bradman loved having Harvey in the Test twelve, for his fielding was very much a trump card. Harvey did not mind twelfth man duties – he was happy to be in the dressing-room, getting to know the established players. He was not bothered by the prospect of carrying the drinks. In fact, he embraced it. 'Being twelfth man on two occasions really helped, for I gained some experience of the Test match atmosphere. This is most important, for a player who is pitch-forked straight into a Test match without any previous experience of the atmosphere can find himself a little overawed by the occasion.'

There was atmosphere aplenty when Vinoo Mankad once again ran out Bill Brown at the bowler's end, who was once again backing up too far, although this time, there had been no warning. Everyone had an opinion, including Harvey – but let's return to that contentious topic after first following Harvey's season. The Second Test was a draw, ruined by rain, and Harvey served again as twelfth man in the Third Test, starting New Year's Day at the MCG, which Australia won handsomely, thanks to centuries in each innings by Bradman, making the series score 2-0.

And so to Adelaide for the Fourth Test – and the Test debut of Robert Neil Harvey. It's hard to imagine, but Harvey still did not own a cricket bat. He thought back to that junior grand final, when just thirteen years old – and decided it was time he owned a bat.

'I had saved up £10 and now that I was about to play my first Test match I thought it time I owned my own cricket bat,' Neil said.

The young Harvey walked into the Melbourne Sports Depot, owned by Clive Fairbairn, one of the legendary Rats of Tobruk, who himself would play one Shield match for Victoria the following season, alongside Harvey. Harvey selected his new bat; the gleaming straight grain of the willow caught his eye. It was a Gunn & Moore Autograph. Just the ticket for his debut Test innings.

Harvey received generous applause from the knowledgeable Adelaide spectators when he walked to the crease to join fellow Victorian Lindsay Hassett. Sid Barnes had played a chanceless innings of 112, Bradman had fallen for 201 and the mercurial Keith Miller hit grandly for 67. The Australians had savaged the Indian attack and the stage was set for Harvey to make merry in the middle. However, the Madras-based fast-medium bowler

Commandur Rajagopalachari (mercifully reduced to his initials, 'C.H.') Rangachari, also making his Test debut, trapped Neil dead in front when he had scored a modest 13.

'I was disappointed with my first Test effort and was not at all confident of retaining my place in the Fifth Test in Melbourne. While we won the Adelaide Test easily by an innings, I was most impressed with Vijay Hazare's batting. The Indian tamed our attack and hit two glorious hundreds – 116 and 145. He did so against our well balanced, talented attack.'

Australia didn't have the services of Bill Johnston for the Adelaide Test, but this line-up – Ray Lindwall, Keith Miller, Ernie Toshack, Colin McCool and Ian Johnson – was world-class that summer.

'Hazare's batting in both innings was brilliant. Two lovely knocks. He played all the shots with great balance, poise and ease of stroke-play,' Neil enthused.

There is a strong Australian link with Hazare. When Clarrie Grimmett was controversially left out of the 1938 Test squad bound for England, the little leg-spin wizard accepted an offer of £2000, plus fares to and from India by ocean liner and a generous expense account, to coach His Highness the Raja of Jath. Apart from coaching the Raja of Jath and His Highness's younger brother, Grimmett also took a young, enthusiastic all-rounder under his wing. That youngster was Vijay Hazare.

Years after his masterclass of batting on the Adelaide Oval in 1947/48, Hazare was quoted in *The Telegraph* in Calcutta: 'Although I was the first to score a Test hundred on successive days, I also became the first to do so and finish on the losing side. But I had the greatest satisfaction of playing those two knocks in the presence of my mentor, Clarrie Grimmett, who had coached me thoroughly in 1938 and had held high hopes for me. An ideal coach, Grimmett did not change my rather unorthodox grip or my unusual stance but bowling with a tennis ball from a shorter distance helped me tighten my defence and execute all strokes.'

Despite his doubts, Neil Harvey was retained for the final Test match at the MCG.

Captain Bradman continued his habit of winning the toss and batting. Again the side began well, but Bradman retired hurt (a suspected torn rib muscle) and Harvey strode to the crease.

And boy did he get stuck into the Indian bowling. So much so, he destroyed his bat. When he had scored about 30 the Gunn & Moore bat Neil had bought for £10 just weeks before fell apart.

'The low part of the bat handle simply broke in two just two inches from the top of the blade. So I had to pick another bat from the old Victorian Cricket Association kit bag which usually lay in a corner of the MCG home dressing-room gathering dust. I selected a pretty well-used RM Crockett bat. This one didn't let me down.'

Harvey punched his way to 78 not out at the end of the first day's play, his good mate Sam Loxton up the other end. It gave him plenty to contemplate overnight. No worries – he completed his century the next day.

'I will never forget the noise that disturbed the peace on that warm Saturday afternoon when Ray Lindwall and I galloped up and down the pitch to run a five and bring up my century. I should think this was one of the few times in Test history that a batsman had reached his hundred with an all-run five,' Neil said.

'Amarnath had just taken the new ball at the time and had a silly mid-on and fine leg. He bowled a shortish ball which I turned forward of square leg, and the fieldsman at silly mid-on had to turn and chase it. The ball stopped a few feet short of the fence in front of the score board and Ray and I ran like the wind.'

Harvey wasn't satisfied with simply a century, but kept going for 153. He was now the youngest Australian to score a Test match century, a tad younger than Archie Jackson was when he hit his debut hundred at the Adelaide Oval in 1928.

Ray 'Sugar' Robinson was a great players' favourite at the SCG during the 1974/75 Ashes series. And Dennis Lillee was Sugar's favourite. We knew of Ray's form. Sugar was Australia's most prolific and best cricket writer between the wars and beyond. He saw Neil Harvey from the outset and he once penned beautiful words to describe Neil's batting. I quizzed him: 'Sugar, you likened Harvey to Michelangelo. How so?' 'Well, Rowdy, I reckoned if Michelangelo played cricket he would bat like Harvey, making the chips of marble fly in all directions on his way to creating a masterpiece; a great piece of sculpture.'

Neil looks back with a mix of his usual humility, but also pride, at his brilliant, attacking first Test century. He had the pleasure of making it at his home ground, the Melbourne Cricket Ground, before his immediate family and an adoring home-town crowd.

In the minds of most people throughout the land, young Harvey's 153 made him a certainty to be selected in the 1948 Australian team soon to head off to England.

'Although I suppose I gave the selectors 153 good reasons why I should be on the boat to England, I was like a cat on hot bricks during the weeks leading up to the announcement of the touring team.'

Neil couldn't sit still. Making an England tour with the Australian team, especially a side led by Don Bradman, was something too precious to contemplate missing. Waiting to hear his fate was agonising.

On the appointed day the youngster decided to get some fresh air and exercise. He gathered his four golf clubs, slotted them into his quiver-like canvas bag, placed the clubs across the handlebars and rode his bike to the nearest nine-hole public golf course. Just the act of hitting the ball and walking the course helped Neil calm down. When he got home from the golf course he saw his mother, Elsie, and father, Horace, at the front gate. 'Mum and Dad were beaming. I knew then that I was in the team.'

Much as cricket fans were thrilled by the emergence of the young Harvey, and seeing Bradman score four centuries in what would be his last Test series at home, the topic that dominated conversation was the way Bill Brown was run out in the Second Test by Vinoo Mankad, which left cricket with a new verb – 'to mankad'.

After Arthur Morris and Brown cruised to 25 for the first wicket, all hell broke loose. The exuberant Indian all-rounder Mankad, a clever exponent of left-arm orthodox spin, suddenly stopped in his delivery stride and whipped off the bails at the non-striker's end. Brown had moved down the pitch before the ball was delivered, and was clearly out of his ground when Mankad struck.

Mankad had done the honourable thing by warning Brown in the India-Australia XI match a few weeks earlier; Brown had not heeded the warning and lost his wicket in the same fashion in that match. When Brown did it again in the Test, he did not get a warning.

The players in the Australian dressing-room were aghast.

'We all thought it (Mankad's action) was a low act,' said Harvey, who of course watched the whole episode while serving as twelfth man.

But by the rules of the game, Brown was fairly and legitimately dismissed; yet Mankad was instantly labelled the villain of the piece. John 'Ginty' Lush, a former NSW all-rounder turned reporter, made his feelings clear in print: 'Brown's dismissal caused heated discussion in the members' stand. Even the press box was the scene of debate as to whether Mankad was guilty of a sporting breach. But in light of a previous warning, and a dismissal, Brown was foolish to take liberties with Mankad.' The dismissal was considered unsporting in the extreme by other furious members of the Australian media. The stigma of his controversial dismissal of Bill Brown lingers in the minds and memories of many.

Yet it really was as simple as this: Brown had once again transgressed, stealing a few yards down the pitch, so Mankad dismissed him. For many years there had been an unwritten law among cricketers that the player at the non-striker's end must be warned that he is transgressing. Mankad had warned Brown in a previous game.

Don Bradman had of course been witness to both incidents, having led in both the Australian XI match and the Second Test. A shade or two towards the pragmatic in anything likely to cause controversy, he did not make public comment on the Mankad incident until years later. Over more than twenty years I had many conversations with Don Bradman. Regarding Mankad, Bradman told me that the Indian had 'every right' to dismiss Bill Brown in the manner he did. 'I cannot understand why the press questioned his sportsmanship. The Laws of Cricket make it quite clear that the non-striker must keep within his ground until the ball has been delivered. If not, why is the provision there which enables the bowler to run him out? By backing up too far or too early, the non-striker is very obviously gaining an unfair advantage.'

The rules are clear, but such a dismissal inflames the passions. It long had, ever since the first known such instance, during an impromptu cricket match on the Victorian goldfields in 1853.

A cricket match was arranged there between a team of students from Oxford (the dark Blues) and Cambridge (the light Blues) on a field near Ballarat. In the wake of the game, a description of an 'incident' in the match was printed in a small limited-edition book – *The Old Fogey* – published by Ronald Cardwell of The Cricket Publishing Company, Pennant Hills, NSW. Oxford was all out for 43. Cambridge was 3/20 when 'in walked a stout fellow who could run like a hare and wield the willow with some style. The old Cantab revealed as correct play as could be shown on our peculiar wicket and the score increased to 35. Here a crisis occurred. One of the batsmen, not the Cantab, you may be sure, was very eager in backing up, and once when at my end he overshot the mark before the ball was delivered, and I, turning suddenly, knocked the stumps flying while the batsmen was fully a foot out of his ground. The umpire of course gave him out, and the batsman made tracks for the tent. The crowd, however, shouted out "swindle", and several stopped the batsman and told him to go back. The hum of voices soon swelled into a deafening roar. Oh! What a row, what a rumpus, what a rioting it was to be sure. After a lengthy explanation, it was admitted by all that the player was out. Then the wild excitement died gradually away; harmony and pleasantness reigned once more.'

The run-out of the non-striker, universally referred to now as a mankad, has happened a few times over the years. I recall the day at Adelaide Oval in the summer of 1968/69 when Australian batsman Ian Redpath, at the non-striker's end, went wandering aimlessly down the wicket as West Indian fast bowler Charlie Griffith moved in to bowl. Redders must have been three yards out of his ground when Griffiths stopped suddenly at delivery and hit the middle stump with such force that it went sailing down the wicket. At that time Harvey was in his second year of a twelve-year stint as a Test selector and was at the ground that day.

While Harvey, along with most of the Australia squad, believed Mankad's action was 'a low act', he reckons one other incident involving Australian opener Andrew Hilditch was 'the worst thing I have seen done on a cricket field'. It was 29 March 1979 and Australia was heading for a good win against Pakistan in the Test match at the WACA Ground in Perth. There was a great deal of feeling between the teams and the Pakistani fast bowler Sarfraz Nawaz was the most volatile of any player in either side. On that last morning the Pakistanis were battling to bat themselves into a position where they could mount a defendable tally for the Australians to chase. The last man, Sikander Bakht, played and missed, mishit and bumbled about, but he survived and did so for more than half an hour. Time was ticking. Alan Hurst, the fiery Victorian quick, who took five wickets in the Pakistani first innings, was bowling. Midway through his approach to the wicket Hurst noticed the stubborn number eleven wandering about outside the crease. Hurst stopped at delivery and whipped off the bails – the dreaded mankad raised its head again. Australia now needed just 236 runs to win. Andrew Hilditch and Rick Darling put on 87 for the first wicket and Allan Border's men were cruising to an easy victory when Darling drove Sarfraz firmly to Sikander at mid-off.

Sikander threw the ball at the non-striker's wicket and Hilditch leant down, picked up the ball and tossed it to the bowler. Sarfraz caught the ball and immediately appealed to umpire Tony Crafter. The umpire had no option but to give Hilditch out handled ball. Australia went on to win the Test easily, but it was these dismal dismissals everyone remembers. Hurst's mankad was one thing, Hilditch's handled ball another – the game would be forever remembered as a day of infamy for two incidents that were within the rules of the game, but not within a bull's roar of the spirit of cricket. Test selector Neil Harvey was not amused.

*Thos Hodgson, describing an evening spent with Neil Harvey and Sam Loxton*

There was however one tense moment when I innocently brought up the infamous underarm bowling incident where Trevor Chappell was instructed by his captain and older brother, Greg, to bowl the final ball of the New Zealand innings underarm in a one-day international. Trevor duly obeyed his captain. Australia won and outrage in the cricketing world followed. Neil and Sam (Loxton) were Australian selectors at the time. Sam told me that at the end of the match, with the situation in uproar, he had gone to the Australian dressing-room and said to Greg Chappell, 'You may have won the bloody game, but you have broken the hearts of every cricket lover in Australia'. Having said that, Sam with tears in his eyes stood up and without saying another word to Neil or me, stormed out of the room and went to bed.

I felt very embarrassed that I had raised this subject and apologised to Neil and asked whether I should go and apologise to Sam, as I had no idea my questions would upset him so much. Neil responded, 'Don't worry. Just leave him. He will be fine in the morning. It still upsets him so much and you weren't to know. I feel the same way as he does but I don't get quite so emotional.' Neil paused and then said, 'Anyway, we have still got half a bottle of port to finish off and we are not going to bed until we do that.' Thereafter, I had a private audience with RN Harvey for a few more hours and during this time, he shared some stories with me.

There was something majestic about the way Neil played. To see Neil Harvey dancing down the wicket to dispatch a spinner, which he did so frequently, was something special to behold. Incidentally, he was never stumped in a Test match.

A wise English friend once said to me that one must be careful about hero worship because often our heroes have feet of clay. In other words when or if we may meet our heroes, we may be disappointed because they may have flaws or weaknesses in their character, which were not otherwise contemplated by us. Neil Harvey however has never disappointed me. He was, is and will always be a hero. His outstanding cricketing achievements are matched by his decency, generosity, humility, modesty and good humour. He certainly holds forthright opinions about the way and the spirit in which cricket should be played. This is an entitlement which he has earnt from his long involvement and service to the game for which he deserves respect. I count myself most fortunate and privileged to have shared a friendship with Neil over many years. I am honoured to have been asked to contribute some observations about a good man and cricketing great.

*Thos Hodgson is a leading Sydney barrister. He is also a long-time member of the Australian Cricket Society and has a long and happy association with Neil Harvey.*

CHAPTER FIVE

# HARVEY HITS THE VELD RUNNING

*'Jeez, how long have I been batting? I am only 60. Merv (Harvey) will not believe that I could have batted for so long and score so slowly.'* – Neil Harvey

NEIL HARVEY'S GREAT Ashes adventure with Don Bradman's Invincibles stamped him as a future Test star. More than one thousand runs on tour, plus his heroic 112 in the first innings of the Leeds Fourth Test in 1948 which helped turn the match, confirmed what good judges thought: this young bloke Harvey is the real deal. After the 1948 England tour, the talented young left-hander settled back with the Fitzroy Cricket Club to prepare for Sheffield Shield season in the summer of 1948/49. No touring side came to Australia that season and it was purely a domestic affair. Such seasons were always a bonus for the emerging players, for all the state sides were at full strength with every fit Test incumbent available for all the matches. However, the summer was not a memorable one for Harvey. He did not score a single century all season. He did manage a score of 87 in a Test trial game, but his first-class season realised just 530 runs at the modest average of 33.68.

When they sat down to pick the Test team to tour South Africa in 1949/50, the Australian selectors – Sir Donald Bradman, Edmund 'Chappie' Dwyer and Jack Ryder – were confident that Harvey would spring back into top form. He was in.

Most of the usual suspects found their way onto the touring list, but one name – then the greatest all-rounder in Test cricket – was missing. Keith Miller had been omitted. There was a huge hue and cry among the press and former players.

Jack Fingleton was livid. He wrote in a Sydney tabloid: 'Australian cricket is reeling ... I would not hesitate to place Miller in the top cricketers in the world today.' Bill O'Reilly, the famous leg-spinner of the Bradman era, later said: 'I was heartbroken when Clarrie Grimmett was passed over for the 1938 tour of England. I have always placed that dereliction of selection responsibilities on a par with the omission of Keith Miller for the Australian team to tour South Africa in 1949/50.'

There were a few changes to the 1948 team. Don Bradman had retired; wicketkeeper Don Tallon withdrew just before the team departed, to be replaced by Ron Saggers, and, of course, Miller's omission was the mother of all bombshells.

Amid the speculation about who would become Bradman's successor as captain, there were two obvious candidates – Lindsay Hassett and Arthur Morris.

Hassett had led the Australian Services team which competed against England in the Victory Tests in England in 1945. He had a lot of experience in leading Victoria and was one of those leaders who could build a rapport with his team, building their confidence, commanding the utmost respect, while still being one of the boys. He was a natural humourist and often had his charges in stitches.

The diminutive Hassett – five foot six in the old measure, or if you prefer 168 centimetres – was a thin little chap, who brought to mind Puck, the mischievous fairy jester in Shakespeare's romp *A Midsummer Night's Dream.* To wit, during a trip to England, the Australians disembarked for a day's outing to stretch their legs and have a quick look around Aden before returning to their ship. Hassett was introduced to an Arab sheikh, who boasted 199 wives. In those days a new ball fell due when 200 runs had been scored. Hassett, quick as a flash, said to the sheikh: 'Ah, good sir. One more and you get a new ball.'

Arthur Morris first played for NSW as an eighteen-year-old in 1941. In his debut match he scored a century in each innings. Then the war intervened. Like Hassett, Morris served in the Australian Army. His batting during the 1948 tour was exceptional, hitting three centuries, including his 196 at The Oval in Bradman's last Test match.

Morris too had a dry and quick sense of humour. Fellow Test player Ken Archer told me: 'It was the first morning of a Sheffield Shield match in Brisbane. Morris confided in me. "I am not feeling too well, dear boy. Don't think I will want to bat too long today." A couple of quick wickets fell and Arthur looked at me with a resigned look on his face. He then proceeded to hit a rapid 253 out of 400. His last fifty came in just seventeen minutes.'

Hassett got the nod by, apparently, the smallest margin, board members voting by telegram. Board secretary Bill Jeanes ran the vote from his office in Adelaide at the weekend, with the final two votes, which confirmed the winner, not received until the Monday.

In taking up the position, Hassett became the first Catholic Test captain since Percy McDonnell in 1888. There had been more than a bit of hostility between the Protestants and the Catholics within the Australian Test team between the wars. It seemed the likes of Bradman on one hand and Catholics Bill O'Reilly, Jack Fingleton and Stan McCabe on the other, were ever at loggerheads. Hassett was all about fostering good relations among the players with his dry humour and gentlemanly ways. He had seen first-hand the tragedy of war. To such men death had been an everyday experience; they knew the cruel and bitter taste of the life and death struggle that was WWII. Cricket to them was just a game, even at the highest level an enjoyable pastime, a game to embrace and to celebrate over a beer with their teammates and the opposition at day's end, but, in the final analysis, a game and nothing more.

It did not hurt Hassett's chances that Bradman held him in high esteem. 'His knowledge of the game and views on tactics [were] extremely sound.'

An unknown correspondent from *The Canberra Times* was altogether more colourful in his description: 'To see Hassett field was to see balanced crispness; not for him the goalkeeper's dive with flannels at the end of the day looking like camouflage trousers. He was known to bowl, approaching the wicket with small measured steps, his hands clasping the ball as a mouse grasps a piece of cheese.'

And so it was that the good ship SS *Nestor* – a small but steady steamer which also had served as a troop carrier during both world wars – left Fremantle on 22 September and docked in Durban just over two weeks later on Friday 7 October 1949, one day before Robert Neil Harvey turned the ripe old age of twenty-one.

'The team put on a little party to celebrate my twenty-first,' Neil said. 'The party was held in Lindsay Hassett's room at Durban's Edward Hotel, then the top-shelf best hotel in the city. The celebrations went for an hour or so, then everyone dispersed. It was a nice gesture by Lindsay and my teammates.'

As was the case on the 1948 Invincibles tour under Don Bradman, Sam Loxton was Neil's cabin mate at sea and roommate on land.

'Sam was my best friend. He remained a close mate throughout my career as a cricketer and Test selector and we stayed in close contact right up until the day he died.'

The tourists soon had a problem on their hand. Bill Johnston, the left-handed quick who could bowl spin when the ball got old, had met a young lady who took his fancy. On the day before a match against Natal, he drove to meet her. Near Rossburgh, he failed to negotiate a corner and had a serious car accident. His mother, a widow who had lost a son in the war, fainted when she heard the news on the radio. Such were intercontinental communications in 1949, it took six days for Johnston to get in touch with his mother to assure her that he was all right. His injury opened up a place – and Keith Miller was on his way.

Neil Harvey's earlier first impression of Hassett had been not altogether favourable. 'I always thought Lindsay to wear a superior air; especially towards the likes of me. I was educated in a state school and Hassett was of the Geelong College set. I guess he felt a bit superior in that regard.'

However, Neil's impressions of Hassett the Test captain were far different. 'Lindsay (Hassett) was easily the best captain I played under and I played under five Test captains – Don Bradman, Lindsay, Ian Johnson, Ian Craig and Richie Benaud. Hassett's flair was such that he read games brilliantly and he made decisions to turn a game on its head with extraordinary vision.'

From the outset of the tour Harvey was getting runs as if they were going out of fashion, but managed only a modest 34 in the First Test in Johannesburg, in which Australia amassed 413, and did not have to bat a second time. Ironically it was Miller who took the honours in the first innings bowling, taking 5/40. By now Bill

Johnston had recovered – the tour had been proceeding for two and a half months before the First Test began – and he returned 6/44 in the second innings.

Now it was time for Harvey to hit the veld running. A rich vein of form saw the left-hander thrash the Springboks to the tune of 178 in the Second Test at Newlands, Cape Town. Australia won easily by eight wickets. Harvey and Loxton put on 130 for the fifth wicket, Sam lamenting his lack of strike. 'Ninna found a way to keep the strike by hitting a three off the last ball of every over and I couldn't get a hit for a long time. I reckon I lost form out in the middle because of it and I ended up having a slog at Tayfield.' Loxton, bowled Tayfield, 35.

Kingsmead Durban was the venue for the Third Test. The weather was to be a key factor, so too Hassett's captaincy and, more importantly to the outcome of an amazing game, the remarkable batting of Neil Harvey. It was January 1950. Durban's weather can be like Brisbane's, humid in summer and prone to heavy rain showers. There was mayhem afoot. The team's luggage truck was marooned in floodwaters en route to Port Elizabeth from Cape Town and the long-term baggage master–cum–scorer, Bill 'Fergie' Ferguson, had to work his magic to arrange a railway bus for the remaining 200-mile (320-kilometre) journey to finish in Durban.

South Africa batted first and was solidly placed at 2/240 at stumps on day one when the heavens opened. Kingsmead was awash amid a furious downpour. The respective captains Dudley Nourse and Lindsay Hassett inspected the ground the next morning and agreed to postpone play for forty-five minutes.

Bill Johnston's last ball of his first over of the day stood straight up and Nourse was good enough to catch up with the ball only to edge it to the 'keeper, Ron Saggers.

'Lindsay had a real problem on his hands,' Neil recalled. 'Of course he needed Australia to dismiss the South Africans for as little as possible, but not so quickly that we had to bat on a pitch playing tricks. Hassett came up with a brilliant strategy. He instructed Johnston and Keith Miller to bowl as full a length as possible and to continue operating with the old ball. Big Bill and 'Nugget' bowled ramrod-straight to a deep-set field. The strategy worked a treat from the outset and the South Africans scored only 14 in the morning session. Mind you we dropped a few easy catches which helped the cause to keep the opposition in batting, so long as they were not scoring too freely.'

But the weather and the wicket conspired to make damaging inroads into the South African batting line-up almost impossible to prevent. Dudley Nourse's men were dismissed for 311, losing 7/57 in the period between lunch and tea. Ray Lindwall (3/47) and Bill Johnston (4/75) were the main wicket-takers.

Hassett's strategy had gained the Australians valuable time for the wicket to show some improvement. The opening partnership between Morris and Jack Moroney lasted for about an hour. The rest of the innings did not take as long.

Moroney played on to the young Springbok off-spinner Hugh Tayfield, and in the wake of his dismissal, Australia lost the remaining nine wickets in less than an hour: Australia all out 75 – 236 runs behind as the day's play ended.

Standing on the steps of the Edward Hotel in Marine Parade, Durban, Keith Miller predicted an Australian victory. He advised his mate, cricketer-turned-journalist Dick Whitington – the two had opened the batting for the Services XI at Lord's in 1945 – to bet on Hassett's men to win.

'In fact, I will bet you £5 on an Australian win.'

Even though he knew that only a miracle could save Australia in the Third Test, Whitington was instinctively wary. Later to be Miller's biographer, Whitington chose not to bet Miller the £5. He knew all too well about 'Miller's luck'.

Hassett's dilemma with weather and pitch on the Sunday became Nourse's problem. He had the whole of the Sunday rest day to ponder. Would he enforce the follow-on and thus risk a last-day chase or would he decide to have another bat and set Australia an unassailable runs target on the last day? Nourse visited the bureau of meteorology with teammate and opening bowler John Watkins – and what he gleaned there decided him. The two men learnt that the forecast was for a possible thunderstorm developing late on the Monday afternoon. He inspected the Kingsmead pitch on the Monday morning before play and decided to bat.

Nourse asked for the heavy roller in the hope that the moisture below would be driven to the surface and batting would be fine until such time as the wind and the sun combined to do their thing. In the days of yore, uncovered wickets turned into a quagmire – a 'sticky dog' – after the combined ravages of rain, wind and sun.

There had been the sort of drying wind that blows up hill and down dale across the broad stretches of the veld in other parts as the Transvaal, but suddenly after lunch, with South Africa nicely placed at 3/85, the wind dropped. Kingsmead, in a flash, became clammy; dripping sweat permeated every nook and cranny of every player's body and the pitch went from a pleasant stroll in the park for all batsmen to being suddenly transformed into their worst nightmare.

In the wake of the wind disappearing, within a few overs the Springboks found themselves in dire trouble. Thanks to inspired spells by off-spinner Ian Johnson (5/34) and Bill Johnston (4/39) an astonishing seven wickets fell for just 14 runs. The Springboks were all out for 99.

'His decision in not enforcing the follow-on cost the Springboks the game,' Harvey said.

Australia now needed 336 runs for victory. The target was at first glance not unassailable, but given the manner in which the track was playing, few people outside the Australian team gave Hassett's men a hope in hell of victory. Hassett asked for the heavy roller, again hoping it would flatten the pitch and bring the moisture to the surface. Since the rains had come, some twenty-eight wickets had fallen for just 245 runs. Before the day was over three key Australian batsmen were back in the dressing-room – Moroney (10), Miller (10) and Hassett (11) – and Australia was teetering at 3/80. Australia needed a further 256 on the last day to win. Arthur Morris was batting solidly and Neil Harvey was just starting to settle in when stumps were drawn. Harvey was used to getting to the wicket and announcing to his partner 'let's get stuck into them' – but the challenge here was vastly different.

'The wicket was a shocker,' he said. 'After the rain showers, the sun baked the surface, but left the mud underneath and when the ball hit the hard top it caused the ball to bounce almost vertically. The heavy roller helped, but there were holes in the surface where the balls had dug in. When the ball pitched in those holes you never knew what it would do. For the first time in my life I had to be very careful about which ball I could hit.'

The Australians added but 15 runs before the dismissal of Arthur Morris (44). At a precarious 4/95, it was now up to Harvey and the incoming batsman, Sam Loxton, to rescue the situation. They batted slowly, hitting the odd boundary, but mindful that the team couldn't afford to lose another wicket.

Harvey knew that scoring would prove difficult and he would have to get his head down and grind out the runs. The left-arm spinner 'Tufty' Mann, who bowled for a long time in tandem with first-innings destroyer Hugh Tayfield, beat Harvey in flight. The left-hander had taken his score to 40.

'I can still see it. To me it was the perfect delivery. It pitched outside off and spun back finding the gap between bat and pad. I thought, "Oh, that's out. I am gone!" I was just about to walk. But I heard nothing and, when I turned around, (Billy) Wade was standing there with his gloved hands above his head. The ball must have bounced over the stumps and Sam (Loxton) called me through for two byes.'

It was tense, riveting cricket. The runs were coming first at a trickle, then as Mann and Tayfield began to tire, the odd loose ball came along. Harvey and his mate took 137 minutes to put on 50. The runs came in ones and twos. It was tough, exacting cricket; physically challenging, mentally draining. Those Durbanites present for the last day kill were to roar their disapproval with each Australian run. Local spectators who had turned out to witness a famous Test victory were becoming anxious.

'When I walked into the change-room unconquered on 50, I heard Keith Miller utter, "Ahem, fellas, we are going to win this!"'

The fifth-wicket stand ended when Loxton had a slog at Mann and was clean bowled for 54. The pair had put on 135, advancing the score to 5/230. A further 106 runs were needed. Colin McCool joined Harvey and the dashing left-hander said: 'Now, Col, can I cut loose and start getting into them?'

'No, Ninna. We have got plenty of time. We can get these runs with sensible batting, ones, twos, rotate the strike and break their rhythm. Mann and Tayfield are tired. They have bowled almost all the overs and there will be a good deal more loose stuff as the game wears on. We have to be patient.'

Soon after at an interval, Harvey said to twelfth man Ken Archer, 'Jeez, how long have I been batting? I am only 60. Merv will not believe that I could have batted for so long and scored so slowly.'

Nevertheless, Harvey kept batting. And batting. Eventually he ended the match by smashing Mann's sixth ball of his 52nd to the mid-wicket boundary. This brought Harvey to 151. He was unbeaten after 325 patient minutes at the crease, and Australia had won by five wickets. What a victory.

Dudley Nourse looked a lost and defeated man. He scanned the sky as if to beseech the cricketing gods. On a turning, twisting pitch of uneven bounce, holes all over a good length, his spinners (Mann 3/101 off 51.6 overs and Tayfield 2/144 off 49 overs) bowled their hearts out – but failed miserably. The forecast rain did not eventuate. Whitington thanked the Lord above that he didn't take Miller on that £5 wager and the Australians celebrated a magnificent, miraculous victory. Hassett knew all too well that the Durban victory would knock the socks off the South African team's morale. Such a shattering loss would see the Springboks as putty in Hassett's hands for the remaining two Tests, especially now that Australia was up 3-0, making a South African series victory impossible. The Australians were happy beyond belief. Theirs was one of the greatest escapes in Test cricket history.

In all first-class matches Harvey scored eight centuries. He scored hundreds all over South Africa. He scored hundreds in the next two Tests: an even hundred in Johannesburg in a drawn match, then 116 in Australia's only innings at Port Elizabeth, where an innings victory made the score 4-0. In tour matches Harvey scored 100 against North East Transvaal at Benoni; 145 not out versus Orange Free State at Bloemfontein; 100 versus a South African XI at Durban; and 100 not out versus Griqualand West at Kimberley.

In the preceding South African summer, England champion Denis Compton starred for his country in the same sort of run-making manner Harvey had. Compton was rested in the tour match against Border in East London, much to the annoyance of local fans. When the Australian team was announced for the corresponding game, Harvey was similarly rested, prompting this headline: No Compton, No Harvey, No Nothing. Wise heads prevailed amid the touring party. Harvey was reinstated in the team to play Border. He fell for a modest 29. In all first-class games Harvey scored 1526 runs and a monumental 660 runs in eight Test knocks, for a Bradman-like average of 132.

One evening during the match against Griqualand West at Kimberley, South Africa's foremost industrialist, Harry Oppenheimer, invited Hassett and his men to his luxurious home for cocktails and canapes. Now, Kimberley is synonymous with almost inexhaustible deposits of high-quality diamonds and Oppenheimer was a leading light at De Beers, the world's best-known diamond merchant. From1888 and into the 21st century De Beers has controlled the vast bulk of the world's rough diamond production. For years De Beers ran its business as a cartel, manipulating the world price. Oppenheimer personally directed that the newly formed state of Israel receive the necessary raw diamond products from De Beers to establish itself as one of the world's leading diamond and polishing exporting countries. The Australians, who were paid £450 for the six-month tour of South Africa, could never in their wildest dreams have known such wealth as surrounded them at the Oppenheimer mansion.

Ken Archer, who had batted so well for 134 in the tour match just played, was at his most watchful best. The party was grand enough, the company good and there was plenty for the players to eat and to drink, yet Ken noticed his captain to be a little distracted. Was our Puck about to weave his mischief?

'I don't know whether Lindsay got bored with the function or thought the mood needed to lift in the room. Whatever his thoughts our captain suddenly sprang into action. He decided to hold an impromptu bit of fielding practice.'

Standing in front of a polished round mahogany table with ornately carved legs and laden with expensive glassware, Lindsay began throwing priceless brandy balloons to his ring of catchers. The inevitable happened. One of the brandy balloons fell to the marble floor with that dreaded sound of shattered glass.

Silence.

There was a brief moment for reflection. Faces turned toward their host, then the Australian captain. Hassett took over. He roared laughing. 'Plenty more where that came from, eh, Harry?'

Oppenheimer too roared laughing. 'Next we saw Hassett and Oppenheimer bounding about arm in arm singing dirty ditties.'

It was a long, tough tour, and a highly successful one. Hassett's men agreed to play a baseball match in Johannesburg as a fund-raiser for the benefit of the highly respected scorer–cum–baggage master, Bill 'Fergie' Ferguson, from which he received the princely sum of £1000.

All the cricket had finished, but the players could not come home immediately. They had to wait for their ship to arrive. The players did their own thing.

Some spent time at the beach; others such as Miller, Johnson and Morris went to the famous Kruger National Park, where Hassett, team manager 'Chappie' Dwyer and Ron Saggers were taken on a tour by Sid Pegler, former Springbok cricketer who played against Australia Down Under in 1910/11 – the summer of great triumph for Victor Trumper.

The trip concluded with a visit to the House of Assemblies in Cape Town, where Lindsay took a wrong turn. He raised dozens of political eyebrows when the Australian wandered into the middle of the chamber when it was in session.

But the most momentous event of the tour was playing out now, although its denouement was some way down the track. Months earlier Neil Harvey had met Iris Greenish, a sixteen-year-old girl, at a dance in Johannesburg. He had two weeks waiting for the ship to take them home – during which he got to know Iris better.

Iris's parents liked Neil, but her father said there could be no thought of an engagement until his daughter reached the age of eighteen. 'If you are still serious at that time, we'll even bring Iris to Australia.' Neil would have to bide his time.

During the voyage home on the *Athenic*, Lindsay Hassett told Harvey that he wanted him to bat in the coveted number three spot for the Australian Test team. And he offered the talented left-hander a job in his sports store.

Due to his busy schedule of club, state and Test matches, Neil's employment history wasn't all that flash. He took nearly six years to complete an apprenticeship in the Melbourne City Council's electric supply department, when the ticket would usually have taken three years. Trying to marry work with cricket was a never-ending problem for most cricketers, so the job at the sports store was a godsend. Neil gladly accepted Lindsay's offer.

Record Test runs against the Springboks, a new and stable job back home and meeting Iris – things were moving ahead for Robert Neil Harvey. Life was good.

*Greg Chappell*

Neil Harvey was a great inspiration to me. My dad, Martin, used to say: 'When you watch NSW or Australia at the Adelaide Oval never take your eyes off Neil Harvey. Watch how he goes about it – his batting, his fielding.'

Martin advised Ian (Chappell) to 'never take your eyes off Keith Miller …'

I took my dad's advice. I watched Harvey like a hawk.

When he went to the nets, I walked round the back of the oval and had my eyes glued on his every move. He had time against the fast bowlers and moved swiftly and with great balance to get down the track to drive the slow bowlers. Playing in the backyard by myself, I'd emulate my heroes. I'd toss a ball up against a wall and hit the rebound. To imitate Harvey, I batted left-handed. And do you know, Neil never failed to score a hundred.

*Greg Chappell was a stylish right-handed batsman, many believe the best Australia has produced since Don Bradman. He played 87 Tests, hitting 7110 runs at 53.86. Highest score 247 not out. Test captain and Australian selector.*

CHAPTER SIX

# BROWN'S COWS AND BIG JAKE

*'I will prove that my bent finger flicking of a cricket ball will take me to the very top of the game.'* – Jack Iverson

FREDDIE BROWN'S ENGLAND team of the 1950/51 Australian summer floundered in the Test matches like a bunch of Brown's cows. Despite England's indifferent bowling, a batting line-up that depended on Len Hutton almost exclusively and a bunch of hopeless fieldsmen, the Australian public somehow warmed to Freddie Brown's men.

Brown himself struck a remarkable figure in the field. He wore a wide-brimmed sun hat and a silk kerchief, which was not dissimilar to those luxurious cravats the gentry wore at summer events in England between the wars. Had his on-field attire been complemented with a hay seed between his teeth, he could have been the perfect fit as the original Farmer Brown. But the nation embraced the forty-year-old Freddie Brown who played with a cheerful competitive spirit throughout the entire Ashes series.

'Freddie was a fine all-round cricketer,' Neil Harvey asserted. 'He gave the ball a bit of a clout scoring invaluable runs down the order. And he could bowl the medium fast stuff and also some pretty good-quality leg breaks.'

Lindsay Hassett was demonstrably less strict than Bradman as a captain, and the players who previously had served under The Don revelled in the warmer atmosphere, both on and off the field of play.

The series proved outstanding for two of the Englishmen – batsman Len Hutton and fast-medium bowler Alec Bedser.

Hutton was described as a batting 'Titan among minnows', scoring 533 runs at an average of 83, while Bedser took thirty wickets at the very good average of 16.06. England was at a disadvantage thanks to an injured knee that restricted star batsman Denis Compton, who averaged just 7.57 in the Tests. England probably erred in the tour selection, leaving out off-spinner Jim Laker, left-armer Tony Lock and all-rounder Bill Edrich.

'Len Hutton was the best England batsman of my experience,' Neil said, 'and (Alec) Bedser was the best bowler I faced.' He cites as evidence *that ball* to Bradman in Adelaide in the Adelaide Test of 1946/47, which of course 'Bradman reckoned was the best that ever dismissed him'.

Harvey also asserts that captain Lindsay Hassett excelled in that role, especially in the First Test in Brisbane.

Australia won the toss on a placid Gabba wicket, but were bundled out for a modest 228. Neil Harvey – batting at first drop just as Hassett had promised – top scored with a dashing 74, made in a smidge over two hours with ten fours.

Then rain intervened. And how it came down. A good old Brisbane downpour, not dissimilar to the sort of rain Hassett's men had experienced in Durban when they turned that first-innings 75 into a miracle victory.

England batted poorly in the miserable conditions, where rain and sun had produced a sticky dog of a track. Brown declared the innings closed at 7/68. He thought it best to get the hosts in the dodgy track as fast as possible. England bowled brilliantly on the Gabba track and Hassett, now playing the Brown game, declared Australia's innings closed at 7/32. England batting last needed a shade under 200 to win, but the wicket had the last word.

Brown juggled his order, hoping to buy time so that his best batsman got to the crease when the pitch had calmed. So the great Len Hutton batted at number eight. But the ploy backfired – when the Yorkshireman got to the wicket, little time had passed and a mere 30 runs had been scored. Hutton hit an unconquered 62, but his efforts were to no avail for he ran out of partners, England all out 122. Alec Bedser, the big Surrey medium fast bowler, took 7/54 for the match (4/45 and 3/9) and he claimed Harvey's wicket in both innings.

'Hassett's captaincy in this match was outstanding. It confirmed to me that he was the best captain I'd played under to that time,' Harvey said.

Australia played a debutant in this match – Big Jake Iverson, aged 35, who took 4/43 in the second innings, impressing all and sundry with his finger-flicking magic. They called Iverson 'the Freak', and the way he bowled his unique finger-flick spin was indeed freakish. But he hadn't always been a spinner – in his school days at Geelong Grammar, where coincidentally he had once bowled Lindsay Hassett, with a big inswinging yorker, he was a quick. But Jack Iverson the schoolboy fast bowler soon tired of cricket and at the age of eighteen became a jackaroo in the Mallee, eventually becoming assistant manager on a big station at Tallarook. Jack preferred golf. By the age of twenty-one he had reached a reasonably high standard, winning the Maldon Club Championship in 1936, and signed up for service in 1940.

He emerged from the war zones of the Middle East and then New Guinea to bring an entirely different aspect to the art of spin bowling.

During his service in the Middle East with the Australian Anti-Aircraft regiment, Iverson suffered from a series of ailments, including jaundice and sand-fly fever, while trying to man the fort in a variety of roles – driver, mechanic and gunner. He returned to Australia – this was when Prime Minister John Curtin was getting his men back, fearing a Japanese invasion – and was thereafter dispatched to New Guinea. Meantime Neil Harvey was making his way with the Fitzroy Cricket Club, while his eldest brother, Mervyn, was an airframe fitter for the RAAF and Mick Harvey was also in New Guinea, serving as an infantryman on the infamous Kokoda Trail.

One day Jack found himself sitting on an ammunition box under the canvas awning of his tent listening to the relentless sound of rain on the roof. Between periods of hostility and fearsome battle, there were long stints of boredom. There was nothing to do. That is, until a large batch of ping pong balls arrived. The rain sounded remarkably like the constant chatter of machine-gun fire and Jack wondered whether the sound would make it impossible for the sentries stationed on the perimeter of the jungle clearing to spot a Japanese attack. As the rain continued to pelt down, Jack flicked a ping pong ball. It began as idle play.

Jack was intrigued by how the ping pong ball reacted to pressure. He found that if he held the ball between his thumb and middle finger of his right hand, he could spin it. He could make the ball twist and curve. Depending on which side of the ball he applied the middle finger to, it dipped and spun differently. When he flicked the right side of the ball and bowled it, the ball swerved late and dramatically to the left, then upon landing it spun in like a big off-break. After hours of testing his skill he decided to try out his method on a few of his army mates. He was unplayable.

'I woke up to the fact that whichever direction I had my thumb pointing, so would the ball break. If my thumb was pointing to the left or off-side as I let the ball go, the result would be a leg break. If it pointed to the right or leg-side it would be a wrong'un. If it pointed directly at the batsman, it would be a top-spinner.'

Best of all, Jack found he could deliver a leg break, an off-break and a top spinner all with the same flicking method, without any obvious change in how he released the ball, thus giving the batsman no clue which way the ball was turning.

Next he tried it out with a tennis ball – but he knew he needed to try this with a real regulation four-piece cricket ball, if he ever managed to get back to Australia in one piece.

He did, of course, and at age thirty-three joined Brighton Cricket Club in Melbourne, declaring to his wife, Dorothy Jean, when he was picked to play in the third XI: 'I plan to prove that my bent finger flicking of a cricket ball will take me to the very top of the game.'

That was late 1946. He went on to the Melbourne Cricket Club in 1948 and a year later, the Victorian state team. While Harvey was away carving up the Springboks, Jack cleaned up for Victoria, taking forty-six wickets at the remarkably low average of 16.42. In the autumn of 1950 Iverson toured New Zealand with Bill Brown's team, taking seventy-five wickets during the tour at an average of 7 runs apiece. And indeed, when he took those four wickets at the Gabba on debut, his promise to his wife had come good.

'Jake was a terrific bowler,' Harvey said. 'He had huge hands and could give the ball a big rip. And he had great control.'

The Australians won the first four Test matches, in no small measure thanks to the spell cast by Iverson, before Freddie Brown's men won the nation over by winning the Fifth and final Test at the MCG. Hassett made the most runs – 366 runs at 40.66 – just pipping Harvey's 362 runs at 40.22. Bill Johnston took the most wickets – twenty-two wickets at 19.18 – followed closely by Iverson's twenty-one wickets at 15.23. His best bowling performance was 6/27 in England second innings at the SCG Third Test.

'The Englishmen had no idea which ball was turning. Jake was to prove a sensation in this series,' Harvey said, before adding that he himself could not pick Iverson's spin. 'No, but then I never picked the wrist spinners very well. I always thought if you got to the pitch of the ball, it didn't matter.

'Nothing seemed to worry him, although he was a big worry in the field. We had to "hide" him. And he couldn't bat much at all. But his bowling was magnificent and the Poms had no idea.'

Iverson would usually not bother to bend over to field the ball, but instead stopped it with his boot – which injured his ankle in the Fourth Test in Adelaide.

Iverson moved to the beat of a different drum. He was a slightly odd chap, given to taking offence.

'Jack was a very strange bloke. I never got to know him. He was pretty much aloof. He didn't say much and did not mix. He didn't grow up with a particular team, got into the game late and never really fitted in. But, he could bowl. He was the first of the blokes who bowled this "funny" stuff. He bowled at a brisk pace. Not as quick through the air as Laker, but quick enough to make it difficult for batsmen to get down the track to him. I was lucky to be very swift on my feet. I never tried to pick the direction of spin so I went after him, down the track to hit him on the full or half volley.

'Jack couldn't bat for nuts and was a terrible fieldsman, but he could bowl and I reckon had he been available to tour England in 1953 we would have beaten them easily. I batted against him once when I was playing for Fitzroy and we met in a grade final against Melbourne. How did I fare? I was lucky to have nimble footwork.'

Iverson had eccentric ways, and indeed his cricket bat moved the one-time great leg-spinner and wordsmith Bill 'Tiger' O'Reilly to pen these words:

'Jack Iverson, last man in, arrived on the scene with his old battle-axe bat. This bat, which must be one of the strangest to make an appearance in a Test match, is bolstered by a solid slab of leather bound firmly round the blade. It has the colour of a very old violin. Its handle is so pliable that it was to be twisted in all directions. It must have seen its best days when the owner was a little boy at school. It has been a scrap-heap job for years. But Iverson seldom places much strain on it.'

After this series, Jack Iverson never again played a Test match. He ruled himself out, losing confidence in himself, especially after Arthur Morris and Keith Miller set about flaying him in a Sheffield Shield match. He couldn't come to terms with simply having a bad day. To him a failing was a permanent thing: one failure and to his seemingly tortured mind he was a total failure.

He left cricket as suddenly as he had arrived. He took over from his father managing a real estate agency. He later became an ABC radio commentator for a time. When he reached his early fifties, Iverson developed atherosclerosis of the brain – plaque hardening its arteries. The disease caused him to suffer frequent fits of depression. At the age of fifty-eight, Iverson was found dead in his Brighton home – a spent shell of a .22 calibre rifle lying on his office desk where he had slumped.

*Tim Lane*

In my childhood, Neil Harvey was a name with a magic aura. One of my first cricket memories is of Dad observing that Harvey had made a duck in each innings at Old Trafford in 1956. I seem to recall bursting into tears at the breakfast table and suspect such spontaneous grief was expressed partly at the fact that Jim Laker had destroyed Australia but also because so terrible a fate had befallen an Australian hero.

Years later, when I found a career which brought me into contact with heroes of my past, I discovered Neil to be approachable, generous and candid. This was most evident to me when he became the bogey-man of a world-beating Australian team in the 1990s. Like him, I wasn't always impressed at the bulldozing ways of these great teams and I recall discussing this with him one evening during the Ashes series of 1998/99. It was the fiftieth anniversary of the all-conquering tour of England by Bradman's Invincibles and the survivors had been taken on a national circuit. Before interviewing some of them at a dinner during the Melbourne Test, I talked with Neil about more recent events and saw a look of hurt – bewilderment almost – in his eyes. He said journalists had been asking him for his opinion and he gave it. He hadn't set out to be a critic of the team that was fast becoming the best since 1948, but the players were now seeing him in that light.

He felt there were plenty of other observers who held similar views but that he was the only one prepared to identify himself. He was prepared to call it as he saw it and the backlash hurt him.

Over the years since, even into his nineties, Neil has always been open to a chat. Something I invariably seek to entertain him with is a reminder that he reached his maiden Test century with an all-run five. It was against India in early 1948 at the MCG, and I add knowingly that he was batting with Ray Lindwall. I think he enjoys that.

I know this fact because the story is told in Neil's 1963 autobiography, *My World of Cricket*, which I read in my teenage years. Decades later, while browsing in a second-hand bookshop in Hobart, I spotted another copy of that old book. Upon picking it up I discovered the original owner had hand-written his name inside the back cover: K.R. Miller, Nullaburra Rd, Newport, Sydney. A coincidence like that meant I just had to buy the book and it still sits in my library. The writing of two Australian cricket giants for the price of one.

*Tim Lane, longtime multi-media personality, Test cricket and AFL television and radio commentator and the man who gave Australia the most brilliant broadcast of Cathy Freeman's gold medal run at the Sydney Olympic Games.*

CHAPTER SEVEN

# COME IN SPINNERS

*'Good day, Ram. I hope you will be bowling when I get in. I want to get off the mark with a six.'* – daily greeting from Keith Miller to Sonny Ramadhin

THE WEST INDIAN spin twins Alf Valentine and Sonny Ramadhin took England by storm in the northern summer of 1950 – and they were on their way to Australia.

In England, Valentine, a bespectacled left-arm orthodox spinner who wore an ever-engaging prominent toothy smile, had taken thirty-three Test wickets. Ramadhin, standing just five foot four inches in his socks (that's 162 centimetres, still in his socks), his shirt buttoned to the wrist; there was purpose in the manner in which he approached the crease. On the England Tests Ramadhin had taken twenty-six wickets.

Ramadhin was very much like a dog with a bone when he sensed a kill. He homed in on the batsman with cleverly disguised fizzing off-breaks and leg-spinners, ever ready to pounce. Every now and then he would introduce a little straight ball, for variety. Ramadhin wheeled his right arm in a windmill fashion. His arm was fast and that in itself helped his deception. That his bowling arm came over so fast made it difficult for the batsman to gauge what his hand was doing, and thus which direction the ball was turning.

The Windies were travelling well, for what would be their first tour to Australia in almost two decades. No less than four of the West Indian tourists were included in *Wisden*'s Five Cricketers of the Year that year – Valentine, Ramadhin, Everton Weekes and Frank Worrell. They had beaten England well, 3-1. It was as convincing a victory as it was unexpected.

After his moderate Test series against England the previous summer, Harvey started the international summer of 1951/52 with 18 and 42 in the First Test, in Brisbane. He fell victim both times to the spin duo: Valentine trapped him lbw in the first dig, Ramadhin clean bowled him in the second. Valentine and Ramadhin worried the Australian batsmen and both bagged six wickets for the match, but the First Test of the 1951/52 summer went Australia's way, the margin three wickets.

In the Sydney Second Test Harvey was out relatively cheaply with a double of 39 and 1. Australia won easily by seven wickets, thanks to Lindsay Hassett's 132 and 46 not out and Keith Miller's first-innings 129, plus a good all-round performance by the Australian bowlers.

The West Indians turned things around in the Third Test in Adelaide, winning by six wickets, on a pitch badly affected by rain. Australia was all out for 82 in its first innings (Harvey 10) and the Windies replied with 105. However, a second innings of 255 (Doug Ring top-scoring with 67, Harvey 9), was not enough to prevent a West Indian victory, achieved with four wickets to spare, on Christmas Day.

It is a largely forgotten fact that Test cricket was played on this Christmas Day. It was the first time it had happened, and has happened but three times since.

'Yes, it happened that once against the West Indian,' Neil recalled. 'I was like everyone else in the side. We didn't think too much about Christmas Day. It coincided with a day in the Test. It was within the scheduled Test and quite frankly we didn't care. It was just another cricket day. We didn't know any different. We just went along with what was scheduled.'

It was customary at the time for South Australia to play Queensland in Adelaide in a Shield game on Christmas Day, a custom that extended from the 1920s to the 1960s.

The next Test match played on Christmas Day was also in Adelaide: the first Test against India in 1967/68. Australia won that match by 146 runs, but when questioned years later the Australian players had all forgotten they had played on Christmas Day, Ian Chappell, Bill Lawry, Alan Connolly, Dave Renneberg and captain Bob Simpson among them. That's unusual for Chappelli, who has marvellous recall of events during his time in the game.

It happened again two years later for Bill Lawry's team in the Fifth Test in Madras (now Chennai). Strangely, the day after Christmas Day was a Friday and was deemed the rest day, even though there had been only two days' play. Your author played in that match, and vividly recalls team manager Fred Bennett promising steaks would be flown in from South Africa for a slap-up Christmas dinner after play. That very notion made no sense then nor in hindsight. Anyway we did dine on steak, but I doubt it came from anywhere else but Chennai. A few of us contracted food poisoning. Alan Connolly was particularly crook, so too a few others, including yours truly. Imagine the board sanctioning steaks for us flown all the way from South Africa when our lives were insured for a mere $400. The board couldn't care less about our welfare. Having taken five wickets in both innings in Australia's win there, I rather enjoyed Christmas Day Test cricket.

The last time it happened was in 1972, when England played India in Delhi and hit the winning runs on Christmas Day care of Tony Lewis.

From Adelaide at Christmas Harvey and co. moved on to Melbourne for the new year. There were runs for Harvey in his home town: a brilliant 83 in the first innings, 33 in the second. Despite 102 by Hassett in the second innings Australia looked down for the count when the ninth wicket fell with a further 39 runs required to win. Doug Ring was at the crease with Bill Johnston. Ring hit out boldly while Johnston somehow survived with nicks and nudges, misses and squirts, all the while making rushes to the other end to ensure his partner kept the strike. Ring's 32 not out made him the hero of the hour, and Johnston had the pleasure of the winning run, an inside edge to leg off paceman Gerry Gomez. Australia easily won the Fifth Test by 202 runs, thus taking the series 4-1. Harvey contributed a modest 18 and 8.

Keith Miller made it his business to chide Ramadhin on each morning of a Test match day.

'Good day, Ram,' was the normal opening, 'I hope you will be bowling when I get in. I want to get off the mark with a six.' Good old Miller bluff, but he did fare pretty well against West Indian teams. In ten Tests he scored 801 runs at 53.40 with four hundreds.

Harvey finished the series with a very middling total of 261 runs for the five Tests at an average of 26.10, disappointed, with two so-so summers in a row.

He needed to make amends. And boy did he. Look out South Africa.

*Richie Benaud*

The last thing Harvey was interested in was statistics. Tell him that he was 0.2 behind the tour averages and he would look at you in amazement … provide a challenge for him with the bat and he would accept it faster than you could sight his twinkling feet dancing down the pitch.

Neil was a terrific friend and teammate. He made my job so much easier in his being an ever confident and loyal deputy. I was so confident that he would handle the captaincy well at Lord's in 1961 that I happily gave him free rein.

*Richie Benaud was Australia's charismatic Test captain from 1958/59 to 1962/63. A leg-spinning all-rounder, Benaud played 63 Tests scoring 2201 runs at 24.45 with three centuries and he took 248 wickets at 27.03. He also excelled as a journalist, author and cricket commentator with Channel Nine in Australia and the BBC in England. Benaud was the master of the pregnant pause.*

CHAPTER EIGHT

# SPRINGBOK SURPRISE

*'When are you going to beat that 196?'* – Horace Harvey

As South Africa's best cricketers set sail for Australia on 3 October 1952, few here gave Jack Cheetham's charges much of a chance. They had won just one match in their past 33 Tests while the Australians were a confident, settled side, well led, mighty strong in batting and equally strong in bowling.

'Jack Cheetham was never really a great cricketer, but he was a wonderful leader,' Neil recalled. 'Jack brought out a much-maligned side. Many of the critics were convinced that the South African tour of Australia would be a huge financial flop. The South Africans didn't do well in England in 1951 and it was generally thought that their cricket didn't warrant an Australian tour.'

Cheetham was an engineer and former army officer. He and team manager Ken Viljoen, a veteran of 27 Tests between 1930 and 1949, believed in discipline, and there was no better place for discipline than aboard ship. They figured that fitness was essential to compete against the all-powerful Australians.

So Messrs Cheetham and Viljoen set a tough program, beginning with a daily team meeting from 7.45 am sharp! Then at 11.45 compulsory physical training sessions, designed specifically for the tour by Springbok rugby great and legendary coach Danie Craven. Craven was a top man in his field, having created the physical training division for the South African Defence Force in 1941.

Then there was the fines regime, which was not as bad as it sounds. Fines included a two shilling and sixpence impost for anyone late to a function aboard ship; missing church incurred a one shilling and sixpence fine; those players who turned up anywhere on board without having shaved were fined one shilling; and moving in on a colleague's girlfriend drew the equal heaviest fine, two shillings and sixpence. Cheetham appointed bailiffs to keep tally of the misdemeanours and report them to every daily team meeting.

Discipline was maintained once the ship docked. An 11 pm curfew was imposed. Golf was banned in the days leading up to the First Test match. Cheetham's theory was that hitting a stationary little white ball was poor preparation for trying to negotiate a moving cricket ball.

The discipline did not pay dividends in the First Test. Hassett's men batted first and hit a modest 280. Neil Harvey was the star, hitting a grand 109, before being caught at slip off Michael Melle (6/71), the most experienced of the Springbok fast bowlers, who also included Eddie Fuller, Anton Murray and John Watkins. South Africa responded with 221, Doug Ring snaffling 6/72. Harvey was run out for 52 as Australia managed 277. The combined forces of Ray Lindwall (5/60), Ian Johnson (3/52) and Bill Johnston (2/62) saw Australia win by 96 runs. Neil Harvey looked back to his best.

The Springboks came back strongly in the Second Test at the MCG. Springbok off-spinner Hugh Tayfield, who had for so long tormented various Australian batting line-ups, was more than a handful on turning tracks, and also a master of flight and spin on good, firm wickets – so the MCG track suited him down to the ground. He snared Neil Harvey in both innings, caught Cheetham for 11 in the first dig and caught Watkins for 60 in the second.

Russell Endean turned the match on its head with an unconquered 162 in the South African second innings, but it was left to Tayfield to make the killer blow.

He had already taken 6/84 in the first innings, restricting Australia to 243. One of those wickets was Keith Miller, who had charged down the wicket and lifted him high to square leg. The ball appeared to be heading well over the fence for a huge six; square to the wicket at the MCG is a long, long way. Miller had tossed back his hair in his customary style and wore a big smile as the ball sailed out of sight. Then from nowhere a hand thrust upwards. It was the hand of Russell Endean thrust high and he grabbed the ball as it was about to clear the square-leg boundary fence. As Endean stood on the boundary fence, the ball held high in the right hand of his upstretched arm like some sort of modern take on the Statue of Liberty, Miller stopped in his tracks. There he stood, transfixed; his utter disbelief and dismay was soon overcome with astonishment and admiration.

Tayfield backed up with 7/81. It was a breathtaking performance on a good batting wicket. 'Toey' Tayfield – he had the unusual habit of tapping his right toe at the top of his run just before he moved in to bowl – had won the Test, making it one Test all.

'Hugh Tayfield was the best slow bowler I faced on Australian wickets,' Neil said. 'Tayfield was the backbone of the Springbok bowling throughout the early 1950s until Neil Adcock and Peter Heine, those men of fire and brimstone, came along to help him. He was a grand bowler with superb control of flight and spin. On the turning wickets of England, Jim Laker was easily the toughest to combat, but when Laker came to Australia he struggled and, at times, his bowling was quite innocuous. But in South Africa and Australia, Hugh Tayfield was the best off-spinner of the time.

'His four wickets in the Test in Brisbane cost him plenty (4/116), but his bowling in Melbourne was sensational. He was always hard to hit and he mixed his deliveries cleverly to make the best use of a two-man leg trap.'

Toey's leg trap lured many an Australian to his doom. He had a man at straight mid-wicket, but no more than ten paces from the bat. Standing almost in a straight line with that man was another standing right on the cut portion of the pitch. The idea was to have the batsman drive and any slight misjudgement of length could, and did, result in a low catch to one of the leg traps.

Leading into the Third Test in Sydney, the series was wide open – one win apiece. The South Africans had already proved themselves tougher competitors than expected. Cheetham made sure his players did the basics right – fitness, discipline and fielding, telling his men that 'rarely does a batsman make a Test century without giving at least one chance during his innings'. He placed an emphasis on the importance of good fielding. 'If we field like demons and grab hold of every possible catch, we must stand a chance of bowling these blokes out for a reasonable tally.'

Harvey is full of praise for the South African fielding. 'The biggest factor of all in the wonderful showing of Cheetham's side here was the spectacular, jack-in-the-box fielding of the visitors. During the tour men like Endean, Jackie McGlew and Ken Funston caught some fantastic catches close to the wicket off Tayfield's bowling.'

The crucial Third Test in Sydney saw the Springboks bowled out for 173, Lindwall and Miller sharing seven cheap wickets. Australian began badly with the early loss of Arthur Morris (18) and Lindsay Hassett (2), but then a fighting third wicket stand between Colin McDonald and Harvey righted the ship. McDonald fell for 67 and Harvey was joined by Keith Miller, who scored a typically dashing 55, but Harvey was even more dashing up the other end, as the two shared a partnership of 168. Harvey went on to score 190, a magnificent display of deft footwork, drives, cuts, hooks and pulls. He took the Springbok attack to the cleaners. Australia's 443 was enough to set up an innings victory inside four days, before it was off to Adelaide.

Australia proceeded to hit a mammoth 530 in the first dig – Colin McDonald 154 and Hassett 163. Harvey had to satisfy himself with 84. In the second knock Harvey scored a scintillating 116 – in just 106 minutes. It was the pocket dynamo at his scintillating best, as the Australians batted as fast as they could to allow themselves enough time to bowl out South Africa.

Cheetham's men batted with disciplined doggedness on the last day. Harvey took just three Test wickets with his right-arm off-breaks in his Test career. One of them came this day, Russell Endean clean bowled with a perfectly pitched off-break that curved away slightly, beating the batsman in flight, and then spinning back to hit the middle and off stumps. Australia tried everything on the last day, but Miller could not bowl due to a back injury, nor Lindwall, because of a leg injury, and the match ended in a draw.

The two quicks did not recover in time for the Fifth Test. The score was 2-1 – giving the South Africans the chance to draw the series. In came South Australia medium-fast merchant Geff Noblet, for his third and final Test, and Queenslander Ron Archer, in the first of his nineteen. The Springboks knew they were in with a chance.

Then Australia came out guns blazing, led by Harvey, who amassed 205 runs in just under five hours at the crease. It was, and would remain, his highest Test score. Perhaps just as importantly, it beat Horace Harvey's famous family highest score of 196, made all those years before. 'When are you going to beat that 196?' the old man would say with a smile to his boys. Neil had been hearing the old line since he was seven years old.

As it happened, Neil was not the first in the family to beat 196. A couple of years earlier brother Ray scored 205 for Fitzroy against University. There at the gate to welcome Ray home was Horace Harvey, wearing a huge grin. 'Congratulations, son. I just knew one of you blokes would beat my record … one day.' So now Ray and Neil shared the family highest score.

Australia made 520. Arthur Morris made 99 run out – and there hangs a tale.

Harvey had stroked the ball into the covers and called for a single, which one correspondent on the day wrote 'was not on'. Morris obeyed the call – and was way out of his ground when the Springbok fieldsman pounced. It was described as 'Morris's great sacrifice'.

Meanwhile all eyes were on seventeen-year-old Ian Craig. Earlier that season Craig had become the youngest batsman to score a double century (291) and already he was being hailed as 'the new Bradman'. Here he was now, the youngest player to represent Australia at Test cricket. Harvey and Craig put on a century partnership and the pundits were extolling the 'mature outlook of young Ian Craig'. He followed his neatly compiled 53 in the first innings with a similarly compact 47 in the second innings.

The Springboks scored 435 in their first innings with a long list of contributors. Noblet and Archer struggled. Without Lindwall and Miller, the attack looked decidedly ordinary. Medium-fast merchant Eddie Fuller bowled Australia out (209) in its second innings. Among his victims Neil Harvey, bowled for 7. Set a tough assignment to score 297 runs for victory, Russell Endean (70),

Watkins (50), McLean (76 not out) and Headley Keith (40 not out) saw South Africa home comfortably. Harvey had made a double century, but the Springboks had played magnificently, securing the win and drawing the series. It was a great Springbok victory, like David bouncing out Goliath.

Harvey finished the series with a colossal 834 runs at an average of 92.66 in the five Tests, with four centuries to his name. His tally beat Don Bradman's long-held record of 806 series runs against South Africa in the summer of 1931/32.

Harvey loved playing South Africa: in his ten Tests against them he had hit 1494 runs at an average of 106.71.

There was another of Bradman's records in the offing. Harvey's 1646 runs for the first-class summer so far was the closest anyone had ever come to beating Bradman's long-standing record of 1690 runs for a season.

The last first-class match of the summer was played by the 1953 Australians against WA in Perth. It was the final big match for Lindsay Hassett's men before they departed for England. WA captain Wally Langdon closed the WA innings early on the last afternoon and gave the Australians 10 overs to win. Really it was Langdon giving Harvey the chance of hitting the required 45 runs to break Bradman's all-time record. But Harvey would have none of it. Neil said as he walked out to bat in the second innings, 'I wouldn't want to break a record that way.' He holed out to swing bowler Ray Strauss for 13 and the record stayed with The Don.

So it stood Bradman 1690; Harvey 1659.

While Harvey wasn't interested in getting any records served to him on a platter, Don Bradman never looked a gift horse in the mouth.

In 1930 Bradman needed 46 runs on the last day of the month to complete the coveted achievement of scoring 1000 runs by the end of May. With his score on 28 at tea, the heavens opened up. On any normal day the game would have been abandoned, however, the Hampshire skipper, Lord Tennyson, orchestrated a ploy for Bradman to get the necessary runs. After tea the rain came down in sheets. When Bradman needed just 7 runs to complete his 1000, the players were huddled in the pavilion. The ground was a near quagmire, everything sodden, including the ends of flannels and the players' familiar thick county grey socks. Suddenly the rain stopped dead. With just 7 runs to get, Lord Tennyson winked at his bowler, Newman. The bowler did the right thing, a slow full toss which Bradman thumped to the mid-on boundary. Three to get. The rain began again, heavily. Another Lord Tennyson wink and this time a Newman long hop.

Everyone knew where that one was heading. As the ball crashed over the rope the players bolted for shelter; Bradman got his 1000, just in the nick of time. He wasn't shy in taking advantage of the situation. As for Neil Harvey, as Richie Benaud said, he never cared for statistics.

*Ken Archer*

I have Neil at the top of the tree. He was to my mind a great player, right up there with Len Hutton, Denis Compton, Everton Weekes, Arthur Morris and Keith Miller.

Whenever Neil walked to the wicket at the fall of a fellow opener, he would say, 'G'day mate. Let's get stuck into these blokes – they can't bowl.' Neil was always positive. There was never any negativity about him. His stats were good, but his average would have been vastly better had he not continued his attacking way in the midst of negative tactics, especially the leg-theory tactics Trevor Bailey employed.

*Ken Archer – at the time of writing – is Australian cricket's oldest Test player, some nine months older than Neil Harvey. Ken was an opener and played five Tests, scoring 234 runs at 26 with a highest score of 48. He was a champion baseballer.*

CHAPTER NINE

# BACK TO ENGLAND 1953

*'Trevor Bailey's bowling was absolutely disgusting.'*
– Neil Harvey

LONDON AWOKE TO light rain on Tuesday 2 June 1953, and under the canopy of that early summer's cloudy day thousands of coronation campers bunkered in along the royal route to watch Princess Elizabeth ride in the Gold State Coach from Buckingham Palace to Westminster Abbey to be coronated Queen Elizabeth II.

Hundreds of thousands had slept along the route, under raincoats and blankets, to secure a good viewing spot. The Australian team was fortunate, for they would watch the royal procession sitting together in a temporary stand erected in a prime spot in the Haymarket. The Haymarket is a street in the St James's area of London, within the precinct of the City of Westminster, running from Piccadilly Circus in the north to Pall Mall in the south.

Lindsay Hassett's Australians sat in comfort and watched the coronation procession from start to finish. NSW all-rounder Alan Davidson, one of a number of England tour debutants, including Richie Benaud and the seventeen-year-old Ian Craig, fondly remembers that special day. 'We played a two-day game against

Nottingham at Trent Bridge. The plan was that the captains would agree to a shortened game, so the Australians had time to drive to London and arrive in time to watch the coronation procession.'

Nottingham batted first and captain Reg Simpson scored a solid 60-odd and the ex-South Australian and Test leg-spinner Bruce Dooland scored 49 to help the home side to limp to a total of 208. Australia was 6/290 in reply when the game finished.

The players had to shower, dress and have everything packed and ready for the coach trip to London. This was pre-motorway days in England, so the 130-odd miles from Nottingham to London was a long haul. The coach would have to negotiate narrow lanes and tiny villages en route. Also, with the likes of Hassett, Keith Miller, Bill Johnston and Ray Lindwall aboard, there was always the prospect of regular stops at a variety of public houses on the way.

'We drove all night,' recalled Davidson, 'And we got there on time to be comfortably seated in our brilliant vantage point overlooking the edge of the street in Haymarket.'

It was a perfect vantage point from which to view the procession from close quarters. The princess and soon-to-be queen was borne by the magnificent Gold State Coach. Built by Samuel Butler in 1792, the coach had been used by every British monarch since King George IV. Because of its great age, colossal weight and lack of maneuverability, the coach is used only for coronations, weddings and the jubilee of the monarch.

'The coach passed below almost within touching distance,' Davidson enthused. 'It was fantastic. You could almost have tossed a bouquet right into the laps of the royals in the carriage.'

Hassett's men could plainly see the Queen and the Duke of Edinburgh as the splendid coach rolled past. Princess Elizabeth wore a gown by renowned designer Norman Hartnell, covered in beads and needlework. The rose of England, the thistle of Scotland

and all the other flowers representing Ireland and Wales – all the symbols representing the colonies of the British Empire – were beautifully embroidered on her gown, considered one of the most magnificent creations of the Royal School of Needlework.

The coach was escorted by the Yeoman of the Guard, the household cavalry and the Queen's aides-de-camp. Hundreds of thousands of Britons lined the route. Some 30,000 soldiers featured in the procession. The people cheered, a sea of Union Jacks waved with glee. They reserved a special cheer for World War II hero Field Marshal Viscount Montgomery.

The ceremony over, the players boarded their less salubrious, but possibly more comfortable, coach. They had to drive straight to Hove for the county match against Sussex the next day. Street parties in London abounded. The traffic was horrendous. There was a joy, a gaiety that had not been about in the English capital since the day the war ended eight years earlier.

Hassett's men took hours to get through the crowds. 'And once we got out of greater London and were on our way, I reckon we stopped off at every pub along the way,' Davidson laughed. 'What a great occasion. A day to remember fondly forever.' Neil Harvey then had a match to remember, scoring 82 and an undefeated 137, followed not long after by a double century against Leicester.

The Australians had already had an even closer encounter with royalty, when invited to Buckingham Palace for cocktails in the first weeks of the tour. The coach stopped and the players alighted, wandering in a group through the designated entrance for visitors. Lindsay Hassett noticed Keith Miller had broken formation and began walking down a darkened walkway. There were rumours that Miller had been more than a little friendly with Princess Margaret, even suggestions from some quarters that the couple had enjoyed an intimate liaison.

'Where are you going Nugget?' Hassett enquired.

'Ahem, it's okay, Lindsay. I know of a different entrance here.'

Debonair, with film star looks, war hero and international sports star Miller attracted the ladies. All the young women in England wanted to be with him, and all the young men wanted to be like him. At Arundel Castle in the traditional one-day opening match, Miller's keen eye spotted an attractive young lady playing trombone in the Salvation Army band. Baby of the touring side, seventeen-year-old Ian Craig, was nearby.

'Well then young Craig. See that well-built, attractive brunette over there? I am taking her to dinner tonight.'

'Oh, Keith. You know the girl?'

'Never set eyes on her before now.'

Miller and the Salvation Army band member went to dinner that evening.

Craig was having all manner of trouble adapting to the English conditions while Harvey was scoring runs like they were going out of fashion. During the tea interval of the fourth day of the Second Test, the players of both sides were introduced to the new Queen and the Duke of Edinburgh.

When Hassett introduced Ian Craig to Her Majesty, the Queen asked, 'This is your first England tour, Ian?'

'Yes, ma'am, and if I don't get some runs pretty soon it will be my last.'

The 1953 tour under Hassett was in stark contrast to the 1948 experience under the watchful eye of Don Bradman. Although Hassett was a jovial cove, given to spontaneous public displays of good humour, he could be tough as nails as a captain. In the main, however, Hassett was fun to be with and to be around. The players warmed to Hassett and they roared that night at the Park Lane Hotel in 1953 when a waiter clumsily dumped a hot dish topped with steaming gravy over his jacket and trousers. He called for the head waiter, took off his jacket, then he dropped his trousers: 'These could do with a clean and a press. And make sure they are back here before the dinner ends.' Hassett resumed his seat in a neatly pressed white shirt, black tie and his underpants, his face deadpan.

Harvey enjoyed a bumper harvest of runs in England in that summer of 1953, scoring 2040 runs in 25 first-class matches at an average of 65.80. He hit ten centuries for the summer: 202 not out v Leicester; 109 v Minor Counties at Stoke; 103 v Lancashire; 137 not out v Sussex; 109 v Hampshire; 141 v Gloucester; 118 v Northants; 113 v Surrey and 180 v Glamorgan. Plus 122 v England at Manchester.

Harvey's dashing 180 for Australia against Glamorgan at Swansea was an innings to behold. He thrashed the Glamorgan attack and delighted the crowd, including one Douglas Davies, a staunch cricket lover, of Porthcawl, Glamorgan. In a letter to the *Daily Mail* sixty-seven years later, 23 September 2020, Davies recalled it as 'the finest innings I've ever seen'. And Davies has seen a few, including the time the Australians scored an amazing tally of 721 runs in one day against Essex in 1948, of which Don Bradman hit a quick-fire 187. Davies had a thirty-eight-year long correspondence with Bradman, and was flown to Australia for The Don's memorial service in Adelaide after his death in 2001.

Sir Donald and Lady Jessie Bradman arrived in England on 5 June 1953, where he would write for none other than the said *Daily Mail*, for the not inconsiderable amount of £10,000. In his first piece he predicted a close series with England a '50-50 chance to win the series'.

The first Test at Trent Bridge, Nottingham was a low scoring, dull draw. Weather and some poor cricket conspired to ruin the match, in which Harvey contributed just 0 and 2. Big Alex Bedser had match figures of 14/99, getting Harvey both times, as he did in the next Test, at Lord's.

Australia should have won at Lord's. With England 3/20 at stumps on the fourth day, chasing 343, Australia were a better than even chance. Only a painstakingly slow fifth-wicket stand of 163 by Willy Watson (109) and Trevor Bailey (71) saved the match for England. 'Barnacle' Bailey joined Watson with England at a precarious 4/73 and the pair batted without a skerrick of flair for most of the rest of the day. Their defence was impregnable. Hassett's men threw everything at them. Lindwall, Miller, Johnston, Davidson led the pace attack, while Doug Ring and Richie Benaud provided quality slow stuff. Watson, a dour Yorkshireman who was also a fine footballer, representing England in the 1950 World Cup, took 346 minutes for his 109, while Bailey laboured for 257 minutes over his 71. Bailey too played football, turning out for Walthamstow Avenue amateurs when they drew 1-1 against Manchester United in the fourth round of that year's FA Cup. (United won the replay.) How different it might have been had not Lindwall dropped a sitter off Watson when he was in single figures. The Lord's crowd, not always ready to applaud all-out defence, clapped in a collective frenzy with every Watson or Bailey block as stumps approached. Rain ruined the Third Test at Old Trafford, but not before Neil Harvey scored his only hundred (122) of the series in Australia's first innings of 318. England replied with 276 and the Australians collapsed to be 8/35 when rain had the final say.

The Fourth Test at Leeds left a bad taste in the mouth of the Australians. Australia dismissed England for 167 (Lindwall 5/54) and Australia managed 266 (Harvey 71) before England was dismissed in its second innings for 275. The slow batting of Lord's was catching on: the swashbuckling Denis Compton took almost five hours to make 61 and Bill Edrich a little over four hours for his 64. Bailey was worse still: four hours and twenty-one minutes for 38. Needing 177 runs for victory in two hours, Australia's Arthur Morris (38 in even time) and Neil Harvey (34 in 31 minutes) batted brilliantly, so well that just 66 runs were required in the final forty-five minutes. Then along came the Australians' ogre, Trevor 'Barnacle' Bailey, to England's rescue.

The England all-rounder bowled his medium-pacers from the Kirkstall end. He deliberately speared the ball wide of leg stump and his tactics slowed the game almost to the very point of inertia. The Australians were shocked, disappointed and left believing that a win was denied them by Bailey's tactics, which were, in the least, unsporting and very much against the spirit of the game.

Neil Harvey was livid. 'Trevor Bailey's bowling was absolutely disgusting. He bowled around the wicket to me and speared them diagonally yards down leg side. Godfrey Evans was standing eight feet wide of leg stump taking the ball. If one-day rules were in force they would have been wides. I made 34 in about even time and if they'd've bowled properly, we'd have got them. But they got away with it.' Bailey bowled 6 overs for 9 runs.

Hassett's men joined the Englishmen for a drink after the game, when relations were a little frosty. England wicketkeeper Evans saw the injustice of it all, later saying: 'The Australians, every single one of them, were absolutely livid and I think rightly so. They had been cheated of victory, they said, by the worst kind of negative cricket. They were right.' Bailey's tactics should have been stopped by even the smallest dollop of commonsense by the two umpires, Frank Lee and Frank Chester. Every single Bailey wide one down leg side should have been called a wide.

Neil Harvey reckons Bailey's tactics were 'the worst piece of bad sportsmanship I have seen on the cricket field'.

'He was the most dislikeable bloke on the field,' Neil recalled of Bailey. 'He was one of those pompous, public school blokes, an amateur who didn't mix with the professionals all that well. Yet after he finished playing I got to know him better and he seemed to fit in okay and I found him to be a decent bloke.'

During the 1972 Australian tour of England I was among a few teammates invited to Bailey's house for drinks. There was a giant macaw perched on a stand in the kitchen and there was Bailey, resplendent in a gaudy striped blazer, holding one of those long cigarette holders you see in movies made in the 1930s. As the ash on the cigarette got longer there was mild fascination among our group as to when the ash would fall to the floor and mix with the macaw's scatterings which had spilled over half the area of the kitchen. Yes, Bailey was in pompous form. We didn't stay long. Bailey couldn't say a good word about Australians, past or present.

And so as the players set off for the Fifth Test at The Oval, the score was 0-0. One person who would watch the game on TV, bought like so many others in order to watch the coronation of Queen Elizabeth II, was brilliant British lyricist, writer and poet Tim Rice, at the time an eight-year-old boy. 'When I set eyes on a copy of the 1954 *Wisden*, I felt pretty much as I suspect Keats did on his first reading of Chapman's Homer,' Sir Tim laughed a couple of years back when we spoke in the comfy confines of Adelaide's Intercontinental Hotel when he was in Adelaide for a Test match. Tim once dismissed the great English bat Colin Cowdrey in a charity match. 'The ball took the edge of his bat and was brilliantly caught by Willie Rushton. Colin said later: "I think that was the message that I really should give up."'

Tim would have been disappointed by the first day's play, on which one run was scored before it was washed out. There were even fewer runs scored the next day, the Sunday rest day, but the rest of the match fired his lifelong passion for the game. England knew the wicket would turn late in the game and they had included off-spinner Jim Laker and left-arm spinner Tony Lock. These men knew The Oval wicket like the back of their hand. England picked two specialist spinners while Australia inexplicably failed to pick one. The fast bowlers excelled in Australia's first dig of 275 (Fred Trueman 4/86 and Alec Bedser 3/88), and England replied with 306. Batting a second time, Australia collapsed to the spin of the Surrey twins: Lock 21 overs 9 maidens 5 wickets for 45 runs; Laker 16.3 overs, 3 maidens 4 wickets for 75. The other wicket (Jim de Courcy) was run-out.

Leg-spinner Doug Ring later wrote: 'That last day was so frustrating. The wicket was spinning like a top. A couple of the quicks tried bowling slow. Keith Miller tried his offies, Bill Johnston his left-arm slows, but neither did much. And there we were – Australia's three specialist spinners, Richie Benaud, Jack Hill and me – sitting on the sidelines twiddling our thumbs.'

In the previous two matches the Australians played at The Oval, the wicket was hard and fast, perfect for the faster men and not helping the spinners at all. But the Englishmen knew their onions and they may also have known the groundsman, Bert Flack, who three years later produced that dreadful dust bowl at Old Trafford, perfect for both the Surrey men, Laker and Lock. The Englishmen chased the 132 runs they needed, won the match by eight wickets, taking the series 1-0, and regaining the Ashes after 19 years.

There were three spinners sitting in the dressing-room – and one who was not there at all: Big Jake Iverson. All the good judges reckoned if Iverson had toured the result would have been different. Hassett said that with Iverson Australia would have won matches in a couple of days.

Harvey agrees. 'With big Jake in our attack, we would have cleaned 'em up.'

Most Australians, including Neil Harvey, were amazed to learn that Iverson had accepted an invitation to join a Commonwealth XI, which toured India in the summer of 1953/54. The team played provincial matches and five unofficial Tests. Iverson did extremely well, picking up wickets galore.

In one provincial match, Sam Loxton, who was fielding at short cover, watched from the side as six Iverson deliveries on the trot beat the batsman's outside edge. A little frustrated, Iverson mumbled something along the lines, 'Jeez I'd better give him something he might be able to hit.'

Loxton takes up the story: 'Big Jake announced, "Mr Umpire, I am going to bowl underarm." I thought, "this will be interesting". The players had seen big Jake mucking around with flicking spin, sometimes overarm and sometimes underarm. Jake used to practise these deliveries in the change-rooms, but never before in a match. There was something magical about the manner in which Jake spun a ball. Few batsmen could pick his direction of spin. If they could not do so when he bowled overarm, how would they cope with his underarm special?

'He ran in from a few paces and up she went, high into the air. The fella played forward, it bounced high up on the splice of the bat and popped up in the air to be caught close in by Alan Watkins standing next to me. He put the ball in his pocket and we all walked off.'

The champagne corks may not have been popping in England's favour had Jake Iverson been in Hassett's team. As it was, this was Hassett's last Test, as he was retiring at 40, like his predecessor, Bradman, and unlike Bradman making a humorous speech on the way out. The Fifth Test lost at The Oval was one of only four

Hassett lost as captain of Australia, winning fourteen, drawing six – statistics that support Harvey's view of how good a captain he was.

The year to come would be domestic cricket only – but something larger loomed for Neil Harvey.

*Neil 'Harpo' Marks*

One day, we (Northern District) played Balmain and we batted against mystery spinner John Gleeson. I asked Harv how I should play Gleeson. Harv said: 'Don't let the ball land. Get down the track and hit him on the full or the half volley.' Boy, did Harv give Gleeson a pasting that afternoon.

Even by the mid to late 1960s, a few years after his first-class retirement, Neil Harvey was that good he could have walked into the Australian Test team of the day.

Sometimes he went so far down you had the feeling that he was hitting the ball out of the bowler's hand. Playing against Randwick, Harv jumped down the wicket to their spinner and he mistimed the ball and drove it into his own foot. It flew back over his head to the 'keeper, Barry Wood, before Harv realised what had happened. Wood grabbed the ball and knocked the bails off with the batsman out of his ground. Over a beer later, Harv told a few of us that it was the first time he had been stumped since the game against Worcester on the tour of England in 1953. He then laughed and said, 'And today, what made it worse. I stumped myself.'

*Neil 'Harpo' Marks was an emerging batting star whose first-class career ended after just ten games for NSW when he underwent surgery to fix a congenital heart condition commonly known as a 'hole in the heart'. Harpo became a brilliant writer on sport – short stories, all with side-splitting humour.*

CHAPTER TEN

# OUT OF AFRICA

*'I just love cricket, but I love this cricketer most of all.'*
– newly-wed Iris Harvey

As the SS *Athenic* had steamed its way across the vast stretch of Indian Ocean on its 8300-kilometre voyage from South Africa to Fremantle back in 1950, the then twenty-one-year-old Neil Harvey would have been gazing on the past and dreaming of the future.

Four Test centuries at an average of 106 were one thing, but there was something more on his mind. Neil Harvey held in his mind memories of cruising past the battlefields and bastions of the Boer and Zulu wars, visions of the strange long-tailed widowbirds and white-billed tick birds that seemed to be forever squatting peacefully upon the broad backs of huge oxen. His mind drifted to the Valley of a Thousand Hills, situated in all its rolling glory between Durban and Pietermaritzburg, a feast for the eyes. The huts of the Zulu people were spotlessly clean. Their highly polished ebony floors were magnificent examples of Zulu knowhow. Whites and blacks mingled happily together in the marketplaces of dozens of villages throughout the valley, many lazing in the sun.

The biggest thing that was preying on Harvey's mind was confirmation that the pretty young blond he had met during the Second Test match had sent word of her intention to set sail for Australia that very winter.

They had met in Johannesburg, where Hassett's men were the guests for dinner at the city's favourite dancing venue, the SA Club. Howard Greenish, a longtime member of the Australia-New Zealand Association, persuaded his wife, Peggy, and their sixteen-year-old daughter, Iris, to accompany him to the function.

Let's hear how Iris recalls the evening:

*The dinner was a great success. I can still remember the wit and humour of Lindsay Hassett's speech. The evening progressed very nicely and as more and more toasts were proposed eventually it degenerated into songs and ditties from the Australians, all suitably sanitised for the ladies present.*

*As the evening wound down my father, who was very 'merry', decided to invite some folks home. Because Neil was then a teetotaller, Dad gave him the keys to drive our new Studebaker, and with me as navigator we were to set off for my home and therein lies a tale.*

*The car had no obvious starter button, as most cars did then. It was concealed under the accelerator. While Neil was working this out, with me standing at the open driver's door, one of Johannesburg's finest, a very young inexperienced, Afrikaans policeman, decided we were attempting to steal the car. He asked Neil for his address, decided he was being a 'smart Alec, man' and was about to cart us off to the fearsome police headquarters.*

*Fortunately, my father and mother arrived at this point, and after even more confusion, because my father's Afrikaans was as bad as the policeman's English, we were finally allowed to depart, provided my dad drove.*

*I found out years later this episode had reached the Melbourne papers and my future mother-in-law, the matriarch of the Harvey family, was not amused.*

*My father and mother decided to be among the families to invite an Aussie cricketer home for Christmas. On such small decisions can lives be changed and mine certainly was from there on, because the cricketer we invited home was Neil Harvey and the rest, as they say, is history.*

*Neil invited me to the cricket at Ellis Park in Johannesburg. A special area was set aside for the players' guests and to my acute embarrassment, I found myself seated near a former school mistress of mine, whose husband was in the Transvaal team. Remember this was 1949. I wasn't used to being in such places. She, however, was kindness itself.*

*So began my years of watching cricket, attempting to learn as much as possible from the sidelines. I did, however, and learned how to catch correctly. For example I was only allowed to put the vegetables in with the roast after I had caught them correctly in front of the oven.*

I asked Neil: 'I guess you underarmed the vegetables to Iris?'

'Not necessarily,' he said with a hint of mischief in his voice.

'I tossed them over hand. Iris had to learn to catch 'em. I didn't believe in making this easy. Hard school at the Harveys'.'

Neil and Iris married on 5 February 1954 at Holy Trinity Church, East Melbourne. It was a quiet wedding with only the closest friends and family on hand. Iris wore a gown of white organza, trimmed with guipure lace. After the wedding ceremony, conducted by the Reverend G. Gilder, the reception was held at Ascot House, Essendon, with rather more attendees, among them Test and Victorian teammates Lindsay Hassett and Ian Johnson. From there, the handsome young couple honeymooned in Tasmania.

Mr and Mrs Howard Greenish ('formerly of Johannesburg, South Africa') were happy attendees. Neil's brother Harold was best man and Brian the groomsman, while the matrons of honour were Mrs Alan Twitt and Marcia Benaud, then wife of Richie. The new Mrs Harvey said with a smile: 'I just love cricket, but I love this cricketer most of all.'

*Graeme Pollock*

My first hero was Neil Harvey. Obviously my greatest hero was Don Bradman, but I never saw him play. I heard about Harvey for the first time on radio and read about him in newspaper reports when Jack Cheetham led South Africa in Australia in 1952/53. I saw Harvey play and get a lot of runs against South Africa. In those days teams hardly had any left-handers, so he was quite special. He was a smallish guy, but he used his feet very nicely. He went down the wicket, got on top of the ball and scored his runs quickly. Batsmen who stand out have always been those who've taken it to the bowlers – those are the guys who turn games in a couple of hours. When I rate a batsman, he needs to have those attributes and Harvey certainly had them.

I got to see him live in 1961, when I went to the UK to visit my parents. I also played for Sussex seconds that year. My coach at school in Pretoria, George Cox, was with the county and as a seventeen-year-old, in my first year out of school, I took up the opportunity. I watched the Second Test at Lord's in 1961, when Harvey took over the captaincy because of a shoulder injury to Richie Benaud. He didn't get too many runs, but it was good to see the Aussies beat the English.

I met Harvey for the first time on my first tour of Australia when he led the Prime Minister's XI. I was nineteen and felt awkward about telling him that he was my hero. I was just happy that he was around.

*Graeme Pollock – great South African left-hand batsman. He played just 23 Tests, scoring 2256 runs at an average of 60.97. He scored seven Test centuries with a highest score of 274.*

CHAPTER ELEVEN

# HUTTON v JOHNSON

*'Don't worry Arthur. You stay there even if you don't make another run before Monday.'* – spectator, to Arthur Morris

WHEN THE TWO captains walked to the centre of the Gabba to toss the coin to get the First Test of the 1954/55 Ashes under way, it was a changing of the guard.

England's captain was Len Hutton – a 'professional' in the old parlance. One who made his money playing cricket. No professional had ever captained England before.

Hutton was ever on the move, walking up and down the Test wicket, stopping frequently, bending down on one knee to prod the surface. Hutton called correctly. He continued this inspection before breaking the silence.

'Ian,' Hutton said.

'Yes, Len.'

'You can have a strike!'

Ian was Ian Johnson. He had not even made the touring party for the Ashes series the year before, three spinners being picked before him. Johnson won the Test captaincy over the players' and fans' favourite Keith Miller, as the leader to replace Lindsay Hassett.

Those holier than thou personages on the cricket board deemed Miller too great a risk to hold the captaincy. Arthur Morris was another contender, but he too was looked over. Had a younger man been wanted, it would have been Neil Harvey, but it wasn't to be.

The Test selection committee comprised Sir Donald Bradman, Jack Ryder and Dudley Seddon. The three wise men opted for Johnson, who appeared to be a favourite of Bradman's. Ryder would opt for a Victorian before anyone else. After all, in 1953 Ryder tried to pressgang a Collingwood club spin bowler, who had never played a first-class match in his life, into the Australian team about to leave for England.

Just eight days after his appointment, and two years since his last Test, Johnson was out in the middle, the leader of his team. Whereas Hutton was a professional, Johnson had a little bit of the amateur about him. Hutton was a shrewd captain; Yorkshire born and bred, more than a little stubborn, a man not for giving up. Johnson was a slow off-spinner and down-the-list batsman; not the type of player to win a Test match on his own, but solid and dependable. He kept plugging away with his slow, dipping off-spinners and at times he hit a useful score down the order. He was seen as a usurper by many, who thought the captaincy should have gone to Keith Miller. And if not Miller, then Neil Harvey. But Johnson it was.

Hutton was by nature cautious and reserved. He tended to take his time over almost every decision he had to make. He decided to go into that first Test without a spin bowler. His attack centred on Lancashire stalwart Brian Statham, the indefatigable but now slower and less effective Alec Bedser, medium-pacer all-rounder Trevor Bailey, and the tearaway fast bowler, Frank Tyson. There were three spinners in the squad, two of them good – Johnny Wardle and Bob Appleyard – the other, off-spinner Jim McConnon, not so much. Despite their heroics in spinning England to Ashes glory at

The Oval in the deciding Test in 1953, neither Jim Laker nor Tony Lock were picked for the Australian tour. The last time England went into a Test match in Australia without a recognised spinner was during the Bodyline series of 1932/33 when, in Melbourne, the Australians – thanks to a second innings century by Don Bradman and brilliant bowling by Bill O'Reilly – stormed to a rare Test victory that summer. So Hutton had no choice, really, but to bowl.

To Hutton's horror, Australia promptly piled on 601 runs. The innings ended with a declaration, eight wickets down.

Neil Harvey and Arthur Morris had a long, productive partnership. They dug in stoically at times and flayed the attack intermittently, hitting 202 runs in 232 minutes for the third wicket. Normally a free-scoring stroke-maker, Morris was unusually subdued. AG 'Johnnie' Moyes, then the doyen of the Australian media, wrote of Morris's slow going: 'One dear old soul called out, "Don't worry Arthur. You stay there even if you don't make another run before Monday." And a tough, old cattleman replied, "Good gracious, Mum! Don't make it Monday. Let him get another one tomorrow, as we wouldn't be here after the weekend."'

Morris eventually shrugged off his defensive mode and began to play his shots. He even outshone the normally free-hitting Harvey, whose nimble footwork became increasingly apparent as he began to hook, drive and cut with his usual flair.

The Englishmen were sluggish in the field. They dropped at least twelve catches, six of them off the tireless Alec Bedser, who finished with 1/131 off 37 overs. Bedser had a bad rash that covered almost the entire length and width of his broad back. He was later diagnosed with shingles and this serious health episode would ruin his Australian tour.

Morris eventually fell to the medium pace of Trevor Bailey, out for 153 made in 419 minutes. He hit eighteen fours and two sixes.

Once Harvey brought up his first Test century against England in Australia, he continued to attack grandly. As Moyes put it: 'Harvey was now in tremendous form and cover hit and drove with atomic power.'

Harvey eventually fell for 162, caught at slip by Colin Cowdrey off Bedser. The explosive left-hander had occupied the crease for 380 minutes, caressing and smiting seventeen fours. Australia won easily by an innings, and England limped away from the Gabba in seeming disarray.

Hutton remained confident. He believed in his fast bowlers. Immediately after the Brisbane debacle the England team wandered back to the team's base, Lennon's Hotel, in the heart of the city. Hutton called for champagne all round. 'Don't worry,' he said. 'We may have lost this Test match, but we are going to beat them. This is the first time I've ever been with an English side where we have the quicker bowlers.'

Johnson was later generous in describing Hutton's error at the toss.

Johnson did hand his English adversary some slack, saying that Hutton's choice in batting first wasn't so bad a decision after all, for in the previous games at the Gabba that early summer the wicket was generally hard and fast and was expected to be even quicker by the time of the First Test match.

In the long run, Hutton was right. His fast bowlers prevailed. Tyson did indeed bowl like a typhoon, bowling his team to victory in the next Test in Sydney – the one I was lucky to attend with my grandfather, where Harvey made that undefeated 92, running out of partners.

After routing Australia in Sydney, Tyson then blitzed Australia on a dodgy MCG wicket. He reckoned that the toughest batsman to dismiss among the Australians was Harvey. 'You always knew that if you didn't get him out early, he'd soon hurt you on the scoreboard. People labelled him a great player of spin, which he was, but he was also a very sound player against everyone else.'

Hutton rotated his fast bowlers shrewdly and ensured that the Australians didn't receive too many balls per hour. In fact, the trio of Tyson, Statham and Bailey rarely bowled more than 12 eight-ball overs per hour. As Tyson pointed out: 'The ploy slowed the run rate down tremendously. I remember chatting to Bill Johnston about it one day and he said how the cricket was dull because of the diminished over rate. "But, Bill," I said to him, "we got you out!"'

England won the Second, Third and Fourth Tests to deservedly take the series 3-1.

After his brilliant batting in the first two Tests, Harvey had a lean run in the final three – 31 and 11 at the MCG; 25 and 7 in Adelaide and 13 and 1 in the SCG Fifth Test. In five Tests Harvey had scored a total of 354 runs at 44.25.

There was no time to rest: a tour of the West Indies beckoned.

*Ray Illingworth*

One of my first meetings with Neil was at Sheffield in 1953 when Yorkshire were hosting the touring Australians. I was young, in my twenties, and only just established in the Yorkshire side, when I was taught a very valuable cricketing lesson. Early in my innings I pushed the ball towards extra cover and confidently called for a quick single. I had only just passed my partner halfway down the wicket when the ball whistled past and narrowly missed the stumps at the bowler's end. I made a mental note that would benefit me well over my career: remember just how quick Neil was over the ground, how good his arm was and never to risk a quick single if the ball was within 10 yards of him.

The second time I witnessed Neil's phenomenal fielding skills was during the Fifth Ashes Test in Sydney in 1963. I was opening the batting with the Reverend David Sheppard in the second innings and although I was out pretty early, we were going well, comfortably passing the 100 mark, before Neil produced another piece of magic. I remember the Reverend playing a decent drive off Richie Benaud out towards extra cover and although it was maybe a foot or so off the ground thinking to myself that's going to be four. Sadly for the Reverend, the next thing I saw was Neil take off and flying through the air to intercept the ball and take a stunning one-handed, full-length diving catch.

With our latter years I have had the pleasure of catching up with Neil on several occasions, usually during the Ashes tours and generally every four years or so at Lord's.

Neil captained his country for the only time in the Second Test at Lord's in 1961. Neil started the series in good form with a hundred in the first drawn Test and was the obvious choice to replace the injured Richie Benaud as captain at Lord's. On a seamer-friendly pitch with runs hard to come by, the Australians, with a big first innings lead, required just 71 runs in their second innings to win the game. It should have been straightforward, but a hostile opening spell from Brian Statham and Fred Trueman, it was game on with Australia reeling at 4/19 and then 5/58, before they got over the line to leave a somewhat sweaty and nervous Neil with a 100 per cent winning record as captain.

This memory reminded me of everything great about Neil – he was a truly great player with a fantastic record and a seriously tough opponent, who played the game aggressively and hard, but always in the right spirit. He was and still is a great man and I look forward to the next time we can share another drink and reminisce over many great memories.

*Ray Illingworth was a great England captain and a top-class all-rounder for Yorkshire and England. In 61 Tests he scored 1853 runs at 23.24 with two centuries and he took 122 wickets at 31.20 with his accurate off-spinners with a best innings bowling performance of 7/29.*

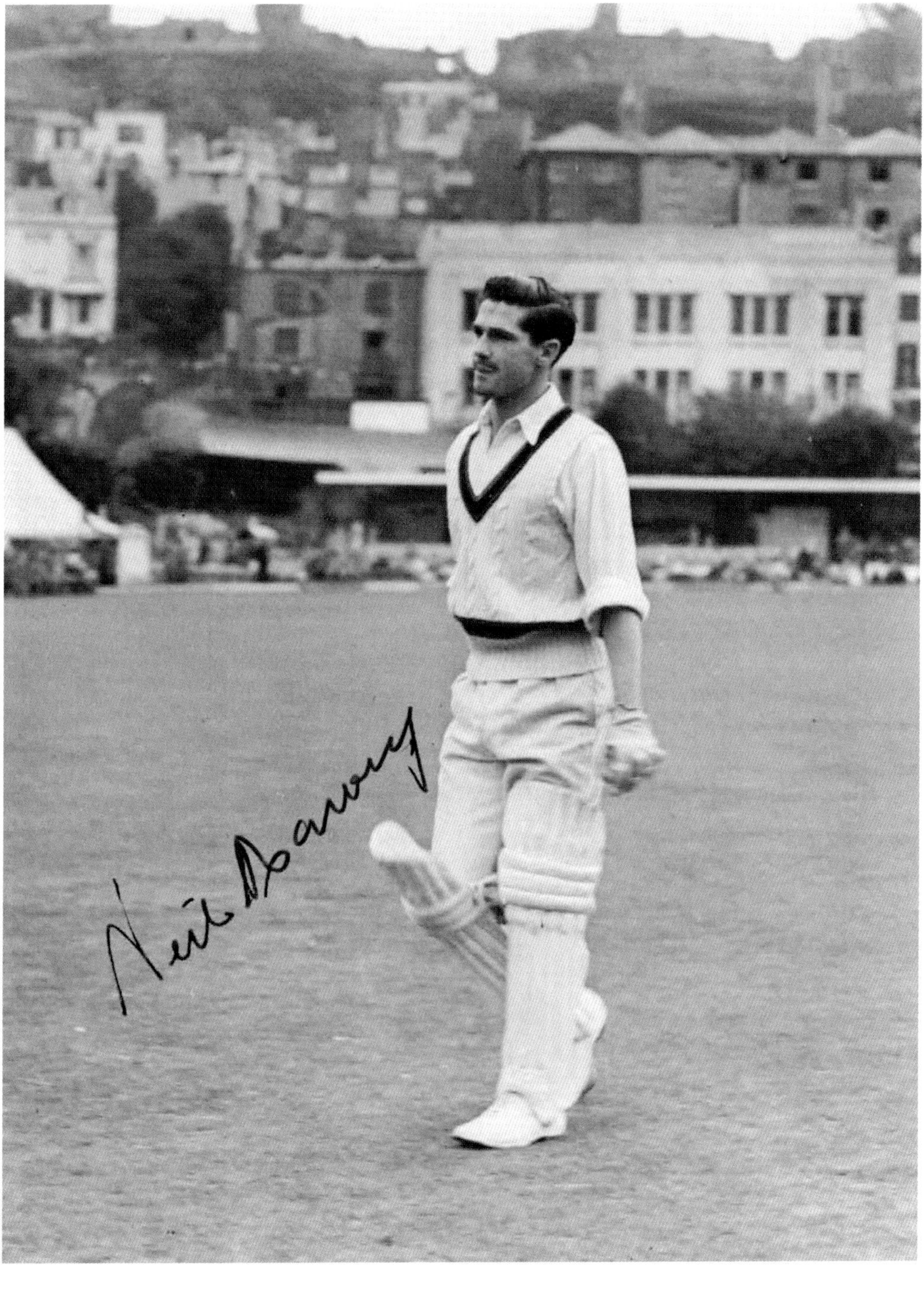

Neil Harvey completes the last of his four centuries with 110 versus South of England at Hastings in 1948.

IMAGE: Ronald Cardwell collection

IMAGES: Ronald Cardwell collection (top left); Popperfoto/Getty Images (bottom left); private collection (top right); Lindsay Hassett collection (bottom right)

TOP LEFT: Sam Loxton rushes to congratulate Neil Harvey on his brilliant 112 in the Leeds Fourth Test, 1948. Jim Laker (in background) applauds his young rival.

BOTTOM LEFT: The Australian cricket team on 28 April 1948. Back row, left to right: Ian Johnson, Arthur Morris, Ernie Toshack, Keith Miller, Don Tallon, Ray Lindwall and Neil Harvey; front row, left to right: Bill Brown, Lindsay Hassett, Don Bradman, Colin McCool and Sid Barnes.

TOP RIGHT: Lindsay Hassett's 1953 Australian team arrives in London. Front row from left: Alan Davidson, Keith Miller, Neil Harvey, George Davies, Lindsay Hassett, Don Tallon and Ray Lindwall.

BOTTOM RIGHT: Lindsay Hassett (left) and Neil Harvey chat with old-time champion leg spinner and newspaper columnist Arthur Mailey on the 1953 tour.

TOP: Neil Harvey hits England left-arm spinner Tony Lock for four during his first innings score of 36 in the Fifth Test at The Oval in 1953; Lock got his revenge second innings, clean bowling Harvey for 1.

BOTTOM: Neil Harvey and Iris Greenish on their wedding day in February 1954.

IMAGES: private collection

TOP: Neil Harvey – baby of the 1948 team, Bradman's Invincibles – was at twenty-eight the oldest player in the Ian Craig-led Australian team to New Zealand in 1957. Norm O'Neill (pictured back row, second from left) was the youngest at nineteen. Harvey topped the runs aggregate with 448 at 49.27.

BOTTOM: The Australian cricket team, England 1961. Captain Richie Benaud and vice-captain Neil Harvey flank the team manager, Sid Webb (front row).

IMAGES: private collection (this page, bottom right page, last page); Malcolm Linke collection (top right)

TOP: Neil Harvey leads Australia in the 1961 Second Test at Lord's – his first Test match as captain. To his right are Wally Grout and Norm O'Neill, behind him is Peter Burge.

BOTTOM LEFT: Neil Harvey in his final Test Series versus England in Australia, 1962/63.

BOTTOM RIGHT: Harvey bowled Brian Statham 39, First Test Australia versus England, Gabba 1962/63.

TOP: Neil Harvey (left) joins the old guard, Jack Ryder (centre) and Sir Donald Bradman, as one of the three Test selectors in the summer of 1967/68.

BOTTOM: Neil Harvey (centre) and Richie Benaud have 'started early' during a reunion of Test players who have toured England with an Australian Test side.

RIGHT: A special day for Neil Harvey and his children, celebrating the unveiling of his statue at the MCG in 2014. From left: Bruce, Neil, Anne and Robert Harvey.

LEFT: Happy times for the Harveys – Neil and Barbara are all smiles.

BOTTOM: Some grand old hands get together on Sydney Harbour. Back row, from left: Lindsay Kline, Colin McDonald, Graham McKenzie, Frank Mission, Neil Harvey. Front row, from left: Brian Booth, Bob Simpson, Barry Jarman, Alan Davidson and Richie Benaud.

CHAPTER TWELVE

# WINDIES PUT TO THE SWORD

*'Johnno, you couldn't captain a team of schoolboys.'*
– Keith Miller to Ian Johnson

BARELY TWO WEEKS after this torrid Ashes series, Ian Johnson's team left Sydney's Kingsford Smith Airport on their epic fifty-four-hour journey to Kingston, Jamaica.

Their route went thus: Fiji, Canton Island, Honolulu, San Francisco, Vancouver, Calgary, Regina, Winnipeg, Toronto, Nassau and Montego Bay, Jamaica. Phew! That's six different nations, with a stop in Kiribati and five stops in Canada.

It was approaching midnight on the third day out from Sydney when the tourists disembarked at Palisadoes Airport in Kingston, Jamaica, and were driven around the harbour. They drove through the dimly lit streets of Captain Morgan Town, past his old pirate stronghold, Port Royal, and on to the fashionable Courtleigh Manor Hotel.

From the moment of his arrival in the Caribbean, Ian Johnson's mood changed dramatically. He reckoned his men were dispirited and demoralised in the wake of the Tyson-Statham attack

Down Under. He thought the England pair's assault had played with his batsmen's minds. While most of his men were still sleeping off jet lag from the flight from Australia, Johnson went to the hotel pool for an early morning dip.

He had already scanned the newspaper left outside his hotel room door and read an article entitled 'Aussies favoured for Tests'. George Hedley, the legendary West Indian batsman of the 1930s who was dubbed the 'Black Bradman' and was now the chairman of the Windies' Test selection committee, was quoted predicting an Australian series win. 'Australia will win because it will establish a moral ascendancy and hold it.' Johnson could hardly believe his eyes.

At the side of the pool chatting animatedly were a number of Australian pressmen. Johnson put a question to them: 'How long is it since an Australian cricket side received real discipline from its captain?' Keith Butler of Adelaide's *Advertiser* fired back: 'You should know, Johnno, you played under Bradman.'

'I'm talking about *real* discipline, the kind you get at public schools. That's what my team is about to get right now.'

Butler and his fellow scribes wondered how the team would react, especially the old hands and more especially Keith Miller. Johnson set the tone: 'We will practise for three hours every morning and afternoon leading up to the Jamaican game in three days.'

Shortly after, Miller bumped into the reporter Butler in a corridor of the hotel: 'What's Johnno up to, Stemmy? Three hours training morning and afternoon. They say the afternoon temperature is 100 degrees in the shade. He can't be serious.'

'Keith, you'd better believe it. He is serious.'

True to his word, Johnson drilled his men in the nets like a regimental sergeant major. Initially just about every man in the squad resented Johnson's strategy. Resentment subsided somewhat when the players found they felt fitter, stronger and ready to take on the might of the Windies. When Arthur Morris and Colin McDonald were about to take the field at the top of the Australian batting order in the First Test, Johnson said loudly: 'As Horatio Nelson flagged to his fleet off Cape Trafalgar in 1805, "England expects that every man will do his duty!"' The two openers exchanged glances before leaving the dressing-room. They got the message. The public school–educated Ian Johnson was well pleased by the time his opening pair had put on 150 by mid-afternoon.

After Johnson's seeming bizarre behaviour in the days leading up to the first Jamaican tour match, there was no love lost between him and Miller. Johnson, however, was winning over the West Indians.

Ian Johnson raised more than a few eyebrows when he first arrived in the Caribbean. He had the famous run-in with Keith Miller; however, Johnson stuck to his guns. Team discipline was his go, and more than that was his aim to win the hearts and minds of the West Indian people. Johnson's diplomacy won through. There was one particular gesture that struck a chord: as the Australians walked off after ending an innings at Sabina Park, a bunch of barefooted local urchins ran onto the field to meet them. Johnson didn't brush past the boys, but stopped to gather up a toddler in his arms and, sporting a wide grin, he talked to the boy as he carried him from the field. The Jamaicans loved every second of Johnson's action. They were delighted. They sang and clapped and danced with joy. Never before had the Caribbean media known a more cooperative visiting Test captain.

But Johnson's demanding tone as captain on the field did not sit well with some of his men, especially Miller. During one stint Miller was operating in a crosswind, bowling medium-paced swingers, and took two wickets in one over. Yet Johnson went to Miller and in an angry voice told him, 'I want some speed!'

Those terse words led to an inevitable confrontation between the pair as they engaged in a stand-up argument on the field of play. Johnson stood by his demand. 'I'll say who bowls and what they bowl … if I throw you the ball will you throw it back?' Johnson immediately took Miller out of the attack and threw the ball to Ray Lindwall. As the players wandered off the field at the close of play, Miller was muttering under his breath. Although these words were clearly heard: 'Johnno, you couldn't captain a team of schoolboys.' Johnson threatened to 'knock your block off' in a challenge with Miller to a punch-up behind the grandstand. Happily they simmered down and never came to blows.

Harvey said he believed the Australian Cricket Board of Control for International Cricket believed 'diplomacy came first for this tour. That's why Johnson was retained as the Australian captain. He wasn't the greatest player or the best strategist in his rotation of bowlers and the setting of fields. However, we had a great rapport with the West Indian fans. In three and a half months in the Caribbean, unlike the Englishmen a year earlier, there was not a single incident.'

The Australians won the hearts and minds of the fans by playing exciting cricket in the same sort of happy, attacking way of their hosts. 'They gave us a grand time wherever we went. Their hospitality was overwhelming to the point of being embarrassing,' Neil enthused. But there was work to be done: 'If we lost this series our cricket stocks would have slumped far lower than they had ever been. We started the tour determined to make a good showing. Our batsmen had failed before the speed of Tyson and Statham on our home wickets.'

Harvey carved 133 in the First Test at Sabina Park, Kingston, and Keith Miller showed all his old flair in hitting 147. Australia scored 515 and bowled the Windies out twice for moderate scores in their two innings.

Clyde Walcott got 108 in the West Indian first dig and Collie Smith, the dashing all-rounder, hit a blazing 104 in the second innings.

There were Australian runs aplenty in the Second Test at Queen's Park Port-of-Spain with Colin McDonald (110), Arthur Morris (111) and Neil Harvey (133) scoring centuries. The match was drawn, thanks to great resistance from Clyde Walcott (126) and Everton Weekes (139) in the Windies' first innings. Walcott completed the double with a resolute 110 in the second dig. Weekes was unconquered on 87.

In the Third Test at Georgetown, Harvey fell for just 38, caught off the bowling of Sonny Ramadhin, the spin bowler who had troubled him in the past. He scored 41 not out in the second innings as Australia won the Test by eight wickets. Ian Johnson took 7/44 with his off-breaks to shatter the Windies' second innings.

Thanks to a long, arduous world-record 347-run seventh-wicket partnership between Dennis Atkinson (219) and Clairmonte Depeiaza (122), the Windies drew the Fourth Test. Harvey scored 74 and 27, which also saw Ray Lindwall score 118 and Keith Miller a grand 137.

Harvey had such a brilliant run of big scores that it seemed the law of averages might decree a rare failure in the Fifth Test at Sabina Park. To the contrary – Harvey hit a brilliant 204. All his brilliance was on display.

His getting down the track to the spinners delighted all and sundry. The constant hum of the crowd and the thrill of the steel bands complemented Harvey's shots all round the wicket. Miller and Ron Archer both hit centuries, but this was Harvey's day.

He was on 162 at lunch on the second day when a local planter, Douglas Vaughn, offered him ten shillings a run if he could go on and beat Len Hutton's record Test score of 364. But Harvey had batted for more than seven hours and he said: 'Won't be doing that, it's too hot. I'll be playing my shots, not grinding it out.' And he did, reaching 204 before he holed out to mid-wicket.

'I didn't feel like hanging around after I passed the 200 mark. A very careless swish saw me holing out to Collie Smith when I was just two runs short of Arthur Morris's Test record for a left-hander of 206.'

Neil Harvey was never besotted with figures. Some players are, but the Neil Harveys of this world reckon a good 70 on a dodgy track against the best bowling was always a better and more satisfying innings that belting average bowling about on a feather-bed wicket. After his brilliant 204 in the Fifth Test, Harvey finished the series with 650 runs at an average of 108.33 in six completed Test match innings. He was now undoubtedly one of the world's best batsmen, one whom many fans the world over loved watching bat.

Aged 26, Harvey still retained that exuberance of youth in his stroke-play and his footwork. At cover he was like a Jack Russell on the hunt: fast across the turf with a lightning pick-up and unerring throw, right into the keeper's gloves just above the bails.

During the series Harvey got to see first-hand the brilliance of newcomer Collie Smith. An attacking right-hand batsman and useful off-spinner, Smith was earmarked to become as good as the Three Ws – Clyde Walcott, Frank Worrell and Everton Weekes. Then in 1959, while playing in the Lancashire League, tragedy struck. Collie Smith was killed in a car crash on a dual motorway near Staffordshire. Garry Sobers was driving Smith and medium-pacer Tom Dewdney to play in a charity match when the car plummeted into a truck.

'Collie Smith was a fine attacking player,' Neil said. 'He learned his cricket at the Boys' Town Centre in Kingston on pitches that were rough and uneven, but he learned his cricket lessons very well. It was a great pity that he didn't live long enough to show his wares to Australian crowds. They would have loved his vigorous approach to the game.'

Harvey had taken a shine to the Caribbean, the weather, the friendliness of the people, the hard, bouncy wickets and the way West Indians played attacking cricket. He loved playing cricket in the Caribbean. He loved the people, the atmosphere in the towns and cities and the joy and enthusiasm of the spectators at the big matches.

'Of all the cricketing countries in the world there is none quite like the West Indies,' Neil recalls. 'Cricket in the Caribbean is one long, unbroken calypso of spontaneous excitement. We got on famously with the West Indian players. Denis Atkinson, who was the Windies' vice-captain for the series, was most considerate. He used to loan us his Mayflower car and took various members of the side on fishing excursions in his little outboard motorboat. Mind you we did see rather too much of him during that 347-run partnership with Clairmonte Depeiaza in the Fourth Test.'

Thanks to mainly Harvey and Miller, the twin spin threat of Sonny Ramadhin and Alf Valentine was largely tamed in the Caribbean. After their resounding success in Australia just four years earlier, Neil was amazed how little impact they had on the 1955 series on their home wickets.

'Sonny was hard to read when John Goddard's side was in Australia four years earlier. He bowled with his shirtsleeves buttoned at the wrist and he had a fast arm. But this time in the Windies he was not the same bowler.

'We Australians scored twelve centuries in the Test series and the West Indians, nine. Miller hit three hundreds, so did yours truly, Colin McDonald hit two centuries and there was one century apiece to Arthur Morris, Richie Benaud, Ray Lindwall and Ron Archer. Our tour was excellent. We won three of the five Tests – two draws – and we went through the tour undefeated. Clyde Walcott hit five centuries for the Windies.'

Harvey thought there was one major contributing factor to the Australians' resounding batting success.

'This was before Wes Hall, Chester Watson and co. emerged on the Test scene. The Windies had one genuine fast bowler in Frank King. He was fast all right, but he was not a clever bowler. King bowled with more brawn than brain. He had a penchant for bowling bouncers at our heads. He telegraphed his bouncer and more often than not he bowled too short to worry us. I remember batting against him in one Test when he bounced one at me so short that it hit the fence behind the wicketkeeper on the first bounce. I didn't even have to duck and the wicketkeeper standing about twenty yards back couldn't have reached it with a step ladder.

'So apart from the erratic, bouncer-happy fast Frank King, the West Indian attack was pretty pedestrian. All the same we played well and deserved our success.'

While Neil was on the boat back from the Caribbean on the SS *Rangitane,* his and Iris's first child, Robert, was born.

*Ian Chappell*

My father, Martin, told me how good a cricketer Neil Harvey happened to be. He also thought Harvey a magnificent baseballer, having played for SA against Harvey in the 1947 Claxton Shield held in Adelaide. As a batsman Neil was all class, neat in his footwork and with time against the fast bowlers. His footwork against the slow bowlers was a joy to watch. For much of my playing career Harvey was one of the three Australian selectors. In the period when he joined Phil Ridings (chairman) and Sam Loxton, Neil was by far the most knowledgeable of the trio, cricket-wise. His thinking on the game was simple and uncomplicated; you scored runs as quickly as possible and bowled to take wickets, not contain the opposition. In a move that surprised me I was appointed captain when he was on the panel with Bradman and Loxton. Years later, after a round of golf and over a beer, Neil told me the full story.

*Ian Chappell was arguably the greatest Australian Test cricket captain. An attacking batsman, useful leg-spinner and brilliant fieldsman at first slip, Chappell was not unlike Harvey as a leader, for his players loved playing under his attacking captaincy.*

CHAPTER THIRTEEN

# ASHES 1956: HOME SPUN FLACK

*'I does what I'se told. Makes the kind of wicket they wants. The Press gives me hell and then I has to clean the bloody papers off the ground.'* – Bert Flack, curator, Old Trafford, 1956

THE AUSTRALIAN TEAM to tour England in 1956 contained, for the first time, a West Australian, John Rutherford – but only just, and helped along by the intercession of one Neil Harvey.

Ian Johnson's team was scheduled to play two first-class matches in Tasmania before the party sailed to Fremantle. The board thought it would save a penny by leaving Rutherford out of those games, and letting the ship pick him up in Fremantle. Rutherford, naturally, insisted upon being part of the tour proper. 'I am joining the Test touring party in Hobart,' he told any official within cooee. He went above the board secretary's head, contacting tour captain Ian Johnson and board chairman Sir Donald Bradman. Johnson and Bradman were sympathetic to his cause and Rutherford flew to Hobart, ready and willing to play a match. However, when he arrived he received a cool reception, copping a thunderous dressing-down from board chairman Frank Cush.

'You are not supposed to be here, Rutherford,' he demanded. 'You must go back to your home state. You may join the party in Fremantle.' Rutherford stood his ground.

'I am part of the Australian eleven. And I can assure you, Mr Cush, I intend to stay and join the side here.'

'But you can't, Rutherford. The hotel is booked out.'

Luckily for John, Harvey overheard the conversation, and a sense of outrage enveloped him. 'Don't worry, John, it is okay. You can come in with me and Lenny Maddocks. We will order another bed.' Years later Rutherford – who had played cricket alongside Bob Hawke for the WA University first XI – coached me and Terry Jenner, and told us that story after training one night.

During the long voyage on the P&O liner *Himalaya*, vice-skipper Keith Miller made it his business to learn as much as he could about the newcomers in the team. He was intrigued to discover that John Rutherford possessed science and mathematics degrees from the University of WA. Rutherford recalled the day: 'We were on the bridge one day and someone said, "I wonder how far it is to the horizon." So I pulled out my traveller's cheques, drew a triangle estimating that we were about 160 feet above sea level and worked out that the horizon was about eleven miles from where we stood.

'Keith Miller said, "How'd you work that out?"

'And I said, "Well, I just used Pythagoras's theorem."

'"Good Lord," said Miller, "Pythagoras walks among us."'

It was Rutherford's dream to play Test cricket, and he got to play one Test, in Bombay (now Mumbai) against India on the trip home, batting once and making 30.

On the England tour he scored just 630 runs at an average below 23, suffering a lot of bad luck, as if he had crossed a black cat. Indeed, while batting against the Marylebone Cricket Club at

Lord's, where he made 98 while Harvey made 225 up the other end, he saw a black cat. 'When Neil had scored his 200 he came up to me and said, "See that cat over there ... I am going to see if I can hit it." The very next ball, Neil stepped back to a ball pitched on the line of leg stump and cut it ... missing the black cat by a whisker.' I quizzed Neil. 'Don't know anything about it,' he laughed.

From 1952 to 1964 there was indeed a black cat that lived at Lord's Cricket Ground. He was called Peter. Peter had the habit of roaming the Lord's outfield while play was underway. He loved the spotlight and was often found purring to his heart's content in front of the television cameras. Amazingly though not *one* photograph of the famous Marylebone mog has ever been uncovered in either the Lord's Pavilion or nearby Lord's Museum. Peter even got an obituary in *Wisden*: 'CAT, Peter, whose ninth life ended on November 5, 1964, was a well-known cricket watcher at Lord's.'

Most of the team believed Miller should have led the 1956 Australian team in England. Pat Crawford, the NSW pace bowler who played one Ashes Test on this tour, was candid. 'Johnson couldn't get anything out of the players, whereas all of the guys would have busted a gut for Keith.'

Alan Davidson said Johnson relied too heavily on the older players. 'He was still trying to lead from the front, but he wasn't up to it. I guess he was trying to help us, but he should have realised that guys like (Richie) Benaud, (Ron) Archer, Ian (Craig) and me had toured in 1953 and we were not as wet behind the ears as he thought we were.'

Harvey and Benaud were roommates on tour. They resented Johnson's insistence that the whole touring party (seventeen players) attend all matches before the first Test. That decision meant that no-one in the Australian touring squad had a break from cricket in seven weeks.

Johnson was turning into some sort of modern-day Captain Bligh: intractable, resolute, unyielding, and stubborn to the point of manic decision-making. For all that, he was cock-a-hoop with his team's performance in the first two Test matches – a draw at Nottingham and a splendid victory at Lord's. There in the Second Test Keith Miller took a match haul of 10/152 and Richie Benaud hit a blazing 97. The team was bristling with confidence.

Harvey had a poor runs return at Lord's (0 and 10) in that dreadful summer of 1956 for the Australian team. But all was not lost on the fans. As Neil and captain Ian Johnson walked to the team's cars at the back of the main pavilion of that hallowed ground, the gun left-hander probably looked a little 'down'. Then out of the blue, a little old lady sidled up to the Australian pair and said to Neil: 'Never mind this match, young man. You are a beautiful cricketer. I saw your first innings in a Test match in this country at Leeds in 1948, and anyone who can bat in such a lovely way must be a great batsman.'

The old lady was right. You must not always measure greatness by the record book.

Four leading cricket writers covering the series – Brian Chapman (*Daily Mirror*), Crawford White (*News Chronicle*), Charles Bray (*Daily Herald*) and Jack Fingleton (*Sunday Times*) – strongly advised Johnson to stand aside and allow Miller to lead the team in the remaining Test matches. He did not take their advice.

Australia may have just won a Test, but it had won only two county matches – against the lowly varsity teams, Cambridge and Oxford. There were lingering questions about Johnson's team batting against high-quality spin bowling – questions care of Jim Laker, who had taken all ten Australian wickets for Surrey at The Oval. His 10/88 ensured a Surrey victory, the first win by any county over an Australian touring team since 1912. Johnson's high-floating spinning deliveries were not as successful: he took 6/168 off 60.3 overs in the Surrey game.

'Gubby' Allen, the respected ex-player, former captain and selector and the man who stood up to Douglas Jardine in the 1932/33 series in Australia refusing point blank to bowl Bodyline, believed England was going to win the 1956 series easily. He was so confident that he had made dozens of bets to that effect.

Even after Miller had blitzed the England batting to help Australia win the Lord's Second Test match, Gubby was adamant that England would win the series. Soon after that a curious Dick Whitington sidled up to Gubby.

'You must be worried, old man,' he said.

'Worried? Of course not. You (Australia) won't win a Test up north,' he said. 'England will be leading two-one when you get back to The Oval (Fifth Test match).'

'What makes you say that, Gubby?'

'You won't get another wicket like this one at Lord's, not at Headingley and Old Trafford.'

Harvey also vividly recalled that immediately after Australia had claimed victory in the Lord's Test, the England captain, Peter May, told him: 'Well, Neil, that (Lord's) is the last pitch you'll see like that on this tour.'

Plus, two Australians, Jock Livingston and George Tribe, then playing for Northants, told Johnson that May had informed the Northants county administration that they should rest fast bowler Frank Tyson as 'from now on England will be top heavy with spinners'.

So perhaps no-one should have been surprised with Headingley's spin-friendly turner at Leeds. Jim Laker and Tony Lock ran amok. Laker took 5/58 and 6/55 while Lock bagged 4/41 and 3/40, making for an innings victory. By contrast, Johnson bowled 29 overs to take 1/59. With the bat he scored 0 and 3. In Australia's paltry second innings total of 140, Neil Harvey scored a brilliant 69, before he chipped one back to Lock.

And so to Old Trafford, Manchester, where the curator knew his onions.

Bert Flack could prepare any type of wicket. Flack was told to shave all the grass off the pitch. His further instruction was to ensure that the surface had a sufficient coating of marl – heavy black dirt that turned to mud in the wet and powdery dust in the sun. There would be nothing so luxurious as one single blade of grass. Not on your nelly. Flack was completely at ease preparing a wicket to instruction. There was not the hint of embarrassment or guilt in the man. He seemingly had a hide as thick as an elephant and some reckoned the man was thick as a brick. There is a haunting image of Flack, taken on the first morning of the Fourth Test at Old Trafford, in which he is almost completely enveloped in thick, swirling dust as he sweeps the Test pitch. As the members of the press moved into position, the legendary Bill O'Reilly peered out the press-box window and declared: 'Why, I'd get twelve wickets on that scrapheap without removing my coat!'

Of course, England was not the only nation to indulge in such jiggery-pokery. During the 1954/55 Ashes series, water appeared miraculously under the covers before the start of play in the Third Test match at the MCG. The England team was a little taken aback. 'There was no rain, so we wondered if a hose leaked or something else occurred,' Harvey said. If the water was meant to blunt Frank Tyson, it failed. He got a stack of wickets cheaply, and England won the game easily. But what happened at Old Trafford in 1956 was on an altogether different scale.

May won the toss and England batted, amassing 459. Johnson and Benaud bowled manfully, but their flighted deliveries didn't suit the slow, turning surface. Peter Richardson scored 104, Colin Cowdrey 80, and the Reverend David Sheppard, who left his pulpit for the match, hit a splendid 113. Johnson and Benaud both bowled 47 overs, Johnson taking 4/151 and Benaud 2/123. Just how would the quicker, flatter spin of Laker and Lock differ from the stuff Johnson and Benaud dished up?

The Australians, after a fair start by Colin McDonald (33) and Jim Burke (22), fell like nine-pins to the spin of Laker. While Lock was spinning and bouncing and the Australian right-handers were playing and missing, Laker was spearing his off-breaks in towards the right-handers with deadly effect. Laker finished with a staggering 9/37 and Lock 1/37. The England spinners had completely defeated the Australian batsmen. Harvey can still recall a magnificent delivery from Laker.

'The ball curved slightly and landed just outside leg. I thought I had the ball covered, but it evaded the outside edge and it hit the top of off-stump. It was simply too good,' Neil recalled. 'The nearest thing I have seen to that delivery I got from Laker is the ball Shane Warne bowled Mike Gatting at Old Trafford all those years later.'

Laker said later: 'That ball to Harvey won us the Test match!'

After the first-innings rout of 84, the Australians followed on. Curator Flack asked Johnson what roller did he want, 'the light or heavy, captain?'

'Please your fucking self,' roared Johnson, a diplomat no more.

After six second-innings wickets were down and Australia heading for the abyss, Johnson declared: 'We are still in this … we can save it.' Keith Miller poked his head out from reading the form guide in the morning newspaper: 'I'll give you 6-4 we don't. This match is already dead and buried.'

It is a rare thing indeed for a Test cricketer from a vastly different era getting to chat for hours with the usually elusive Keith Miller.

We found ourselves sitting together on a flight from Taiwan to Johannesburg in 1989. Miller was not always easy to catch. When he stood with a few mates for a beer he often slipped away from the bar with the throwaway line, 'could you please hold this (the glass of beer) for a minute'. Then he was gone. I figured that at a height of 35,000 feet over a rough sea, Miller wouldn't be going very far at all. At some stage he would return to his allocated seat. We were part of a party of old cricketers invited to the republic to help South Africa celebrate their 100 years of Test match cricket. There were some luminaries there alright – Keith Miller, Neil Harvey, Bill Johnston, Ian Johnson, Ray Lindwall among the Invincibles invited, and Ian Craig, Australia's youngest Test captain. I quizzed Miller about lots of things. Then we got around to the year 1956, Jim Laker's sensational year on the dodgy English wickets of that summer. We talked about the curator Bert Flack. 'Was he a crook?' I asked. 'No, I don't think so,' Miller replied. 'Perhaps he was a bit naïve. He simply did as he was told by the powers that be, the English cricket heavies. But then my mate, journalist and author, Dick Whitington, who played for SA before the war and was a member of the Australian team which contested the Victory Tests, was like a dog with a bone. Dick wanted to "nail" Flack, whom he believed went way too far in his preparation of pitches perfectly suited for the home team. He even interviewed Flack and had Bert sign what he had quoted before shooting off his story to everyone and anyone who'd print it. One of his quotes simply said it all. Flack said candidly: "I does what I'se told. I makes the kind of wicket 'they' wants. The press give me hell and then I has to clean the bloody papers off the ground."'

Whitington got his story alright – and Neil Harvey got a pair. Bowled by that beauty in the first dig and then Laker served him up a juicy full toss in the second. 'I could have and should have hit the ball into the members' stand. Instead, I holed out lamely to Colin Cowdrey at short mid-wicket. I threw the bat in the air and laughed at my stupidity. But when I got back into the dressing-room, I couldn't see the funny side of it.'

Harvey said all the Australians felt cheated by the state of the wicket. 'No doubt about it,' Harvey said. 'We were dudded alright, conned.' He never spoke to Flack about the crook wicket. 'Never used to talk to curators other than wish them good day.'

Jim Laker's bowling was magnificent: 51.2 overs, 23 maidens, taking all ten wickets for 53 runs. No-one had taken all ten wickets before in a Test. No-one has done it since. He had taken nineteen of a possible twenty wickets.

After the match Laker sat back in the England dressing-room, quietly sipping a pint. The Australians filed in to have a drink with the victors. They knew they had been dudded, but it wasn't the fault of the England players. Their beef was with the England cricket administrators. Harvey was one of the first to thrust out his right hand: 'Well done Jimmy. Great performance.'

Laker left Old Trafford at 8 pm, drove to a local hotel, where the patrons were clustered about the television watching replays of his amazing match effort – 19/90 – while there the man himself sat, eating a sandwich and downing another pint. The hero of the hour sat in mufti, unrecognised. There was no fuss or fanfare; the hotel patrons had no idea who the quiet bloke in the corner happened to be. He was just a bloke sitting alone, minding his own business, quietly washing down a sandwich with a heady pint. Jim was trying to come to terms with what had just occurred. It was the achievement of a cricketing lifetime, and more than a little surreal.

Laker's wife, Lilly, was an Austrian and didn't have a clue about cricket. That day she had taken numerous congratulatory phone calls from friends. When Jim finished his pint and sandwich and arrived home that night, Lilly asked: 'Did you do something good today?'

When the first Australian wicket fell in the next Test – off the bowling of Frank Tyson – Laker announced from his spot in the gully: 'I've nowt to play for now!'

*David Frith*

Neil Harvey was a study in creams: no commercial logos then (least of all affixed to the white boundary pickets or splattered even more intrusively across the sacred turf), just a clean bat wielded by a young chap with shirtsleeves rolled high, pads gleaming white, dark hair unencumbered by a cap or sun hat (let alone helmet).

I played against Neil Harvey. I'd read Arthur Mailey's poignant essay about playing against his hero, Victor Trumper. If I'd earlier found Mailey's near-hysterical countdown a bit over the top, I didn't think it now. So, God, please don't let it rain. I'll keep it brief.

Harvey back cut a ball which I chased. Picking it up near the pickets, I gazed at it. Gosh, this ball had just been stroked by Neil Harvey. Our wicketkeeper was screaming.

'C'mon Frithy! Throw the bloody thing in!' I did, shame-faced, at the silly delay. Then our off-spinner, annoyingly, dismissed Neil for 10. Second day of the match was the following Saturday. My old scrapbook records that I scored 29 in 100 minutes, a dreary effort. What must Neil Harvey have thought? What really matters though, is how my precious innings ended. Neil Harvey bowled a curving off-spinner outside leg stump. I tried to glance it, but the ball was loaded. It swerved, what, two feet? Well, two or three inches anyway. Maybe there's something wrong with me, but I left the field slightly elated.

*David Frith is a journalist, author, cricket historian and long-term managing editor of* Wisden Cricket Monthly. *Born in England and based there for most of the year, he spent many summers in Australia, playing grade cricket in Sydney and writing of his experiences in a variety of newspapers, magazines and books.*

CHAPTER FOURTEEN

# OVERLOOKED

*'Craigy remains the captain. We outvote Ian 2/1. Okay?'*
– Neil Harvey

As the 1956/57 season came around, the door was open at the top of Australian cricket. Captain Ian Johnson and vice-captain Keith Miller had both hung up their boots, so the position of captain was up for grabs – a role often described as second only to the prime ministership in terms of national importance.

Australian cricket was not travelling well: three Ashes series in succession had now been lost, and an expected home win against South Africa had been a draw. By contrast, Lew Hoad and Ken Rosewall dominated Wimbledon and the Davis Cup, while Peter Thompson had won his third British Open Golf Championship.

Neil Harvey was clearly the obvious and logical choice to take over the captaincy from Ian Johnson. He had succeeded Johnson as the Victorian captain. But there were problems.

Ian Johnson had filed his captain's report after the Ashes tour. He had been scathing about Richie Benaud and Harvey. The board members were apparently mightily unimpressed. Neil Harvey said there were rumours in the wind.

'There were whispers that the Australian Board of Control had received a report midway through the 1956 tour that neither Benaud nor myself were fit persons to take charge of an Australian cricket team,' Harvey said. 'I understand the board was told that neither of us had real captaincy material, and that Ian Craig or Ron Archer were better suited to assume the mantle of leadership.

'The first leak of this news from the Board of Control's sanctum surprised Benaud and me, for never at any stage of the England tour had either of us been challenged for not doing our job or for neglect of duty.'

NSW cricket then dropped a bombshell of its own. The association announced that Ian Craig would captain NSW as Miller's replacement. 'Getting the NSW captaincy threw me a bit,' Craig later said. 'Like everyone about the place I expected Richie (Benaud) to be the leader.' Craig, with just six Tests under his belt, and a batting average of 23, even began to believe he might get the Test captaincy. 'I reasoned that I was a 50-50 chance.'

Just who might be the next Australian captain seemed to depend upon how the board saw Benaud and Harvey's behaviour in England in 1956. Craig held Harvey in high regard: 'I thought Neil would make an excellent captain.'

Fast bowler Ian Meckiff had his view. 'You know,' Meckiff volunteered, 'I played under Neil's leadership when he captained Victoria. We were playing South Australia in St Kilda because the MCG was unavailable. The wicket was very slow and a little up and down. To win the match we had to break a middle-order partnership. SA batsman Colin Pinch was blocking everything. The new ball was due and I was itching to have a crack with it. But Neil said he was not going to take the new ball. "The new ball will come off the pitch at an even height and good pace for them to score freely. Stick to the old ball, Meck, and we'll beat them.

While it is a slow deck, there is lots of up and down. You'll bowl Pinch with one." As Harvey predicted, I did clean bowl Pinch with a ball that kept very low and we were home. Harvey did pretty well in both of his innings – 125 and 66 not out – and we won by 152 runs. But we had to get Pinch to ensure a win. As we walked from the ground, Harvey said with a smile, "Now, Meck, that was good captaincy."'

As it happened 1956/57 was a domestic only season, with the exception of a short tour of New Zealand near the end of the Australian summer. The announcement of the team coincided with the Victorian team arriving in Sydney for a Sheffield Shield match against NSW at the SCG.

Ian Craig was announced as the captain of the Australian touring team – and Neil Harvey was named as his vice-captain.

Harvey was livid. 'I was pretty pissed off about it. I reckoned I was entitled. I guess the thinking was that I tended to speak my mind a bit and that I might not be capable of handling the captain's off-field duties. Maybe it is one of my failings. A spade's a spade with me and I have never seen anything wrong with that: the truth never hurt anybody.

'Reflecting back on what had been written back to the board from England made the announcement not quite as surprising as it might have been,' Neil recalled. 'But I must confess that I was bitterly disappointed. I felt I had earned the captaincy, and to know that I had been overlooked hurt me deeply. It made me all the more determined to do well against NSW at the SCG the next day.'

The NSW–Victoria matches of the era were always torrid affairs. Each side was brimful of Test players and they were traditionally fierce contests.

Come the morning of the match, the crowd had already packed the SCG. Harvey and Craig met to exchange team lists and toss the coin. 'Bad luck, Ninna,' Craig said of his shock choice as Australian captain, 'I thought you may have got it.' Harvey lost the coin toss and Craig unexpectedly invited Victoria to bat first.

When Neil got back to the Victorian dressing-room, one of the players said, 'Colin McDonald's been taken to hospital. He was in the nets, top-edged a sweep off Spinner Kline. They reckon his nose is broken.'

Harvey jogged the length of the members' bar and explained the situation to Craig. 'Can we agree for Victoria to replace McDonald with twelfth man, Bill Lawry?'

'No,' said Craig. 'We have tossed, exchanged teams. What are rules for, Ninna?'

The Victorian captain couldn't believe his ears. He was still fuming when he got back to the visitors' dressing-room.

'I had expected a bit of sportsmanship and I didn't get it.'

Harvey decided to open the batting in place of the injured McDonald. He looked about the room, told Len Maddocks to pad up and said, 'C'mon Lenny, let's go in and get stuck right into those bastards.'

As they strode confidently to the middle, Harvey stopped to get Alan Davidson's ear: 'C'mon Lenny, let's give this mob a bit of a tickle.' Davo knew then they were in for a pasting.

Harvey smashed the NSW attack in a savage onslaught, hitting 209 runs in five hours. He was particularly severe on Benaud's leg-spinners and Davidson. Davo recalls: 'We weren't too happy with Craigy not allowing Neil to replace McDonald with Lawry, because I had this nasty feeling that Neil was about to tear us to shreds. He most certainly did so, belting the hell out of us. I took the new ball at one stage and my first ball was a beauty. It pitched about the line of middle and off and it swung late away. I thought, "That's it, another Davo wicket." But no, Harvey has judged the length perfectly. He went back and across and hit the ball with the velocity of a tracer bullet. The ball smashed into the fence at cover point and came back some thirty yards from the fence. Awesome power.'

Benaud said that he had never seen a better Sheffield Shield innings. 'Nin was an angry man that day and boy did he make the NSW bowlers pay.'

Harvey recalled: 'This was my first double century for Victoria and coming right on top of the captaincy issue, gave me as much pleasure as any innings I have ever played. My only disappointment was that I succumbed to fatigue with only twenty minutes to play.'

A very tired Harvey missed one from a very tired Davidson for a classic 209.

'If I hadn't got out then I might have reached 300 the next day. I certainly had my mind set on such a score.'

Sporting two black eyes and a broken nose, Colin McDonald batted bravely down the list, falling cheaply in both innings. The game ended in a tame draw – but the match belonged to Harvey: his double century was one of the Sheffield Shield competition's greatest knocks.

The team that went to New Zealand – where the matches were not designated Test matches – was a new look team. Only three members had toured England in 1956: Harvey, Benaud and Craig. The others were Peter Burge, John Drennan, Les Favell, Ron Gaunt, Barry Jarman, Lindsay Kline, Johnny Martin, Ian Meckiff, Norm O'Neill, Bob Simpson and Bill Watson.

Despite his feelings, Harvey believes Craig, from the outset, did a good job in marshalling his troops.

'All the newcomers did well,' Neil said. 'Norm O'Neill, Lindsay Kline, Ian Meckiff and Barry Jarman had exceptional tours and all of them except for O'Neill were picked for the South African tour.

'I am pleased to say that Ian Craig and I got on famously,' Neil said. 'Ian proved to be an astute leader. He was a willing listener, and he was prepared to consider any advice offered to him by the senior players.'

Harvey confirmed team spirit was better than it had been under the intractable Ian Johnson.

'Team harmony was better than it was for many seasons. Our young side went through the visit undefeated, drawing the first two unofficial Test matches and trouncing New Zealand in the third at Auckland where Norm O'Neill hit a fine undefeated century.'

Immediately upon the team's return from New Zealand, the touring side was picked to tour South Africa. Craig retained the captaincy, Neil remained his deputy.

'If we were going to have any chance of beating England in Australia in 1958/59, we simply had to continue to build our team development in South Africa. Both Ian and I knew that we faced an onerous task. England had proved far too good for us in 1954/55 at home and in England in 1956. Much of the nucleus of their 1956 side would be in Australia in a year's time.'

Most critics, including those within the Australian press, didn't give Ian Craig's side much of a chance of beating Jackie McGlew's Springboks.

'After the New Zealand tour, Ian Craig got special dispensation from the board to further his pharmacy studies in the UK (a few years later he was the boss of the huge chain of pharmacies in the UK, Boots Chemists) and he planned to meet up with us when we landed in South Africa. The day before the main body of the side flew out of Australia, our manager, Jack Jenke, took ill. So, we left our shores minus a captain and a manager.

'A week later, Jack Norton, who had managed the team in New Zealand, arrived in Johannesburg to replace Jenke. Ian Craig had earlier met us when we touched down in Joburg, so we were at full strength once more.'

---

The Springbok pace pair of Peter Heine and Neil Adcock came at the opposition with unrelenting speed and aggression, backed by the clever medium pace of left-hander Trevor Goddard and the spin of Hugh Tayfield, still the best of the world's finger spinners. 'They were genuinely quick and both very aggressive. We had to bat well to counter them,' Harvey said.

Those young players who performed so well in New Zealand all won a place on the South African tour – except O'Neill. Just how O'Neill missed selection had many pundits, including Harvey, nonplussed. 'I was amazed Normie wasn't picked for South Africa. He had done everything right in New Zealand and was a certainty in my book to be picked for South Africa. Just put it down to one of cricket's mysteries.' As the Australians travelled around South Africa from December 1957 to March 1958, O'Neill took the domestic Australian season by storm, scoring a Bradman-like 1005 Sheffield Shield runs at an average of 83.75.

In South Africa meanwhile, Richie Benaud and Alan Davidson were defining themselves, coming of age as cricketers. Both all-rounders had toured England in 1953 and 1956 and had experience behind them, but they had been pretty much bit-part performers. Neither man had been afforded a leading role of responsibility on previous Test tours. They survived on the Test stage through sheer will of making themselves virtually indispensable through their combined skills with bat, ball and in the field. But in 1953 Benaud had received some important advice. Tom Goodman, cricket correspondent of *The Sydney Morning Herald*, arranged a meeting with legendary spinner Bill O'Reilly, who told him: 'Now young Benaud. You are trying to get a wicket every ball. That is ruining your control. The whole point of bowling is to give the batsman nothing. And I mean nothing, not a hint of a chance to build his score.'

From the outset of the tour, Benaud, especially, trained his socks off. From the day the tour started he sprang into action, bowling for three hours a day in an empty net, while his teammates went to the pictures. There was no magic bullet here, just good old-fashioned hard work. Benaud made himself a vow: 'This will be my tour. I can feel it. All I need to do is to practise, practise, practise.'

Benaud had a good repertoire for a leg-spinner – a genuine leg break with over spin and a good top-spinner. He also had begun developing a wrong'un. Just before the team left Australia for South Africa, Benaud approached the old Australian and SA leg-spinner Bruce Dooland, to discover the secrets of the flipper. The flipper is held twixt thumb and forefinger and is spun backwards. Quite difficult to get the knack, but once you cotton it, it is relatively easy.

Harvey had some difficulties early on the tour. He broke a finger at fielding practice and was forced to miss the first three first-class matches. 'We were fielding in Johannesburg,' recalled fast bowler Ian Meckiff. 'Everyone was warned about the rarefied atmosphere in Joburg and we needed to run and catch high flyers, to adjust to the ball going that much further in the atmosphere. I reckon that is when Neil, who usually caught these catches easily, somehow misjudged one and copped a broken finger.' Neil lamented: 'While the side went to Rhodesia to open the tour, I had to stay behind in Johannesburg to have the finger set and give it time to mend. The injury was a bitter pill to swallow, but then I hit 173 in my first innings of the tour against a South African XI at Pretoria; things didn't look half as dismal for me.'

Harvey then scored 78 versus Natal and 63 against Western Province in Cape Town before the team journeyed to Benoni for a two-day second-class fixture. It was a lighthearted affair, as most of those games invariably were, for the visitors should beat such opposition with their eyes closed – but that's when accidents happen. Harvey was bowling his off-breaks when he spilled a return catch – and in so doing he broke the same finger. The broken finger ruled Harvey out of the First Test and he was downcast. Since coming into the Australian Test side at Leeds in 1948, Harvey had played forty-six consecutive Tests and he was hoping to beat a world record, set by the elegant England left-hander Frank Woolley, of fifty-two successive Tests. He took this little injury hiccup in his stride. He felt that he had enjoyed a terrific injury-free career up until this point and he easily rationalised the situation. 'I guess I had to get injured at some point along the way,' he said. 'Apart from one Test score of 68 at Durban, worthwhile scores eluded me, and I had my worst series ever against South Africa.'

Markets abound in the seaside city of Durban. Many of the traders are of Indian descent and, like so many Indian small business owners, they are sharp and clever. Neil discovered a touristy place, where the trader was selling a range of statues, trinkets, carved polished wooden figures and some animal skins. He cast his eye about the shop, focusing on a lion skin, complete with head. The lion looked so lifelike and Neil, never one to procrastinate at any time, was quickly thumbing through his wallet of rand notes. The lion skin was destined to grace the Harvey household in Heidelberg, 25 kilometres north-east of the Melbourne CBD. Then they were moving house, and Neil came to the conclusion that the lion skin he so enthusiastically set about purchasing in Durban barely six months before was suddenly no longer a 'must item'.

Rather than discard the lion skin, Neil hit upon the idea of offering the skin to the Fitzroy Football Club, one of the oldest Victorian Football League clubs, who were known as 'the Lions'. Fitzroy was delighted to accept the gift, but over the years, as Neil had discovered, 'Fitzroy did not look after the lion skin'. In the 1990s Fitzroy merged with the Brisbane Bears, who became the Brisbane Lions. Brisbane got its act together. They embraced the history and tradition of Fitzroy. The lion was emblazoned on the front of Brisbane's jumper. The old lion skin, which the Fitzroy club had allowed to fall into disrepair, suddenly became a wanted item for the Brisbane Lions. 'The club refurbished the lion skin and I believe it now lies proudly under glass in the Brisbane Lions' boardroom,' Neil said.

Despite his largesse in that Indian shopkeeper's stall, Neil Harvey was having misgivings about his working life back in Melbourne. He was thinking seriously about leaving Victoria – even perhaps making the move to leave Australia and make a permanent home in South Africa. Job opportunities in Australia were scarce. Now with two children – first born, Robert, and Anne, who had been born just five days before Neil flew to South Africa – the added family responsibilities weighed heavily on him. Neil loved playing big cricket and he knew he could go on for a few more years at the top, but there would come a time when it was all over, and when that time arrived, he wanted a safe and secure future for his wife and children.

There was no pressure whatsoever on Neil to make a decision either way from his South African–born wife. 'Iris left that sort of decision to me,' Neil said. 'All I knew then is that my job situation in Melbourne was a problem.'

The greatest feature of this series was the exceptional form of Benaud and Davidson. Benaud hammered two centuries, in the First and Fourth Tests, both in Johannesburg, and emerged as the best leg-spinner in the world, taking thirty wickets for the series. Davidson also batted well and he teamed brilliantly with Benaud, taking a total of twenty-five wickets in the five Tests. Newcomer Bobby Simpson revealed his brilliance as a first-slip fieldsman, snaring more than twenty catches on the tour. One stands out in particular.

South African fast bowler Neil Adcock had wandered to the crease in the Second Test in Cape Town. He would be facing left-arm wrist-spinner Lindsay Kline. Kline was on a hat-trick. 'At the top of my mark I decided I would bowl a regulation leg break, or an off-spinner to the right-hander. Then just as I approached the wicket I decided to bowl a wrong'un. The ball pitched round off stump and Adcock obliged with an outside edge. It went past Wally Grout's right glove, but Simmo (Simpson) moved beautifully to his left, like a cat, and he took the ball low to the ground. Talk about making an almost impossible catch look easy ...'

Davidson might have excelled on tour – but one thing bothered him. Team manager Norton had imposed a 10 pm nightly curfew.

One night Davidson said to his roommate and good friend, Les Favell, the South Australian opening batsman: 'Hey, Les. Bugger the curfew. I am going off my rocker sitting about. Forget the blasted curfew. Let's go out for a bite to eat and maybe take in a movie.'

On the way to watching a movie, *Don't Go Near the Water*, Davo and Favell bumped into Springbok batsman Ken Funston, who was surprised to see the pair: 'Thought you blokes are supposed to be tucked up into your little beds by ten.' Funston gave them the keys to his Peugeot and they drove into Pretoria, grabbed a toasted sandwich and a coffee at a café and then drove back to Johannesburg. When they arrived at the team hotel, they were handed a scribbled note from the Australian manager, who seemed none too pleased: 'Report to me. I've got your keys. Norton.'

'We had a quick-fire discussion and decided to walk round to Curt and Natalie Rosenberg's home, just a block away,' Davidson said. 'The Rosenbergs were hosts to the Australian team, celebrating Christmas at their home the night before.'

Learning of the cricketers' situation, the Rosenbergs offered the pair a bed for the night. When the pair arrived at the Australian dressing-room at the Wanderers the next day, they were peppered with questions from their concerned teammates: 'You two will be sorry. First plane home, I reckon.' Davidson bowled like a man possessed, taking 6/34.

Manager Norton checked out their story with the Rosenbergs. Yes, they had indeed stayed there the night. Without offering a hint of an apology, he said simply: 'Okay, I will have to accept what you two blokes have told me in your defence.' Within hours, the curfew was repealed.

Neil's form on tour was indifferent. He had long thought that his eyesight wasn't 100 per cent. He had a habit of squinting. It had got to the stage he had to squint to read the scoreboard.

Neil recalled: 'The optometrist next door to our Johannesburg hotel, The Victoria, was an avid cricket fan. He mixed happily with the blokes and was ever enthusiastic about the game. We got to know him well.'

The optometrist, whose name has been lost to the ravages of memory, approached Norton and offered to check all the players' eyesight. And Norton, a man to the board's liking, another of those administrative Scrooges who scrimped and scraped for every penny saved, was overjoyed by the optometrist's offer to do all the players' tests, *free of charge*.

Harvey wasn't a happy camper: 'When it came to my turn, I was a little concerned. I didn't want the bloke to know that my eyesight wasn't too good, so I don't think I answered his questions comprehensively. The bloke sensed my reluctance and he said he wanted to see me again, the very next day.'

It was impossible for Harvey to hide his faulty eyesight and after a thorough second examination, the optometrist said: 'Neil, you should be wearing glasses.' It was a shattering revelation.

Harvey shrugged. Eventually he agreed to have a pair of glasses made for him.

'I couldn't quite believe what was happening to me. I had much too much stupid pride to let too many people know I had to wear glasses,' Neil said. 'Of course, I had to tell Richie Benaud because he was my roomie and I would try the glasses out at night behind closed doors. When I was alone I would wear them outside and it was a whole new world, but I never considered using them when I batted. It wasn't the done thing in those days and I suppose there was a basic fear of being hit and the glass going into my eyes.'

There was at the time a stigma associated with wearing glasses. Old people wore glasses, not sportsmen. Alan Davidson – for whom the optometrist also recommended glasses – recalled that Jack Ryder, who was a Test selector for more years than the locusts have eaten, once told him over the top of his rimless glasses: 'No player who wears glasses at the wicket will ever get my vote to play for Australia as a batsman.'

'I really know I was a bloody fool,' said Harvey. 'I batted for the last five years of my career with poor eyesight and my form fell away. It's crazy really – the year after I retired South African Eddie Barlow, who wore glasses, ripped off three Test centuries against us and Geoff Boycott, although he switched from glasses to contact lenses – well, he could hardly be regarded as a flop.'

So Neil wore his glasses only in his room and in the darkened theatre. He never thought seriously about wearing them in a big cricket match. But word spread all the same. Maybe it all had some sort of impact on the Harvey psyche.

Ian Meckiff said he never saw Harvey wearing glasses, 'but we did learn that both Ninna and Davo had the spectacles in their coat pocket. And when the lights turned down at the picture theatre they would delve into their coat pockets, and put the glasses on in the dark so they could see the film clearly. Later in the tour we were standing about having a cursory look at the wicket in the middle. It must have been during a game for the scores were still on the scoreboard. We idolised Neil Harvey, but we were curious as to why the optometrist had advised that he wear spectacles. One of the blokes volunteered. "Hey, Ninna. We hear that from the centre wicket you can't read the scoreboard. Can you make out the numbers on the scoreboard now?"

'"No, it is just a blur," he said in his clipped way. Never wasting a word.'

Years later, in 1968, Harvey was a Test selector, along with Bradman and Ryder. If Ryder was true to his word, then it must have been Harvey and Bradman who selected me and Eric Freeman to tour England, for we both wore contact lenses.

'The miracle of the modern age,' wrote old Jack Fingleton, when I took ten wickets in a match and Freeman scored a century against Northants. So even then the stigma was not entirely absent.

The Australians played twenty first-class matches in South Africa, eleven of which were victories and there were nine draws. More importantly the Australians won three Test matches – Cape Town, Port Elizabeth and Johannesburg – while South Africa fought hard to draw the Tests in Durban and the second time in Johannesburg. It was a monumental feat by the now young and eager Test team. Harvey played fourteen first-class matches in South Africa that tour and scored 759 runs at 50.60, with just two centuries. In the four Tests he played he scored 131 runs at 21.83, with a highest score of 68. They weren't great figures, but he did enjoy the tour. 'Living and playing cricket in South Africa, on both tours, I felt completely safe. The people were very welcoming and I felt totally at ease.'

Victorious captain Ian Craig was afforded hero status. But it would all have been very different without the leadership of one Robert Neil Harvey.

After the Fourth Test, Ian Craig put his neck on the line. 'I am not playing well enough and I am dropping myself,' Craig announced to his deputy.

It was a remarkable move. Craig had Sir Donald Bradman's complete trust and his backing as Test captain one hundred per cent, which Harvey well knew. Bradman had admired how Craig had rebuilt this new team in New Zealand. There was a healthy camaraderie among the players and they were going well. Except for Craig.

When Craig made his dramatic declaration to Harvey, the vice-captain immediately called in third selector Peter Burge.

Before they sat to make a final decision, Harvey sensed that Burge was simply going to agree with Craig and drop him, which would mean the captaincy passed to the man Burge most admired in Test cricket – Neil Harvey. Burge was very much a Harvey man. He loved the man for his cricket artistry, his cricket nous, and Burge knew how much Harvey had coveted the role of Test captain.

'It is only logical,' Craig said. 'The right and proper thing to do is to drop myself.'

Then Harvey made his move. He took Burge aside. 'Now, look Peter. No Australian captain has been sacked at any time during a Test series and I do not intend to be party to it happening here,' Harvey said, looking Burge straight in the eye. 'Craigy remains the captain. We outvote Ian 2/1. Okay?'

Burge didn't argue.

He was eyeballing a true leader and he learnt a good deal about leadership in that short conversation. It was something Burge never forgot. As master wordsmith Gideon Haigh was later to write: 'Forty years later he was sure it was the finest act of sportsmanship he's ever seen.'

Years later, Craig confirmed the story, and registered his appreciation. 'I wasn't happy with my own form on the trip to South Africa in 1957/58 and leading into the Fourth Test I put it to my fellow selectors that I be dropped. But Neil wouldn't have a bar of it. A touring captain had never been dropped before. He wasn't going to have anything to do with it. I really did appreciate his support.'

In a rare show of support for the Australian Test leadership, Sir Donald Bradman met the team when the *Dominion Monarch* docked in Sydney in April 1958. Within a few months the battle for the Ashes would be on.

Then a bombshell – Ian Craig had contracted hepatitis. He would never play for Australia again. The captaincy was again open.

*Jack D'Arcy*

I actually only played once against Neil when I played for Canterbury against Ian Craig's Australian team in February 1957. However, I was twelfth man for New Zealand in all three games we played against Australia and as a result got the opportunity to watch and observe him along with his Australian teammates. As twelfth man I was also given the usual job of spending a little time in the Australian dressing room obtaining autographs. I have two distinct memories of Neil Harvey from that time.

The first relates to Canterbury's game played at Lancaster Park. I was twenty years old and an opening batsman and I vividly remember being on edge before the game. This was largely due to the fact that my dad was an Australian from Melbourne who had moved to live in New Zealand. As I was growing up in Christchurch he had hung a framed photo of Don Bradman above my bed and had spent a lot of time telling me how good Australian cricketers were and how they played hard and to win. Just prior to the game I think he realised I was feeling pretty tense and he tried to downplay their capabilities with words like 'you know Australians bowl with the same size cricket ball and from the same twenty-two yards just like every bowler you have faced'. Canterbury won the toss and batted and I was still feeling very nervous when I went out to the middle. After only a couple of overs I realised that one of my boot laces was dragging on the ground, so play was held up while I fixed the problem. I must have looked a little panicky because whilst I was bent over doing this a voice behind me said 'Relax son, just take your time!' I looked around to find it was Neil Harvey. I muttered thanks and although I did not go on and make many runs I remember thinking later, 'Gee that was a nice gesture. Maybe these Aussies are not as hard-nosed as I have been told they are.'

My second memory was at the end of the third and final tour match in Auckland. I went into the Australian dressing-room for final autographs and there was a lot of noise and skylarking going on. After signing the autograph sheets Neil Harvey said: 'Your team is going to England next year. If you are lucky enough to get picked, you will have the greatest time of your life. Good luck.' Again another appreciated gesture.

*Jack D'Arcy was an opening batsman who played five Tests for New Zealand, all on that 1958 tour of England.*

CHAPTER FIFTEEN

# THE BENAUD-HARVEY ALLIANCE

*'It was not so hard missing out to Richie.'* – Neil Harvey

ROUND MID-MORNING ON Tuesday 25 November 1958 Neil Harvey answered his telephone in his plush new office at glassware company John Dynon & Sons, in Kent Street, Sydney.

The Victorian had moved north. Upon returning from South Africa, Harvey had appeared on a Melbourne-produced television show, *Meet the Press*. The members of the board overseeing Australian cricket would have been taken aback when their team's vice-captain spoke of the poor Test match pay: £75, plus £10 out-of-pocket expenses for each Test. Harvey was touting for a job. He had been long complaining about trying to combine work with a life in cricket while raising a family. A decent job was nowhere to be found in Melbourne. He was looking further afield, even considering his wife's South Africa, although the political situation there didn't excite either Neil or Iris. The Harveys got no takers in Melbourne, but a glassware firm in Sydney offered him a good, well-paying and secure job. The Harveys left Melbourne and landed in Sydney: Neil, Iris, Robert and baby Anne arrived ready to enjoy another chapter in their journey.

'Guess who is the new Australian captain?' asked the familiar voice at the other end of the line.

'You are, Richie,' Neil said firmly, not then knowing, but fully expecting Richie Benaud to get the Test captaincy.

'That's right, Ninna,' Benaud said. 'I'm sorry. I thought you may have got it.'

Harvey was disappointed, as he believed he most assuredly should have got the captaincy, but he was pretty relaxed about it. Benaud and Harvey had been good mates for years. They fought many tough campaigns together and to Harv, missing out to Benaud was not like missing out to Craig.

'It wasn't too bad,' Harvey said. 'It was not so hard missing out to Richie. I was glad to have been named vice-captain to Benaud.'

He instinctively knew their new relationship as captain and vice-captain of the Australian Test team would work well. The pair met up at the Cricketers' Club in George Street. There they chatted over a few drinks and laughed as mates do. There was not the hint of stiffness in their conversation, although one suspects that had more to do with Harvey's generosity of spirit, when just an hour or two earlier he missed the dream of a lifetime and would again be confined to being the perennial bridesmaid of Australian cricket when it came to captaincy of the national team.

Gideon Haigh wrote to me recently: 'Going around and interviewing Harv's contemporaries, something else was apparent in the way they spoke of him. He was a cricketer's cricketer. Not like Bradman, to whom the only way to look was up; not like Miller, to whom one looked with a certain masculine envy; no, in his time Harvey was the player to whom others looked across. It always struck me as significant that Benaud, on learning that he had been appointed captain, immediately contacted Harvey, took him to lunch, picked his brain. Because if you had Harvey, you had the team. Benaud could never have been as successful as captain had he not had Harvey's allegiance. The office of vice-captain is an uneasy one, in that your personal ambition can be enhanced by the faltering of the team and its leader.'

Benaud and Harvey knew they had their work cut out. England had picked a mighty strong outfit under the leadership of Peter May. Spinners Jim Laker and Tony Lock, so long thorns in the Australian batting side on their home wickets, were brought together for the first time Down Under.

Apart from the elegant world-class May, the side was festooned with batting talent: openers Arthur Milton and Peter Richardson, Colin Cowdrey, Tom Graveney and Willy Watson. The attack was also formidable with Frank Tyson and Brian Statham still in the frame, that annoying medium-paced all-rounder Trevor Bailey, Peter Loader and Fred Trueman, backed by the feared spin of Laker and Lock. The indefatigable wicketkeeper Godfrey Evans was also among the touring party.

The first Test of the 1958/59 Ashes series was played at the Gabba. It would turn out to be one of the dreariest Tests in history.

England was whisked out for 134; (Alan Davidson 3/36, Ian Meckiff 3/33 and Richie Benaud 3/46) then Australia batted, but could only muster 186. Trevor Bailey bowled tightly, not always bowling within reach of the batsman and often spearing the ball down leg side, thus frustrating the Australian stroke-makers. In the England first innings 'Barnacle' Bailey, usually stuck fast to the crease like a limpet mine, was lured from the crease by a well-flighted Benaud leg break and was done like a dinner; stumped by a laughing Wally Grout for not many. In the second dig it was a different story. Bailey was stuck at the crease for 458 minutes of sheer boredom while he compiled 68.

Bailey's stubborn resistance ensured the Englishmen would salvage a draw. The only highlight in the match was Norman O'Neill's second innings of 71 not out, which he hit in just 113 minutes. All the Australians needed now was to take the series by the scruff of the neck. Forget Bailey and his negativity; Australia must take the attack to this mob. Benaud had brought a new vitality to the side. He introduced a team meeting–cum–dinner the night before the first day's play in each Test. All of the players – the old hands and the newcomers – were considered equals around the table. Benaud encouraged the new chums to have their say, to make a contribution to the meeting. A player might have noticed a kink in the technique of one of the Englishmen, or noticed one disliked being crowded at the crease, or had a poor throwing arm. Importantly, the team meetings were conducted in a light atmosphere.

The Australians were upbeat when they flew into Melbourne for the Second Test match. England batted first. Alan Davidson took the new ball with Ian Meckiff. Davidson opened from the MCC Members end and within a few overs the Englishmen were on the ropes at 3/7. Peter Richardson fell for 3, Willie Watson for nought and Tom Graveney also cleaned up for a duck. It was an unforgettable start of an Ashes Test match and it was made all the more memorable by the commentary of Michael Charlton. For mine, Charlton was the greatest ABC ball-by-ball cricket commentator of them all. He was miles better than anyone today, even better than the man they once dubbed The Voice of Australia, Alan McGilvray. There was a star quality in Charlton's voice. Little wonder the BBC snapped him up a couple of years later and he wowed his British audiences doing top-notch television and radio specials.

England recovered to a respectable 259, thanks to a classy 113 by skipper May. Then came Harvey. From the very first ball Harvey took the attack to England. He savaged the England spinners Jim Laker and Tony Lock.

Out of a team total of 308, Harvey hammered 167 in 370 minutes with sixteen fours.

'It was, I think, Harvey's greatest innings,' proclaimed Ian Meckiff. 'Neil took Laker and Lock apart. The way he moved his feet and climbed into that pair of spinners was something akin to Neil settling a score. After all, Laker got him for a pair at Manchester in 1956.'

Australia won by eight wickets. Davidson took 6/64 and 3/41 and Meckiff 3/69 and 6/38. That's eighteen wickets to the left-handers.

A change had come over the Australians, over the game. Before Benaud's influence, an Australian bowler would take a wicket and there would be the odd tap of acknowledgement on the bowler's back and/or a quiet, almost inaudible 'Well done, mate'. Observers regarded any ostentatious show of passion on the cricket field to be rather infra dig. Even Miller – hardly a straitlaced type – was a little taken aback by Benaud's enthusiasm, rushing to a wicket-taking bowler and smothering him with hugs and slaps on the back. Many people thought the on-field expressions of emotion at the fall of a wicket to be a little over the top. Either way, it was indicative of a team enjoying themselves.

The team's camaraderie was evident, which endeared them to the Australian cricket-loving public.

Thanks to the batting of Harvey and Colin McDonald, plus the inspired bowling of Benaud, Davidson and Meckiff, Australia won the series convincingly, 2-0. It was a great triumph for Benaud and his men. In the five Tests Harvey scored 291 runs at 48.50, with one century, his brilliant 167 in Melbourne. Australia had regained the Ashes.

A tour of India and Pakistan loomed – a prospect that did not entice everyone.

*Ian Meckiff*

What a player was Neil Harvey. I was there in Johannesburg (the summer of 1957/58) when he had his eyes tested by the cricket-mad optometrist, whose practice happened to be situated right next door to our team base, the Victoria Hotel. Neil and Davo (the great all-rounder Alan Davidson) were singled out as blokes who really should have been wearing glasses. It was the first time I realised that Neil struggled to focus on any object a distance away. He couldn't see his score on the scoreboard. He'd squint to try and find some sort of focus on the ball, yet he was still scoring lots of runs at the top level. There was nothing wrong with his eyesight that day in the Third Test at Durban. We were cleaned up by the speedster Neil Adcock (6/43) in the first dig and we were in real danger of losing the match, when Neil strode to the wicket and hauled our sinking ship to safe and calm waters. Neil Harvey's heroics that day, when he scored an unbeaten 68, saved the day. Neil was an astute captain and he batted with so much freedom and confidence. His upbeat attitude rubbed off on his teammates. Harv inspired us all. Even when the going was tough, such as his extraordinary batting against the odds at Dacca in 1959, Neil Harvey proved time and again that he was a wonderful cricketer and a brilliant leader.

*Ian Meckiff was a fiery left-handed fast bowler, who played for Victoria and Australia with distinction. In 18 Tests he took forty-five wickets at 31.62, with two hauls of five wickets in a Test innings. His last Test match ended in sadness, when he was called for throwing. He never bowled another ball in a first-class match.*

*Thos Hodgson*

My first recollection of meeting Neil Harvey was with his great mate Sam Loxton after dinner one evening at a private home in the mid-1970s. In response to my questions about their famous partnership in the Fourth Test at Headingley in 1948, they resolved that an action replay for my sole benefit would be appropriate. Thereupon, using the cardboard cylinder from inside an alfoil roll as a bat, they re-enacted the highlights of their innings by passing it backwards and forwards to one another as they played their respective strokes. In a position even closer than silly mid-off to a batsman, I was able to observe Neil stepping back and imperiously square cutting the imaginary ball past point or nimbly stepping down the wicket and playing his perfectly executed cover drive.

Sam would then take over and start flaying the invisible bowling attack with powerful lofted drives, which cleared the pickets. Occasionally they would take a quick single, calling each other through for the run and passing on the cardboard cylinder in the process. They would simultaneously comment upon the worthiness of the other's stroke-play as well as revealing the strengths and weaknesses of the English bowler they were facing at the time. This was priceless and I was captivated. I did not want the performance to ever end. Neil played the stroke which brought up his maiden Test century and Sam immediately came over and shook his hand as he had done all those years ago. But suddenly and sadly it was all over. Sam advanced down the wicket and took an almighty swing. He missed the ball and was bowled for 93. He then explained to me that he had become impatient and was attempting to hit Norman Yardley 'for a seven' to bring up his century.

I knew at this time I had witnessed something special that these two men shared. An extraordinary relationship and close friendship forged from their mutual love of cricket. When the Victorian team was departing by train on Neil's first interstate tour, Lindsay Hassett had instructed Sam to look after him. Neil was barely eighteen years old at the time. It appears Sam willingly accepted this duty and from that time onwards, they were inseparable.

Neil and Sam played for Victoria and Australia together, toured together, roomed together, shared historic partnerships, shared duties as Australian selectors, shared wonderful memories and in their later years, went on tours to remote country towns together, regaling audiences of cricket lovers with stories of their exploits in a style akin to a stand-up comedy duo. The tour to England in 1948 was their principal subject.

Originally Neil was Sam's straight man, although over time he developed his own laconic style and sometimes achieved more laughs than Sam, which was no easy feat. Although they were not batting together, this was a wonderful partnership to behold. Like the runs they scored together at Headingley in 1948, the stories, jokes and anecdotes came thick and fast. I remember telling Neil that I believed he was responsible for the most famous and well-known batting average in Test cricket, that of Sir Donald Bradman of 99.94.

I suggested to him that if he had not hogged the strike and hit the winning boundary in Australia's second innings of the Headingley Test, and had allowed Bradman, who was at the other end on 173 not out, to do so, The Don would have achieved an average of a perfect one hundred.

Neil chortled and responded that in those days, few if any batsmen ever thought about their batting averages. He was certain that Sir Donald would not have had the slightest awareness of his personal batting statistics. He purely wanted to score as many runs as he could and ensure Australia would win. Neil shared with me that many years later, Sir Donald, as a surprise, had inscribed a beautiful and heartfelt message of appreciation and admiration of Neil's efforts at Headingley on that bat with which Neil had scored his century and the match-winning boundary. It is a possession which he treasures, and I could observe Neil's eyes well up with tears of pride as he told me of Sir Donald's kindness and thoughtfulness.

In the years to come I would often see both Neil and Sam, either separately or with their wives, [Neil's second wife] Barbara and Jo, at various cricket dinners and functions. It was always a delight to spend time with them. Whilst Neil and Sam were often signing autographs and meeting with their admirers, I had the opportunity to spend time talking with Barbara and Jo, who were delightful company. The expression 'Behind every great man is a great woman' certainly applied for both Sam and Neil. Jo was usually hilarious and at times, quite outrageous. She was loved by all who knew her. Barbara was always so elegant, charming and gracious. At times she looked like a princess. She adored Neil and he adored her. They shared a special partnership.

A highlight for me was when I was asked to act as a chaperone for Sam and Neil when they were invited by my cricketing friend, John Geber, to attend an Old Australia versus Old England match at the magnificent Chateau Tanunda cricket ground in the Barossa Valley in 2006 and to stay on for the Adelaide Ashes Test. This was a task I accepted with great relish. In fact, it was not a task at all, but rather a great privilege, as it meant that I shared a cottage with these two great cricketers for a number of days. During this time, there were many opportunities to hear their stories.

I recall coming in after dinner on our first night together and observing that there was a bottle of fine port which had been left for us and that perhaps we might consider sharing a glass as a nightcap before retiring to bed. Neil looked at me in a rather bemused way and replied, 'Forget about just having a glass, we are going to finish the whole bottle tonight.' And we did. The stories flowed even more quickly than the port.

*Thos Hodgson is a leading Sydney-based barrister. He is also a long-time member of the Australian Cricket Society (NSW Branch) and has a long and happy association with Neil Harvey. Thos often takes Neil to lunch on the occasion of Neil's birthday.*

CHAPTER SIXTEEN

# SAM LOXTON

*'I would advise Mr Menzies to have Army and Navy standing by. A week after Sam gets to India, war is bound to break out.'*
– Lindsay Hassett

NOT ONE MEMBER of the board controlling Australian cricket put their hand up to manage the 1959/60 tour of India and Pakistan. An England or South African tour was very different. England was the plum job and there was much clamouring for position by the board members to win the role, for in England the manager would rub shoulders with royalty, film stars, war heroes, sportsmen and -women, with many an opportunity to pontificate at various well-attended events.

Sam Loxton put his hand up for the India job. He half-suspected he was the only applicant for the job. 'What board member would be silly enough to go there?' he quipped. Loxton had not always pleased administrators. He was blunt and forthright and always told it as he saw it. There were no grey areas with Sam, who was an amazing mix of a bloke. One of Bradman's Invincibles, he was an ebullient all-rounder, hard-hitting batsman and a medium-fast bowler, with a penchant for bowling bouncers. He could be just as wilful off the field.

During a speech at a cricket dinner, Sam's former skipper for Victoria and Australia, Lindsay Hassett, joked: 'I would advise Mr (Prime Minister) Menzies to have Army and Navy standing by. A week after Sam gets to India war is bound to break out.'

The players were not especially looking forward to the trip either, for those who had been there before often spoke of the dreadful conditions they faced: the poor food and accommodation, the lack of hygiene, even the most basic cleanliness was absent from everyday life. Hotel rooms were hovels, riddled with cockroaches, rats and mosquitoes. Dysentery was rife. When the players took to the field they would often stuff wads of toilet paper down their pants to try and stem the flow were they to fall foul of the dreaded looseness of bowel.

Coming back from the nets in Adelaide during the Fourth Ashes Test that preceding summer, Alan Davidson bumped into Sir Donald Bradman, then chairman of the Test selection committee.

Davo and Sir Donald had established a pretty good rapport over the years and Sir Donald would have been delighted with Davo's form that series. Davidson came straight to the point. 'Don,' he said, 'is it compulsory to go to India and Pakistan?'

'You have retired, have you Alan?'

'No Sir Donald, I have not.'

'That's good to hear, Alan,' The Don said with his funny little squeak. 'When you get back to the dressing-room you tell the boys what I have just told you!'

Harvey was of like mind and he too had approached The Don with the very same inquiry.

'Same story,' Neil laughed.

So, India and Pakistan, here we come.

Loxton may have been no diplomat, but he was a politician. A real one – he was the Liberal Member for Prahran in the Victorian parliament, a seat he had occupied since 1955 and would continue to hold until 1979. He discovered soon enough that he could read the mood of a room, even if there was nothing smooth and silky about the way he spoke.

He knew how to win support and win loyalty among his constituents. The same went for the players under his managership, and even members of the board. He had many endearing traits, not the least of which was his passion for the contest and his loyalty to his teammates. Sam also had a penchant for telling a damned good yarn. He was indeed an entertainer.

Having travelled to India in the 1953/54 Commonwealth team, a year or two after his last Test match, he was in actuality an inspired choice as manager of Richie Benaud's 1959/60 team.

'All the players, without exception, loved Sam,' said Neil. 'They loved his loyalty, his incredible storytelling and his passion.'

Loxton would need all his experience as a player, selector and politician to arrest a few tight situations on tour, such as the opening day of the fifth and final Test in the oppressive heat of Bombay (now Mumbai). Some 50,000 fans had arrived at Brabourne Stadium that supremely hot day on 1 January 1960. Australia had won in New Delhi and lost in Kanpur; the series, tied at 1-1, was up for grabs.

Loxton had explicit instructions from the board chairman Bill Dowling. 'Sam,' said Dowling, 'on no account are you to let the team participate in a Test match unless you receive a receipt for the £7500 the Indian Board owes us. We want to see a back transfer of the payment in full before even one ball is bowled.'

Sam eyed Dowling quizzically. 'Does that mean what I think it does?'

'You bet it does.'

The Australian Board had set a course for making a financial killing on this tour, which would embrace eight Test matches in just seventy-seven days: gruelling stuff. Each player was paid the princely sum of £650 for the entire tour. Touring expenses and daily allowances, which really were little more than a pittance, did not cut deep into the board's profits. They made a killing. The Indians had kept to their side of the bargain in the first two Tests, but by the morning of the Bombay match no money for the Third Test had been forthcoming.

While most of the players were preparing in the dressing-room for the contest, Loxton, accompanied by skipper Benaud, walked briskly to the official area, seeking to speak with the BCCI's executive secretary, Narayan 'Mama' Karmarkar.

Sam came straight to the point: 'Mama, where is the money? Have you paid up yet?'

Mama was evasive, nervously laughing off the suggestion. 'No, no, Mister Sam. We cannot spoil a perfectly good relationship by talking about money. Don't you trust us?'

'Our relationship will be spoilt sure enough if you don't pay what your terms of the agreement happen to be,' Loxton replied. 'I want to obtain from you the receipt for the telegraphic transfer. I need to have evidence that you have sent the money owing to Australia.'

While Mama mumbled and continued to evade answering the questions Loxton fired at him, and other Indian officials filed into the room and engaged in animated talk in their own lingo, Sam hit Mama with an avalanche of questions. Benaud maintained his silence.

'What about the 50,000 people who might miss seeing any cricket today,' Mama pleaded.

'That is your problem, Mama. The BCCI's problem, because I am going to tell them that it is all your fault.'

Loxton and Benaud then left.

Sam told the players that they were not to get dressed ready to play. 'The match may never get off the ground,' he said. He went back to the BCCI area, sought out Mama, and announced: 'Forget our beautiful friendship. Australia will not play in this match.'

There would be no backdown. 'No money,' Sam said, 'no play!'

The crisis was averted when about twenty minutes later Mama went to the Australian dressing-room and handed Loxton the all-important telegraphic receipt. It may not have been classic diplomatic speak that won the day for Sam, but the board members were delighted. Their man had come through in style.

Before the five-Test Indian part of the tour, the Australians played three matches in Pakistan. They played magnificently to win in Dacca (now Dhaka, the capital of Bangladesh), thanks to a brilliant 96 on the mat by Harvey.

The International Cricket Council had recommended that Pakistan prepare turf wickets. The Australians suspected the Pakistanis would not do so. Before departing Australia, a four-day match was arranged at the Gabba to coincide with the Centenary of Queensland – and during periods before and after play Benaud had his men practise on matting. Benaud was sure the Pakistanis would do their own thing regarding the wickets and he knew that they knew they had a better chance of winning on the matting surfaces, especially if they could doctor the tension of the mat before Australia batted. The Australian captain was delighted that one of his bowlers, Ken 'Slasher' Mackay, took to the mat immediately, getting the ball to move appreciably off the matting surface. His leg-cutters were fabulous.

At the Test in Dacca, Benaud had twelfth man Lindsay Kline and other team members not part of the final XI monitor the ground staff's preparations. It was essential to have the mat as taut as possible, for a slack mat would be deadly for the visitors. Pakistan's gun medium-fast bowler Fazal Mahmood was a master of the mat and unless the mat was pulled into line and was taunt, he would have been expected to run through the Australians like a large dose of Epsom salts. The Australians had seen previously how the locals could stretch and loosen the matting wicket, all to suit their purpose.

Thanks to Kline and company's keen-eyed monitoring, the Pakistanis were not allowed to get away with presenting the tourists with a slack mat. Pakistan batted first, all out for 200. Australia's reply brought the cricket world one of the great Test innings. The day was your typical Subcontinental type of day: hot and shirt-clinging humid; the air hazy, almost as if the sun was eclipsed by a thin blanket of fine dust. Opener Les Favell was soon out for a duck, bowled neck and crop by the medium-pacer, Israr Ali. Enter Harvey.

Norm O'Neill (2) and Peter Burge (0) were both soon out. Up the other end Harvey was running a temperature. He was suffering from a serious bout of dysentery. Despite this, Harvey set about the Pakistani attack as if his life depended upon it.

'We'd been out – at the trade commissioner's place – the night before the game started,' Neil recalled. 'I had only just put my pads on when I heard a roar. I was feeling awful. I could hardly keep my head up. In a way my being unable to lift my head worked for me, as the ball was only bouncing about two feet off the ground. With my head down all the time I felt confident. It made me play forward, whereas normally my first movements would be slightly back and across. It was hard, grinding cricket.'

Harvey was visiting the toilet regularly. When you contract dysentery, it hits you like a runaway train. The great loss of liquid is draining and dangerous if you do not keep the fluids up.

Harvey was the eighth Australian wicket to fall. He had scored 96 out of 151, which in time became 225. It was an innings to behold. Fazal got his man in the end; Harvey tried to loft the Pakistani fast-medium bowler over mid-wicket and was bowled. He may have fallen short of a century, but his innings is remembered as one of Test cricket's best.

Michael Charlton witnessed this grand knock. 'Neil must have been to the toilet at least eight times during his time to bat. I know because the commentary box was directly above the toilet and I would see him scurrying towards me, then disappear. I would hear the familiar sound of an ancient toilet chain being pulled and within a minute or two this small, compact figure would reappear to resume his innings. I asked Richie (Benaud) afterwards, "Well, what does one say about an innings like that?" "I will write it down for you," Richie said.

'I made just one change to what Richie had written. He had called the Harvey innings of 96 "one of the greatest innings of all time." I crossed out, "of all time."'

On the field Australia played grand cricket, against the odds, poor food, dreadful accommodation, lack of hygiene at every turn, slapstick umpiring which bordered on the cheating variety, and sickness, which spread through the group.

In Ahmedabad, India, during a game against a Universities XI, the Australians stayed at a place with the unlikely name of the Hotel Ritz. It was, in fact, a reconditioned prison and the foyer at the Hotel Ritz featured a dubious endorsement from the Duke of Edinburgh. Barry Jarman, the side's deputy 'keeper to Wally Grout, told me of the conditions on that tour.

'Gavin Stevens and I were taken to an area of the Hotel Ritz which was called "the stables". And that is exactly what it was, a stable. There was a dirt floor with a mat on it, no glass in the windows, just rungs of iron bars and two old wooden beds that looked like they would collapse under our weight. We said, "Bugger this. You can shove your stables." We carried our bedding to the foyer of the hotel. The floor was green-painted cement and Gavin and I slept there with Wally Pugh, an Australian journalist, and the ABC commentator, Michael Charlton.'

The heat and constant humidity, the food, hotel rooms infested with rats, cockroaches and overrun nightly with cloudy swarms of mosquitoes, who knows what disease they carried, preyed on mind and flesh. The players feared sickness most of all and soon the inevitable came to pay a visit.

The Australians believed that they were being very diligent in bringing Dr Ian McDonald with the touring party. McDonald was a good cricketer in his own right. He was a wicketkeeper, but missed selection for this tour, so he thought he might be able to help in another capacity. He was brother to Colin McDonald, the gutsy opening batsman, and he had the confidence of the players.

McDonald advocated what foods he thought the players should stick to, however some strayed and ate the salads. The salads – crisp lettuce, tomato and the like – looked marvellous to the players. That they were washed in water taken from the Ganges River, which played host to a variety of pollution, including rotting dead animals and even human beings, did not gladden anyone's take on proceedings. Serious illness was afoot and inevitable.

Lindsay 'Spinner' Kline roomed with Gordon Rorke, a huge man with a big appetite and there came a moment when Rorke declared: 'That salad looks fabulous. I am going to get stuck into it.' Spinner was horrified. He told Rorke of his concerns, but no sooner had he turned his back on the big fast bowler than Rorke was stuffing his face with the Pakistani salad.

Rorke, Kline and Stevens all contracted a virulent strain of hepatitis. Nearly every player in the touring side fell foul of fever and dysentery, but that trio really copped it very badly. Rorke played in the Second Test against India at Kanpur in December 1959, but was so ill he could complete just two overs in the Indian first innings. He had to return to Australia early for medical treatment, and never played another Test. The night before the Madras Test match, Stevens was so ill he had to be withdrawn from the match. Stevens ended up in hospital and likewise never played another Test. He was replaced by South Australia's dashing opener Les Favell, who scored his one and only century in his nineteen-match Test career. 'Spinner' Kline, thank goodness, did recover from his illness and played on for Victoria and Australia.

During a get-together of the 1959/60 tourists, Neil Harvey met up with Stevens for the first time in twenty-five years.

'Hey Gavin, do you realise that you missed a big opportunity to create a record in the Subcontinent?'

'Oh yes, Ninna, what was that?

'Well, you were so ill in India you could have become the first Australian Test cricketer to die on tour.'

So many players were stricken that Sam Loxton had to take the field in one match against Indian Universities in Bangalore. Sam scored 33 – not bad for his first first-class match in two years.

Arguably Sam Loxton was the most popular manager of an Australian team of all time. At the age of thirty-eight he was easily the youngest to have been given the role and Sam knew what the players wanted. They yearned for a cold beer after play. In the Subcontinent tourists could get an alcoholic drink only at the biggest of the hotels. Sometimes you had to apply for a liquor permit and sign a statement which in effect said you agreed that you were an alcoholic. Sam circumvented such asides by bringing dozens of cans of beer into his room. He had done a deal with Melbourne-based brewer Carlton and United. Initially 4000 cans of Fosters were made available, but Sam had more supplies organised about the place. He ensured that the cartons of beer were marked 'fruit juice'. His connections with External Affairs did not hurt; there was beer aplenty provided to the team via the High Commissioners in Karachi and New Delhi.

At night after play the players would inevitably gather around Sam's bed. There they sat drinking copious cans of ice-cold Fosters – Sam had them all submerged in a bath full of ice.

Sam the politician met another politician on this tour: US President Dwight Eisenhower. The Third Test at Karachi was watched by President Eisenhower, the former WWII general, who was afforded quite a welcome by another five-star general, Pakistan President Field Marshall Ayub Khan. President Eisenhower appeared wearing a Pakistan team blazer and team tie. Benaud, fast learning the art of diplomacy, presented the US President with a baggy green cap. The president had however picked a terrible day to come to the cricket: Pakistan scored a miserable 104 runs for the day.

The Australians won the hearts of the people in the Subcontinent. They also won the cricket, beating Pakistan 2-0 over three Tests, and India 2-1 over five tightly contested Tests.

The tour only confirmed the great friendship between Neil Harvey and Sam Loxton. The friendship had been there since they were roommates a decade earlier on the Invincibles tour. And it lasted decades into the future.

Round the year 2000 Neil and Sam were encouraged by Sid Barnes Jnr, the son of the great Test opening batsman, to join forces and do their take on Don Bradman's Invincibles tour of 1948 to the people. They put a show together: Sam was the entertainer, Neil the straight man.

'We did hundreds of shows together,' Neil said. 'All we did was talk about the 1948 tour. Sid Barnes Jnr would introduce us and I'd start with a bit about cricket in general, maybe say something briefly about a certain match, then Sam would take over. He added all the embellishments, making us all laugh. He loved an audience did Sam. I have never come across a better storyteller than Sam. No-one could command the floor like Sammy Loxton.'

*An Evening with the Invincibles* kept Neil and Sam busy and young for a few more years. They loved the interaction with the crowd and, of course, Sam revelled being centre stage.

Sam loved this little tale: 'You know, people ask me how good the 1948 side was and I explain it in this way. "George", you know, Donald George Bradman, the little fella, would pick up the ball the umpires left on the ground as they walked to the wicket and he would simply toss it high in the air behind him, not ever looking where it landed. How good were we? Whoever happened to catch the ball Bradman tossed opened the bowling … that's how good the 1948 team happened to be!'

During those shows, tragedy struck.

By that time Sam had been married for twenty-four years, to Jo. After some function on the NSW South Coast, Jo Loxton, who was a willing helper at the popular functions with Barbara Harvey (Neil's second wife), returned home earlier than the others. Sam expected her, as usual, to collect him at Coolangatta Airport.

Sam waited a few minutes, then he phoned home, only to find himself speaking with a policeman who told him the terrible news.

Jo Loxton had been found dead, floating face down in their swimming pool at their home in Runaway Bay. Jo was seventy-five. It was Tuesday, 12 December 2000.

As if the tragic death of his wife Jo was not enough, within an hour Sam learnt that his eldest son, Michael, had been taken by a shark that very afternoon in Fiji, some 2000 kilometres away. The tragedies happened within minutes of one another. Michael had bled to death after being mauled by a 6-metre shark that tore off his right leg and buttocks as he frantically tried to swim to shore to the safety of the Taveuni Garden Island Resort. Michael was forty-seven.

In 2009 Sam and Neil were in England for the Ashes series. There they were sitting at Lord's in one of the corporate boxes – wined, dined and feted, surrounded by mates old and new, but all of them on common ground in their love of the game of cricket. Let Neil take up the story:

'Barbara took a message from Alec Bedser, MCC president, urging us to come to the Committee Room. "Be there by noon, sharp" was the directive. Sammy had no idea what was going on. Barb and I had been tipped off. We walked through the Long Room to the Committee Room and there was Alec, a pint of beer in his huge right hand. He was beaming. "I have an announcement," Sir Alec said. "My friend Sam Loxton, all the way from Melbourne, Australia is … from today a new life member of MCC." I have never seen anyone so happy. Sam was in tears. He had no idea. It was one of the thrills of his life. And there was more to come. During the Test they asked Sammy to ring the bell to resume play. That capped off maybe the greatest week of all for my closest buddy.'

Neil Harvey wrote a lovely tribute to his mate Sammy Loxton in Martin Roger's delightful biography of Sam, *Invincible, the Life and Times of Sam Loxton.* 'It is hard talking about your best mate. It brings tears to my eyes. I loved everything about Sam, his humour, his strut, his fearlessness, his dedication. His knowledge, his skill, his empathy. Slox was like a big brother to me. We were ever so close. I am so proud to have been his mate.'

Sam Loxton passed away in 2011, aged ninety.

*Gordon Rorke*

A few of the blokes got very sick on the 1959/60 tour of Pakistan. I became ill, alongside Gavin Stevens and Lindsay Kline. We were all eventually sent home for medical treatment. Our manager Sam Loxton knew that the odd tipple might help ward off the bugs, so those of us not playing in the Dacca Test match would all pitch in and help the playing group. We gave the players Scotch and water at every break. It was 110 degrees in the water bag and poor Neil was suffering big time with the trots. He played the most extraordinary knock under the most trying of conditions.

*Gordon Rorke was a big man who could bowl at hurricane velocity. He played four Tests, taking ten wickets at 20.30, but he was never quite right after that Pakistan tour.*

CHAPTER SEVENTEEN

# A CALYPSO SUMMER

*'I've never seen the ball hit so hard. I got down on one knee and it hit me right on the driving muscle. I thought my leg was broken.'*
– Lindsay 'Spinner' Kline

FRANK WORRELL WAS the first black man to captain the West Indies cricket team throughout a series. His appointment to lead his national cricket team came less than two weeks after the inauguration of the 35th President of the United States, John Fitzgerald Kennedy, who replaced the unlikely Pakistan-cricket loving Eisenhower. Things were changing.

Worrell was thirty-six years old, highly intelligent and well-educated. He was pretty much a role model for the Barbadian middle class: respectable and respected. He was a member of the Boy Scout movement as a youngster, became a Mason and later was a Manchester University graduate, earning honours in the social services.

The young Frank Worrell possessed the most laid-back demeanour and the coolest of cool heads. His rise in cricket came before that of the global political champion of black South Africa,

Nelson Mandela, yet both men were destined to reach the pinnacle of their respective pursuits.

Uncannily, Sir Donald Bradman sensed that Worrell's West Indians were destined to have an immediate and dramatic effect on not only Australian cricket, but cricket the world over. The Windies began their calypso summer of 1960/61 Down Under in hot and cold fashion. They lost to Western Australia, beat a strong Combined XI, also at the WACA Ground in Perth, then were lucky to draw against South Australia, before – thanks to a stirring 252 from the exciting Rohan Kanhai – thrashing Victoria at the MCG.

In October 1960 John Rutherford, who we remember toured England with Australia as an opening batsman in 1956, was leading WA against Worrell's men when he started to feel queasy. Worrell was batting at the time and he noticed that something was wrong, terribly wrong, with Rutherford. Frank and John had become good friends when they played in the Lancashire League for two seasons – 1959 and 1960.

Worrell asked: 'John, are you okay?' Rutherford tried to speak. He opened his mouth but could not get the words out. 'This man is ill,' Frank declared, 'he needs to be taken to hospital.' Rutherford was stretchered from the ground and rushed to Royal Perth Hospital where he was assessed immediately – and told that he had suffered a mild stroke.

At the age of thirty-one, Rutherford was warned off playing cricket again. It took months of rehabilitation for him to return to good health and to be able to return to work as a teacher.

Bradman was keeping a close eye on the West Indians' progress. He loved the sheer pace of Wes Hall, the brilliance of young Kanhai and the immense all-round skills of Garfield 'Garry' Sobers. Bradman thought that with the respective teams led by Benaud and Worrell, this series could be something special. Sobers had not set the world on fire leading up to the First Test in Brisbane. Bradman had a few brief discussions with the twenty-four-year-old Sobers, who confessed that he was struggling to find form with the bat. 'Don't worry,' said The Don cheerfully, 'you will get them when you really need to get them.' And get them he certainly did.

Cammie Smith, a hard-hitting opening batsman, had a penchant to hit out at anything at any time and was just as likely to hook Alan Davidson for six first ball of a Test match as he was to let the ball pass harmlessly by the off stump. Benaud, who had studied the West Indian batting line-up and the technique of all of their players, hoped that Worrell would select the erratic Smith in lieu of the more solid and steady Joe Solomon. To that end, in a tour game he said to Davidson, 'Go easy on this bloke today, Davo.' Smith promptly put Davidson's first ball over fine leg for six. A few hooked fours later, Benaud said, 'It is okay Davo. Now, he's all yours.'

'Jeez, Rich, I've been trying to knock him over for two overs or more!'

On the eve of the First Test at Brisbane, Sir Donald Bradman asked Benaud if he could 'speak to the boys' over their team dinner.

Bradman didn't follow the time-honoured traditional route of most cricket administrators of making a rousing speech about playing for team and country and playing well to preserve the brilliance of those players past, whose deeds are set in historical gold. No, Bradman said he hoped that the team ethic was *not* to play a 'win at any cost' strategy, which had born some dreadful, slow and dull cricket throughout the 1950s.

'This Australian side could lead the way to one of the most attractive cricket series seen in this country for a long time – however, fellas, it is entirely up to you.' Bradman knew Benaud would take risks and, from what he had seen of Worrell's captaincy in the lead-up matches, he reckoned between the pair they could fashion a brilliant Test series.

On the first morning of the First Test, Benaud read in the newspapers where his leg-spin bowling had the 'wood' on the brilliant young West Indian all-rounder Sobers. Benaud hated such media hype. Yes, he had dismissed Sobers a couple of times, but that didn't mean that he had Sobers in his pocket.

Benaud and his vice-captain Harvey had seen, and marvelled at, the skill of Sobers when Australia toured the Caribbean in 1955. In February 1958, Sobers broke Len Hutton's record Test score of 364 by hitting 365 not out for the Windies against Pakistan at Sabina Park, Kingston, Jamaica.

In Brisbane the Windies batted first, scoring a highly creditable 453. The start had been shaky at best. Alan Davidson cut through the top order with pacy left-arm swingers, getting Cammie Smith (7), Conrad Hunte (24) and Rohan Kanhai (24) to have the visitors a vulnerable 3/65. Then came the combined forces of Sobers and Worrell. They put on a memorable 174 for the fourth wicket. Sobers finished with 132 – Benaud's misgivings about the hype were justified – and Worrell, 65, but the statistics don't tell us anything about the quality of the stroke-play. No bold statistic can paint a word picture of the majesty of a cover drive, exquisitely executed to a late swinging Davidson delivery, which would have had a player of lesser clay reaching forward in hope. Nor can a statistic describe the way Sobers moved, at first instance to a Benaud leg break, only to swiftly correct himself then sway onto the back foot and hit the ball with awesome power to the point boundary. Mere statistics cannot ever tell the full story of any cricketer's career.

Throughout the Sobers onslaught, the tall and slight Lindsay 'Spinner' Kline fielded at mid-on. There he copped a swag of hard-hit Sobers drives. 'I have never seen a ball hit so hard. I got down on one knee to stop one of Garry's drives and it hit me right on the driving muscle. I thought it had broken my leg.'

Tom Goodman, cricket writer for *The Sydney Morning Herald*, described Sobers' knock as 'one of the greatest Test innings of our time'. Bradman, never one to offer compliments to a player, walked to the Windies' dressing-room and sought to speak with Garry: 'Congratulations. You did not disappoint me.'

Australia replied with 505. Bobby Simpson (92) and Norm O'Neill, who hit a stirring 181, laced with twenty-two powerful boundaries, led the way. Harvey was bowled by Windies left-arm spinner Alf Valentine for 15, which was really the start of a pretty miserable batting series for Neil. After another stirring bowling performance by Davidson (6/67), Australia was left with a very gettable target of 233 for victory. At tea Australia was 6/92, needed 130 runs with three wickets in hand. As they walked off, Bradman said to Benaud: 'What are your thoughts?'

'We are going for a win.'

'Good to hear it,' Sir Donald smiled.

When Benaud returned to the field after the tea break with Davidson, they decided to unsettle the Windies with lots of quick singles: break up the field, break the rhythm of the bowlers and perhaps annoy the bowler to such an extent that more bad balls would present.

'They'll crack, if only we can get the pressure on them,' Richie thought. 'Pressure and more and more pressure and they must crack ... they've done it so often before.'

Yet Benaud sensed something was entirely different with Worrell leading this young, energetic and exciting bunch of cricketers. They were inexperienced and not used to the pressure cooker atmosphere of the Test stage, but Benaud could sense their hunger for the contest.

'This was not the same team as they'd had before, they had a leader this time ... a great player in his own right, a shrewd tactician and a man who had the respect and liking of his side ... and of the opposition, too. A great cricketer this Worrell ... a great cricketer in every sense of the word. A quiet man with a sense of humour, and a throaty laugh, the sort of man one cannot imagine falling into panic.'

The plan worked and kept working. Australia got to 6/226. Davidson was unconquered on 80, and Benaud 52, when he dropped the ball at his feet and called for a run. Davidson reacted swiftly, but little Joe Solomon at mid-wicket swooped, grabbed the ball and threw down the wicket with Davo stranded: Australia 7/226, still seven runs to win. Davo later said the run was a 'suicidal attempt at a single; even Usain Bolt would have struggled to make his ground'.

That very day my Mount Lawley Cricket Club teammate Terry Jenner, aged sixteen, and I, aged fifteen, were at the WACA Ground for training with the WA Colts Squad.

As we meandered our way from the nets to the dressing-room, we noticed players walking from the main ground. It was tea-time in a match involving the Governor's XI. Magically a gleaming black Rolls-Royce cruised slowly alongside us. The vehicle stopped near where we stood and the back door opened.

'Boys, it's the last over in Brisbane ... Australia should win it. Hop in the back and listen with me.'

We didn't hesitate and accepted the invitation to sit in the back seat of the Rolls-Royce of Governor Lieutenant-General Sir Charles Gairdner to listen to the last over. Now Sir Charles as a boy was educated at Repton in Derbyshire, England, and he learnt a lesson in fair play early in the piece. He was once thrashed by the headmaster and future Archbishop of Canterbury William Temple for submitting a poem by Henry Longfellow as his own composition.

He later became a prominent figure in both world wars. In 1945, as personal representative of British PM Winston Churchill, he visited the headquarters of General Douglas MacArthur; became Governor of Western Australia in 1951, and had a hospital – Sir Charles Gairdner Hospital – named in his honour in 1963.

We listened intently as Benaud hooked at a Wes Hall bouncer, got a glove and Gerry Alexander gleefully took the catch behind: 8/228, still five runs to win. Ian Meckiff somehow scraped together two runs and by the last over only three runs were required for victory. Wally Grout negotiated a few balls, then he hooked a Hall bouncer, the ball soaring to the mid-wicket boundary. It seemed a certain four, but Conrad Hunte had other ideas. He chased the ball down and threw magnificently to the end Grout was running.

Grout was well out of his ground when the bails were removed. The batsmen had completed two runs: Australia 9/232. In walked Lindsay Kline, the man they called 'Spinner.' Two balls left. Spinner decided to push and run. He dug the attempted yorker out and ran. Meckiff scampered towards the batting end, but he didn't count on Solomon at mid-wicket.

The story goes that Solomon had honed his throwing skills knocking mangoes out of trees in his home town of Port Mourant, Berbice, British Guiana (these days, Guyana). As Kline ran to the safety of the non-striker's end, Meckiff scampered the other way. The ball had slewed from the bottom of Kline's bat to just in front of square where Peter Lashley was about to field.

Suddenly Solomon, the mid-wicket specialist, appeared. 'Out the way, move, move, it's mine.' Solomon grabbed the ball cleanly and threw down the stumps side-on with Meckiff way out of his ground. Result: the first tied Test in history.

Meckiff was inconsolable. He thought Australia had lost the match; Kline wasn't sure whether it was a win or a loss and most of the players on both sides were bouncing about in an atmosphere of total confusion. Finally, amid all the laughter and tears and almighty din, someone yelled out: 'It's a tie. The first tied Test in history.'

Bradman was delighted: 'That was the greatest Test match of all time.'

Neil Harvey remembers it all. 'The final moments were thrilling and got over fast. Davidson and Benaud came up with a superb partnership in the second innings after O'Neill had scored a splendid century in the first innings. And Joe Solomon's throw from an angle at which only one stump could be seen, was spectacular. I think one of the reasons why we could not win was that the grass had now been mowed on the final morning. The growth was fast and hence the outfield was very slow.'

Never one to dwell on a slice of bad luck or a dodgy umpiring decision, Neil didn't believe he was out, caught Sobers at second slip off Wes Hall, in the Australian second innings. He had scored just 5 and his dismissal left Australia 2/7. 'I still believe Sobers scooped the ball up on the half volley. Later I saw Gerry Alexander, a veterinary surgeon, bandage Garry's dislocated finger.'

Not that Harvey made an incident of the matter. 'No, Sobey never brought it up down the track and I never mentioned it. My attitude was then, as it is now … let sleeping dogs lie.'

As Jenner and I sat rather stunned in the governor's car, he commented: 'Funny thing, you know. Alan McGilvray should have been on air for that final over. I wonder what happened to him.' McGilvray was the doyen of radio commentators, yet this day of the tie proved to be his greatest professional disaster.

When Ken Mackay fell to Sonny Ramadhin for 28 just before tea, Australia was 6/92 and McGilvray announced: 'That's it, the game's over. We've lost it. I'm going home.' Brisbane-based ABC radio commentary veteran Clive Harburg pleaded with Mac to stay and see the game out, but McGilvray was adamant. He caught the 4 pm flight to Sydney and missed all the drama. He was crestfallen when he arrived in Sydney to learn of the game's first Test tie, sick to his stomach. Even a quarter of a century later he was lamenting his lamentable decision.

That left Michael Charlton in commentary box with local boy Harburg. At the death, Harburg attempted to hand the mike over to Charlton to broadcast the final stanza of this epic contest, but Charlton said no. 'He refused to take over at that final stage of the broadcast so I could do it; the hometown boy. What a talent is Michael and what a gentleman,' Harburg said later.

A word about McGilvray. Mac, as everyone called him, did like the odd tipple: a cold beer or two by day, a bottle of scotch by night. One day in 1983 at the Adelaide Oval I was working with the ABC, spending a number of stints alongside him at a one-day match. A local brewery had donated two dozen cans of beer. The ABC commentary team agreed to save the coldies until day's end. When not at the microphone, McGilvray could be seen at the back of the members' stand drinking with his great mate, Keith Miller. When stumps were drawn, we found one full can in the esky. McGilvray had cleaned up the other twenty-three. And in keeping with his iron constitution, McGilvray did not slur one word. By that time, Richie Benaud was in the commentary box himself, for Channel Nine, in the Bradman Stand at the other end of the ground. Can't imagine Richie knocking back twenty-three cans in a day's play at the mic; perhaps a crisp white at day's end.

With all the ebbs and flows of this Test match, the game set up the series. The players were excited, so too the public. The press waxed lyrical for weeks. The entire nation couldn't wait for the Second Test match. Australia won it easily, by seven wickets. NSW left arm spinner Johnny Martin took three key wickets in the West Indian second dig, snaring Kanhai (25), Sobers (0) and Worrell (0).

In the Third Test at the SCG, Sobers led the way for the Windies with a dashing 168. The visitors scored more than 300 in both innings. The 'keeper Alexander continued his good form with the bat, scoring 108 in the second innings. In Australia's second innings Neil Harvey batted beautifully for 85, his lone score of over 50 in the entire series. A tie in Brisbane, an Australian victory in the Second Test at the MCG and a Windies win in the Third in Sydney really set the series up for the looming Fourth Test in Adelaide.

Australia, severely depleted with injuries to three of its stars – Harvey, Davidson and Meckiff – brought in NSW speedster Frank Mission and WA fast bowler Des Hoare for his debut Test match and recalled Lindsay Kline. Hoare struck early, trapping Hunte for six. The game ebbed and flowed. Kanhai slammed a brilliant century in each innings, Lance Gibbs took a hat-trick. The young off-spinner, tall, gangly, bereft of one single ounce of fat, took 6/97 off 35 overs, but it was his hat-trick that helped enrich a West Indian performance, led by Kanhai's mastery at the crease.

Gibbs trapped Ken Mackay lbw for 29, then had Grout groping forward in hope to a dipping, high-bouncing off-break which he edged via bat and pad to Sobers at backward short leg. Mission came in to face the music. He decided that he would prod well forward and keep his bat well back almost behind the front pad. Gibbs wheeled down a fast yorker. Mission's bat was still high in the back lift when the ball crashed into the base of his stumps. From that moment on, every time Gibbs and Mission met up, Lance would say with a smile: 'Thanks, Frank!'

Needing 460 to win in the final innings, Australia slumped to 7/203 at tea on the final day. A number of players escorted Spinner Kline, the 'hope of the side' to the nets for a last-minute 'brush up', for inevitably he would soon be in the middle confronting Hall, Worrell and Gibbs.

In those days the Adelaide Oval nets were situated behind the George Giffen Stand and there arrived Kline, accompanied by Norm O'Neill and Johnny Martin. The pair bowled to Kline and in a quarter of an hour's batting they got Spinner out no less than eleven times. Situation hopeless. A woman watching behind the net had surveyed the scene. She said: 'Well, Mr Kline. I can see it is an absolute waste of time sending you in to bat!'

Kline had had a poor Test, taking 0/109 and 0/40. Was it possible that he would somehow help Mackay defy the West Indian attack for nigh on two hours to save the match?

Neither O'Neill nor Martin thought such a thing to be possible; so too the old lady, whose beady stare matched her cutting remarks, as she shook her head to and fro, every now and then letting her thoughts be known to those spectators cheerfully huddled about her.

The West Indians got through their overs in double quick time, bowling around 100 eight-ball overs for the day. Runs were of no moment. Australia, having been 3/21 overnight, was never in the hunt to win, having a near hopeless task of scoring 460 in the last innings. Fieldsmen were clustered about the bat. Michael Charlton and Johnnie Moyes shared the microphone for the ABC radio coverage as Mackay and Kline continued to defy everything the Windies attack could throw at them. Moyes declared: 'The West Indies are rushing their overs way too much. They need to settle and take their time in working the batsmen over.'

In rushing things the visitors were playing into the batsmen's hands. Somehow the last pair's last stand had reached 50. Yes, there were easy runs to be had as the fieldsmen were all round the bat, no-one out on the boundary. A simple push through the ring of close in fieldsmen could run to the fence. Worrell was bowling tightly. He had already taken three cheap wickets with his left-arm medium-pacers when he caused Mackay to squeeze a delivery uppishly towards Sobers at short leg. Sobers claimed the catch.

But no. Umpire Colin Egar had other ideas.

'No ball!' he bellowed. The late call from Egar was like a dagger to the heart of West Indian cricket. Worrell wanted no complaints to be aired aloud on the field. He had drilled his men well in that regard. He would later say: 'It was a long, hot day. The umpires feel the heat and the tension every bit as much, if not more, than the players. I have no complaints about the incident.'

And so to the last over. Benaud, who in those days was an occasional smoker, found himself chain-smoking. Wally Grout, who loved a cold beer whatever time of night and day, announced with plenty of overs to go: 'Fellas, I plan to down a beer for every over these guys survive. I will be happy if you have to carry me out!' Now with just eight Wes Hall balls to negotiate, Grout found himself anchored to his seat. He dared not move to the fridge to get another beer lest his action prove bad luck. There was, certainly since Benaud's reign as captain, a sort of unwritten law that in a tense situation like this the players must retain their seat: no going to the bathroom, no leaving, however briefly, to grab a beer.

Few among the Australian team could believe how well Kline batted. It was as if a splendid defensive batsman with a blade as wide as the stumps was the incumbent: someone better than Lindsay by far, but a lookalike. Spinner middled everything they bowled at him. He let the ball go when it was just outside off and he batted for a total of 109 minutes, even hitting two fours in an unconquered 15. O'Neill and Martin couldn't believe their eyes, nor could the little old lady Spinner had encountered at the nets.

Hall charged in. He bowled like the wind and he threw everything into every single delivery. Mackay took the final over. A couple of deliveries he let go harmlessly outside off. He nudged one past point for a couple of runs, negotiated a couple of short ones targeting his ribs, until the final ball cometh. 'Slasher' promised himself that if Hall bowled a short one at him he would take the ball flush on the body. All he needed to do was to avoid having his gloves or bat anywhere near the ball.

Here it comes. The last ball. And what a let-down. Wes overstepped the mark. It was a no-ball. Some 20,000 people flooded the ground yelling 'it's a draw, it's a draw'.

Michael Charlton called the action. Mackay yelled desperately: 'Get 'em off, get 'em off.'

The premature flood of the crowd only heightened the tension.

Poor Slasher was beside himself.

Minutes passed.

Now, the final delivery.

Wes Hall pushed off, seemingly so far back in his run that he had used the picket fence as a launch pad. Indeed, the ball was lightning fast and short.

Slasher lifted his arms high. Everything important, bat and gloves, well out of the way. He took the ball mid-ships; it struck him flush on the side of his body.

'It was magnificent,' said Harvey who watched the replay on TV from his Sydney home.

Having pushed their way through the madding crowd, the last pair finally got back into the Australian dressing-room and were greeted with smiles and slaps on the back all round. The bruise on Slasher's side had already developed – a dinner-plate-sized red welt which would soon develop into a multi-coloured bruise splashed with dark blue and purple highlights. A delighted and relieved

Benaud sidled up to Slasher, who was standing with the others proudly showing his bruised side, a prized battlefield trophy, and with a light tap on the shoulder said softly: 'Thanks, Slasher.'

The series was locked in at 1-1, with one tie and one draw, when the teams met for the final Test at the MCG. Former Test opening batsman of the Bradman era, Bill Ponsford, then working at the MCG, asked Victorian Cricket Association secretary Jack Ledward for his take on how many fans were expected to attend the first day.

'Oh, about something up to 50,000,' said Jack.

The day arrived and an extraordinary 90,800 turned up.

'Jeez, Jack, you are some judge,' Ponny quipped.

Test fast bowler Ian Meckiff confided in a friend about the West Indians: 'They're so likeable that it's dangerous for a bowler. I should be building myself up to hate their batsmen.

'When we arrived in Brisbane for the First Test both teams were staying at the big Lennon's Hotel. The West Indies had been in Brisbane for more than a week to play a game against Queensland. When the bulk of the Australian team arrived we had no sooner put our bags down than the West Indian boys were around to welcome us. This won't go down in a "How to Play Cricket" book giving advice to young players, but two nights before the Test started four or five Australians, including myself, and the same number of West Indian players got together in Garry Sobers' room and played calypso records and talked cricket to about 2 am.'

Worrell laid down the law early in the tour. There was to be no drinking in public. What his players did in the privacy of their hotel room was another matter.

The West Indian team was afforded a tickertape parade through the streets of Melbourne and nigh on 100,000 people lined the streets. Those young women who could manage to get within reach planted kisses on the faces, neck and shirt collars of the West Indians.

The last Test went all the way as well, Australia winning by two wickets.

Sir Donald Bradman, so taken with the excitement of the series, offered Sobers a contract to play for South Australia the following Sheffield Shield season. Queensland signed Hall, West Australia Kanhai.

Harvey had a pretty lean time of it. He played in four of the matches, scoring a paltry 143 runs at 17.87 with a highest score of 85, and batted at number six in the last Test. Those figures did not reflect fully the quality of his batting that 1960/61 summer, for overall in all first-class matches he hit three centuries (a high of 229) in compiling 849 runs at 56.60.

Harvey felt Worrell received more than his fair share of accolades for the pace and excitement of the series. 'I would say in many respects Richie contributed more to the spectacular nature of the series than did Worrell,' he said. 'In Brisbane Worrell bowled quite defensively, attacking the leg stump with a leg field of about five or six men. He was often the chief culprit, bowling negatively at one end while Wes Hall really got stuck into us from the other. On the other hand, never once during the series did Richie resort to negative bowling. I do not make this comparison of the tactics adopted by the two captains to discredit Worrell, but I do think that the part Australia played in the immense success of the series deserves at least equal recognition to the job done by the visitors.'

Harvey does not believe all the hype about the tied Test match.

'This Test was not the greatest of all time. I think this assessment is built entirely from the result. I do not think the Brisbane tied Test was anywhere near as good as the Manchester Test match in 1961. The chief difference between the two games was that the drama of the West Indies match is built entirely around the happenings of the final twenty minutes, whereas in Manchester the whole of the final day was played under a spell of drama.'

Despite Harvey's poor batting form in the Test matches of the 1960/61 summer, he still refrained from wearing glasses at any time throughout the season.

'Perhaps I was foolish. Vanity, I guess.'

*Des Hoare*

In my early years Neil Harvey was regarded by most of my playing teammates as Australia's premier batsman. My recollection of his style and technique is that he never seemed to be troubled unduly by even the fastest bowling and, despite having quite a high back lift, was so fast on his feet that he had plenty of time to play his strokes. It was also very difficult for a bowler to restrict his scoring because his range and shot making was so complete. Rightly or wrongly I formed a view that he was possibly more comfortable against sheer speed than a swinging ball. I seem to recall that he was troubled occasionally by Ray Strauss. Perhaps that applied to most batsmen.

Personally, I found him to be very friendly and quietly modest and unassuming.

Although our paths crossed less than those of most first-class players I always regarded him with the highest degree of respect.

Perhaps my most lasting memory of Neil is of the match in which he captained an Australian XI versus the West Indies at the WACA at the beginning of the 1960/61 season. In that match Wes Hall bowled for the first time in Australia in a first-class match and he was quite electrifying. His pace and ferocity was something over and above what most of us had seen before. Those of us in the dressing-room waiting our turn to bat were unusually quiet. He bowled only three balls to Norm O'Neill, the first two of which had gone past him before he got the bat down and the third caught an edge and was caught by the 'keeper. In this situation Neil played a beautiful and untroubled inning of 80 runs then made another 63 in the second innings at a time when the West Indies were pressing for victory.

It was a classic performance. I hope that my memory is not playing me false here but I believe that there was one occurrence during one of Neil's innings in that match which showed how comfortable he was at the crease. Whilst batting he realised that he had forgotten to wear his box but waited until the next drinks break to have one brought out.

*Des Hoare was a fiery fast bowler who bowled in tandem with Ron Gaunt for WA on the fast, bouncy WACA wicket in Perth. He played one Test match, against Frank Worrell's West Indians at Adelaide Oval in the summer of 1960/61, taking 2/68.*

CHAPTER EIGHTEEN

# CAPTAIN AT LORD'S

*'Richie came to me before the toss and he said, "It is all yours!"'*
– Neil Harvey

AFTER A LONG sea journey, during which the players were engaged in daily exercise under the watchful eye of Brian Booth, who was in the touring party but was also a physical trainer, and a stopover in Colombo where the team played a one-day match against Ceylon (now Sri Lanka), the SS *Himalaya* finally docked in Tilbury, Essex. It was 1960, and the Australian team was still travelling to England by ship. It was a new-look team, with just four players who had toured England previously: captain Richie Benaud, deputy Neil Harvey, Alan Davidson and Colin McDonald – and consequently they were not favoured to win.

The traditional joust with the British press was easily dealt with by Benaud, who had spent time working for the *Daily Express* along with his long association with newspapers in Australia. He was not just a cricket columnist but a trained journalist – he had done police rounds, and knew the caper. Benaud was a clever and shrewd customer. He could read the mood of people, and soon had the press eating out of his hand, which can make life a lot more pleasant for a touring captain.

The Australians quickly settled into the Waldorf Hotel, a grand Victorian establishment right in the heart of Covent Garden. Australia House was nearby, just a Neil Harvey cover drive away, the place to catch up with the news via a swag of newspapers from back home. The first fortnight was a packed program: two weeks solid net practice at Lord's and one big show or event night after night. The players invariably had to wear formal attire, partaking in cocktail parties galore, and memorable nights such as the Cricket Writers' Dinner at Fishmongers Hall and, perhaps best of all, The Lord's Taverners spring luncheon, attended by The Duke of Edinburgh and held in the Long Room in the members' Pavilion at Lord's Cricket Ground.

In an early tour match new chum Booth, an elegant NSW right-handed batsman, was chuffed to hear from the region of cover a Worcester player – Tom Graveney – declare: 'Well done Brian. Congratulations on your first run on English soil.' Booth wrote Graveney's words in his tour diary, which he kept up to date throughout the cricket journey in the northern summer of 1961.

On came Benaud to bowl. Before long he cried out in pain as he delivered a wrong'un. Benaud felt shooting pains in his right shoulder. Something was dreadfully wrong. When the players returned from the ground to Droitwich's Raven Hotel, Richie sat on the bed in his room, scarcely able to raise his bowling arm.

Conversely, by mid-May, 1961, Neil Harvey was in good spirits, both with his batting form and with news from Iris back home. Iris had joined Tupperware as a dealer. Within three months she would be a manager, and within two years a distributor, with Neil an administrator (an arrangement that was maintained until Neil remarried in 1976). The news put Neil's mind at ease.

Australia bowled England out for a paltry 195 in the first innings of the First Test at Edgbaston, Birmingham, with Ken Mackay (4/57 off 29 overs) and Benaud (3/15 off 14.3 overs) grabbing the lion's share of the wickets. Australia replied with 9/516. Harvey top-scored with a lovely 114. England made plenty in reply and a draw ensued.

Benaud's injury niggled, and he had other problems, quite unrelated to his shoulder injury. The team manager, Syd Webb, QC, was a stringent cricket board disciple. He possessed all the banter of a top-flight lawyer; some said the man could find a way to win any situation. Just before the First Test, O'Neill had sustained an injury to his right knee. The three Test selectors Benaud, Harvey and McDonald sat down on a bench at Euston Station. The trio were joined by Syd Webb. The manager held a medical report and blurted: 'Well, O'Neill is out of the Test.' 'C'mon, Syd,' Benaud said, 'Normie hasn't had a fitness test yet.'

'I am telling you lot,' Syd's eyes narrowed, 'O'Neill is not playing … and that is that.'

Benaud was in no mood for this nonsense. He told Webb that he was the team manager and had no say in team selection. 'We, the three Australian selectors, Messrs Benaud, Harvey and McDonald, find your move to interfere in team selection to be unacceptable in the extreme. If we deem O'Neill fit to play, he will play in the First Test.'

Webb didn't back down immediately, but he finally relented and Benaud won that little battle.

O'Neill, of course, did play at Edgbaston and hit a scorching 82.

Webb had sent Benaud to a mate of his to treat his shoulder, and the mate started Benaud on a course of radiotherapy, which was not helping. Word of that reached the ear of a medical specialist from Sydney, Dr Brian Corrigan, who had worked for the NSW

Cricket Association as a part-time medical consultant, and had followed the Australians to England, getting work at University College Hospital in Gower Street, London. Corrigan was fuming. He noted that Benaud's injury was a 'terrible tear, very extensive and very unusual'. He'd torn the subscapularis right down to the capsule that contains the shoulder.

Benaud swapped horses – and Webb, of course, was unimpressed that Benaud had quit the medical treatment he had set up for him. In fact, Syd Webb was livid.

In May, Neil Harvey was back to his brilliant best with a scorching, chanceless 120 against Lancashire at Manchester. It was his sixtieth first-class ton, putting him second only to Sir Donald Bradman at the time on the list of Australian century-makers.

Just before the Second Test match was due to be played at Lord's, Dr Corrigan told Benaud: 'You should not play this game.'

'Richie was like a bear with a sore head,' Dr Corrigan later recalled. 'He would have done almost anything to turn out at Lord's. He was crestfallen. I guess every Australian Test captain wants to lead his men in a Test match at Lord's. And this one, in June 1961, was Richie's only chance to do so,' Dr Corrigan said.

The risk was that Benaud may make his injury worse and miss the rest of the tour if he played. He had to pull out.

'Richie came to me before the toss,' Neil recalled, 'and he said, "It is all yours!"

'I asked him "Is there anything you want me to do?"

'"No, Ninna. It's your team. That is the way I want it."'

Benaud had every confidence in Harvey. He knew the players in the team would have run through a brick wall for the man. They idolised him. The injured leader had no concerns about Harvey's ability to take over the captaincy.

There was an article in a local morning newspaper that asserted the Australians were unable to play quality spin bowling. The article also pointed out the Aussies' inability to overcome the threat of England spin twins Jim Laker and Tony Lock. The article mentioned a few Australian batsmen, including Harvey. Benaud made sure a copy of the paper was placed over Harvey's breakfast plate. Just as a little spur.

The two captains – Colin Cowdrey and Harvey – donned their blazers and walked to the centre at Lord's. Cowdrey won the toss and decided that England would bat. Harvey was disappointed to lose the toss, as he thought the pitch looked a good batting surface. Keith Miller, writing for the *Daily Express*, agreed, proclaiming the wicket magnificent: 'We are in for the biggest runs-fest since the war.'

Lord's is a curious little ground. Before the ground grew on him, Miller said his first impression of Lord's was that it was 'a crummy little place'. It has a distinctive slope: the north-west side of the ground is 2.5 metres higher than the south-east side. When Thomas Lord first settled on the land at St John's Wood to be his new Lord's Cricket Ground in 1814, some necessary refinements were done to the top end of the ground, where the St John's Wood duck pond was situated, which may well be connected to the fact that the outfield was notorious for getting waterlogged. The slope, of course, causes appreciable deviation in the bounce of the ball on the pitch, making it easier to move the ball in to the right-hander when bowling from the Pavilion End and to move the ball away when bowling from the Nursery End. The slope was in great form for this match.

Before the team took to the field all the players took time to wish Neil well. 'It made me extremely happy,' Harvey said. 'It makes a world of difference to a captain to know that every one of his players are behind him all the way.'

Davidson would open the bowling, but not before sidling up to his new captain: 'Ninna, I really should be sitting this one out with Richie, but I am doing it for you, mate.'

Only a few balls from Davidson to Geoff Pullar from the Pavilion End were enough to convince Harvey that something was amiss with the pitch – there was a ridge at the Nursery End of the wicket. Soon enough it had acquired a capital letter – it was the Ridge.

'We soon found that balls darted at strange angles and odd heights,' said Harvey. 'Subsequent examination showed that the Ridge was really the top of a drain which was lain under the wicket many years before.'

With the England score at 14, Pullar took a ball high from Davidson on the splice of the bat and the ball spooned gently to Peter Burge in the gully. It was the easiest catch imaginable and Burge, usually a good mover with good hands in the gully, somehow dropped the chance. Harvey muttered quietly, 'I don't believe it!' Burge later admitted: 'My three-year-old could have caught that easily.'

Davidson soon got his man, clean bowling Pullar between bat and pad. England 1/26. By lunch Raman Subba Row (48) and Ted Dexter (27) were out and England's score stood at 3/87. Harvey was well satisfied with the morning's work. An hour before stumps England was all out for 206. Davidson had bowled magnificently, taking 5/42 off 24.3 overs. The last hour of the day saw the England fast bowlers Fred Trueman and Brian Statham give the Australians a terrible battering. In the third over Statham bowled Colin McDonald and then Bobby Simpson, whom Harvey had promoted to bat number three, copped a nasty rising ball straight from the

Ridge and managed only to edge an easy catch to Ray Illingworth in the gully.

'We were really in deep trouble at 2/6. But Bill Lawry who showed tremendous tenacity and courage – he took numerous blows to the body – and I held out to stumps. We were 2/42.'

Next day, a fabulous, courageous 130 by Lawry, playing only his second Test, and great supporting innings by Peter Burge (46), Ken Mackay (54) and a genuine tail wag with Graham McKenzie hitting 34 and Frank Mission an unconquered 25, saw Australia reach 340, a more than handy lead of 134. Harvey scored 27 before falling to the hostile Trueman. Lawry's knock was as courageous an innings as Harvey had ever seen in big cricket. Davo said that after play he was at the massage table and he noticed Lawry next to him.

Lawry winced as he removed his shirt. Davo recalled: 'His side was a mass of black. He had copped a terrible hammering from the England pair, Trueman and Statham. But Bill's innings was all courage and an inspiration.'

The pitch was getting increasingly more dangerous, especially with the bowlers operating from the Pavilion End and aiming at the Ridge. Some deliveries would kick off the Ridge at the batsman's throat and others would scoot low like the old-fashioned grubber.

Before the England second innings began, Harvey made a big decision. After consultation with Davidson, Harvey decided to have the nineteen-year-old debutant Graham McKenzie bowl at the Ridge.

McKenzie was a raw talent. He was a huge man, over six feet, broad of shoulder and so big and strong he was nicknamed 'Garth' after the popular He-Man comic strip character. In the 1960/61 season he came into the Western Australian side more as an opening batsman than opening bowler. Fortunately for Graham, when bowling in the WACA Ground nets before the West Indies tour match against WA, Frank Worrell had watched McKenzie bowl very closely. He predicted a bright future for the youngster as a fast bowler in Test cricket.

McKenzie said: 'I bowled okay in the first innings, getting Colin Cowdrey, my first Test wicket. Alan bowled beautifully. Just before we took the field in the second innings Neil and Alan asked me to join them. Neil had an idea that my bowling would ideally suit bowling to the end which contained the Ridge.

'"Just the right length for Garth," Harvey said.

'Davo agreed and so that is how I got to bowl the other end – into the Ridge – in the second dig.'

'Graham bowled better than any of us thought he could,' said Harvey. 'He operated off a short run and really made the ball fizz at good speed. He picked up a terrific 5/37 off 29 overs claiming the wickets of Peter May, Ted Dexter, John Murray, Tony Lock and Freddie Trueman. He helped tremendously towards England being dismissed for just 202. We needed just 69 runs for victory.'

McKenzie first met Harvey on that last frenetic day of the Tied Test in Brisbane. Western Australia were in town to play a Sheffield Shield match a day or two after the Test finished. Garth thought he might pop out to the Gabba to watch the final stages of the Test. At game's incredible end he found himself in the Australian dressing-room. There he met Benaud and Harvey and the nucleus of the team among which he would soon be touring England.

'In England during the county matches and of course in the Lord's Test, I found Neil a good captain and I always felt comfortable with him. He and Richie worked so well together,' McKenzie recalled. 'They and the other senior players always made the new players feel an integral part of the touring side. They made us feel welcome: ever encouraging and supportive.

'Interestingly when we first got to the Waldorf Hotel, our home away from home in London, Richie stood amongst us and let us know just which journalists could be trusted and those who could not. "Don't trust that bloke", "He's to be avoided", "That fella is terrific" and so on.'

After Australia's top-class bowling and fielding, Harvey's men needed just 69 runs to win, but things got a little dicey with Trueman and Statham bowling with their tails up. The Ridge was worse than ever and gremlins began to appear in the collective psyche of the team when wickets started to tumble alarmingly. McDonald was caught in the gully at 15, Lawry left at the same score trying to hook Trueman, then O'Neill came in, played back and copped an unplayable delivery which seamed off the Ridge. Round that time with Australia 3/19, Harvey called for a pair of replacement batting gloves. Twelfth man Booth dutifully rushed down the stairs from the Australian dressing-room clutching the all-important gloves. He walked through the Long Room until he reached the tall glass doors that led to the walkway to the ground. But he didn't figure about the official who stood by the closed doors.

'No entry here, son,' the man said gruffly. Booth explained that he had to get the replacement gloves to Harvey out in the middle, but the man wouldn't budge.

'Only time these doors are opened is at the start of play, the luncheon interval and tea adjournment, end of play and meantime, of course, when a wicket falls,' the officious gatekeeper said sternly. 'You'll need to go downstairs and find the little gate. Easily found, sir!' Booth desperately rushed downstairs to find a gate to the ground and by the time he got within twenty yards of the fence he heard the crowd roar.

'Oh, no. Harvey's out!'

Australia was on the brink at 4/19. On his way back to the pavilion, Harvey met the incoming batsman, Burge, and instructed him: 'Don't just try and hang about, do what you do best and play your shots, Peter.'

'And that is what Burge did,' recalled Harvey. 'He played many powerful strokes, excelling with the pull and hook, and although he lost (Bobby) Simpson with the score at 58 Peter pulled the game right around. He scored the final 13 runs himself, finishing off proceedings with a smashing short-arm hook off Statham, which crashed into the fence at long-on.'

The Battle of the Ridge is indelibly etched in the memory of those who saw it, and those who read about it. And it left Neil with a great line: 'I have a 100 per cent record as Test captain.'

After the match Burge said: 'I have never been in an Australian side that pulled so hard for its captain. Everyone respected Neil so much. They would have done anything for him.'

Harvey said it was his proudest moment and he confessed that after victory was won he decided it high time to get stuck into the French champagne. 'I knew it would be my only chance to captain the Test side so I decided to make the most of the victory. I did a pretty good job of it ... I was too crook to go anywhere that night.'

Neil's dad was teetotal, and he never had a drink himself until he was twenty-nine. 'It was soon after we moved from Melbourne to Sydney. I had taken a job as a salesman servicing hotels and clubs in and about Sydney. I guess I just eased into having a drink or two along the way. I grew to like it and I reckon the Australian tour of South Africa in 1957/58 was my first tour when I had a drink.' These days Neil likes a cold beer or a shiraz – but it probably never tastes as sweet as that French champagne at Lord's.

The next Test would be at Headingley, Leeds, Yorkshire. Yorkshire chairman Brian Sellers said in a mock tone, 'We know how to prepare a proper wicket up north,' referring to the Ridge. As it turned out the Leeds wicket was a shocker. It was a cacky yellow-brown in colour, devoid of anything resembling grass and looked as though it would offer the bowlers variable bounce from ball one.

Benaud had recovered to lead the Australian team for the Third Test. However, he was rusty: two very expensive wickets to his name and a pair of ducks. Australia's batting was poor. In the first innings Australia hit 237, Harvey pitching in a magnificent 73. The ball was flying everywhere, uneven bounce, some balls scooting ankle high, others at the throat.

It was akin to batting on a ridge at both ends. Trueman took five first-innings wickets for just 58 and in the Australian second innings he ran amok taking 6/30 off 15.5 overs. Harvey again was the lone star for Australia with a fighting 53 out of 120. He alone showed class on a difficult wicket. Score 1-1.

On the eve of the critical Fourth Test at Manchester, Benaud bounced back into good bowling form, grabbing a match haul of 9/70 off 50 overs against a strong Middlesex side at Lord's. In a previous match he bowled 35 overs against Northants and those two performances on the trot really lifted him. Meantime the battle of wills with team manger Webb continued. However, assistant manager Ray Steele, a personable and shrewd Melbourne lawyer, a sportsman at heart and in 1943 a member of Richmond's VFL Grand Final winning side, was there to virtually take over Webb's role.

Colin McDonald praised Steele. 'We were lucky to have a bloke like Ray,' he said. 'He carried the tour for Richie. Ray realised early on, as every player did, that Syd (Webb) simply did not have a clue. Quite frankly, Webb was a joke.'

The English press hammered the Australian team after the loss at Leeds. That let Benaud renew an old ploy: he placed copies of the morning papers on the players' breakfast tables. The general tone of the articles: 'Hopeless, No Good', 'Bye bye Ashes'. Most of the feedback from the players was music to Benaud's ears. He wanted his men to be angry over the Leeds loss and more determined than ever to make amends at Old Trafford, Manchester.

Australia won the toss and batted, but the batting was largely sub-standard. Bill Lawry (74) batted grandly, Harvey hit 19 and then Booth in his debut Test match crafted a lovely 46. However, the Australian total of 190 meant it would be a helluva win from here. England replied with a more than handy 367 – a big lead of 177 runs. The England captain May batted beautifully for 95.

The huge deficit worried Benaud, but the pitch, he thought, was still a good batting one. All his men had to do was to bat out of their skins, get a relatively good lead, say in excess of 200, to have a chance to press for victory. Australia did respond brilliantly. Lawry again excelled with a typically considered and never-say-die attitude – the attitude so aptly characterised by the *Daily Mail*'s intrepid sports reporter Ian Wooldridge in the immortal phrase he coined for Lawry: 'the corpse with pads'. Harvey chipped in with 35, O'Neill hit a brilliant 67 and then came the last wicket. Davidson was in.

Australia had just lost three wickets for no runs to the England off-spinner David Allen. Benaud's team was well short of the runs required to press England in the fourth innings. The players watched last man McKenzie walk out of the dressing-rooms and on to the Manchester turf. They knew he could bat. Did the Englishmen?

Davo stood astride his bat in the middle. He watched young McKenzie stroll to the wicket as if he had not a worry in the world. At least, Davo thought, the nerves haven't got the young bloke. 'There I was at the pitch shaking with anxiety. I knew how valuable late runs would be and there was Garth nonchalantly wandering to the other end as if he was taking the dog for a walk.' Davidson decided to attack.

He reckoned the spinners had to go. He hit Allen for two mighty sixes and then May took off the spinners and bowled the pacemen. Freddie Trueman came on and his first ball hit Davo on the foot.

'Right,' thought Davo, 'this joker has got to go.' He smashed Trueman for four and suddenly went berserk hitting the fast bowlers with savage hooks and pulls and delightful cover and off drives. He was on fire. Up the other end McKenzie was playing with the straightest of straight bats. 'I thought May should have persevered with the spinners, Allen especially, as Garth was playing the quicks well but the spin would have soon sorted him out and ended our partnership,' Davidson later recalled.

As it turned out, the pair put on 98, before medium-pacer Jack Flavell got one past McKenzie's straight bat and he was bowled for 32 of the most valuable runs.

The last couple were mobbed by the players when they returned to the dressing-room. Davo was swamped. 'Davo walked about the room with a smile as big as the Sydney Harbour Bridge,' is how Neil remembers that moment. Harvey recalled that in the wake of the Davidson-McKenzie 98-run last wicket stand, he believed that the side could at least escape with a face-saving draw and even get England out if they panicked. They needed 256 in a shade over a run a minute for victory.

On the night before the last day, Benaud walked to the centre with the fast-bowling great Ray Lindwall, as good a fast bowler as Australia ever produced. Benaud knew Lindwall possessed a good cricket brain. As the pair looked down at the Old Trafford surface, Benaud said: 'Lindy, what do you think about my bowling around the wicket tomorrow. You see where Freddie Trueman has dug a huge hole here ...'

Lindwall stood tall, his crooked index finger pushing under and up at the tip of his nose: 'Well, Rich. I think it is fine against the left-handers. The ball will pitch in the rough outside their eyeline, land and turn. There will be uneven bounce and the lefties will find it very difficult. I think it will work a treat against the lefties.'

'And, Lindy ... the right-handers?'

'Well, Rich. You will have to be very accurate to the right-handers from around. If you are leaking too many runs, you will have to come back over and stop the flow of runs by bowling over.'

With those words ringing in his mind, Benaud led the side out for the final confrontation at Old Trafford. Openers Raman Subba Row and Geoff Pullar hit off 20 runs easily in the available 25 minutes before lunch. The chase was on. And how. Pullar fell for 25, then Ted Dexter took over. The elegant right-hander smashed 76 of the most glorious runs imaginable: blistering cover and off drives, hooks, cuts, you name it, Dexter was masterful, lifting England from 1/40 to 1/150. Twenty thousand English men, women and boys in the crowd roared their delight with every crashing Dexter stroke.

Harvey recalled: 'I passed Richie at the end of an over and he asked me what I thought. I told him that it didn't look too good, which at the time was a masterpiece of understatement.'

'We can't draw it,' Richie said, 'so we'll just have to win it now.'

Benaud came around the wicket once more. Dexter was on 76. The ball turned and bounced. In attempting another slashing cut, Dexter got a faint outside edge and Wally Grout took the catch with glee. England 2/150.

In came England's most elegant and best batsman, the captain, Peter May. Benaud continued bowling around. His second delivery to May pitched outside his leg stump, hit the footmarks and turned appreciably, bowling the England captain around his legs. May bowled Benaud 0. Game on.

The beefy left-hander Brian Close, a hard-hitting off-spinning all-rounder, strode to the wicket boldly. He was a man on a mission. He began to sweep across the line of every Benaud delivery. Remember the ball was landing in the rough outside his eye line and the bounce was variable. A top edge loomed.

Close swept and missed a dozen balls. It was almost comical. Then, suddenly out of sweeping mode, Close came out of his crease and hit Benaud for a big six over long-on. It was a strategy he might, probably should, have followed. But no, a few balls into the next over Close swept once too often and succeeded only in top-edging to the safe hands of O'Neill at backward square leg. England was then 4/158, just five minutes before the tea break. Ken Barrington joined Subba Row. Benaud began the last over before tea. Subba Row worked him for a brace of twos, in front of square. He hit with the spin, but that was a little fraught with danger because of the variable bounce. On the last ball Subba Row fell for 49 – hitting over the top of a Benaud leg break as he pushed forward. England had folded. In just seventeen minutes before tea England had lost 4/13 and Benaud had taken the lot for 9 runs in nineteen deliveries. There was now a feeling that England had given up the chase and they would bat for a draw. With forty minutes to go England was nine down with pacemen Statham and Flavell at the crease. Benaud had 6/66 and had bowled for three hours straight. Harvey was getting restless. He wanted the game over. He said as Benaud handed his cap to the umpire for another over: 'C'mon, Rich. Let's finish this now. Bring back Davo … It's all over.'

'No, not now, Ninna. I am going to continue bowling.'

The first ball of Benaud's over was pushed by Flavell straight to Harvey at cover point. Harvey was the gun fieldsman of world cricket, possessing a bullet arm and amazing accuracy. This time, however, Harvey fielded the ball and instead of throwing it over the bails to the 'keeper Grout, he turned his back and purposely threw the ball like a rocket to the cover fence.

He then sidled up to Benaud and said matter-of-factly: 'Now, will you put Davo back on?'

Davidson returned and his second ball knocked back Statham's off stump.

Australia had won by 54 runs. Benaud had bowled 35 overs to take 6/70, an extraordinary effort.

As captain and vice-captain sat drinking champagne, the sweet success of a remarkable victory was a special moment for them both.

They looked out to the middle where five years before England's Jim Laker had taken nineteen wickets to complete a humiliating defeat for Ian Johnson's Australians. The English crowd swamped the ground that afternoon. Not this time.

To Richie Benaud and Neil Harvey, the Fourth Test victory over a rampaging England was sweet revenge indeed over the olde enemy. The win meant Australia was up 2-1 with one Test to play. No matter the result (it was a draw), Australia had retained the Ashes.

Harvey scored five centuries on the tour – the 114 in the First Test, plus 120 v Lancashire; 117 v Glamorgan; 140 v Nottingham and 115 not out v Warwickshire. In the Test matches he scored 338 runs at an average of 42.25, including a 73 and 53 on a treacherous wicket in the Third Test at Leeds when Freddie Trueman ran amok. In all first-class matches he scored 1452 runs at 44. Good, but not altogether as brilliant as in his many other successful campaigns abroad.

*Graham McKenzie*

I thought Neil was a good captain and I always felt comfortable in his company. Harv worked well with Richie. Like Richie, Neil was loyal and very supportive. My first Test was at Lord's in 1961. Richie was injured and Harv was captain. There was a decided ridge at the Nursery End and Davo (Alan Davidson) got five wickets in the England first dig. After speaking with Davo and me, Neil thought I would be better bowling into the ridge in the second innings. He thought my usual length in a good area was just about right for the conditions. He was proven right. I got 5/37 off 29 overs.

*Graeme McKenzie was a great fast bowler. He played 60 Tests and took 246 wickets at 29.78. Best bowling 8/71.*

CHAPTER NINETEEN

# WHEN ONE DOOR CLOSES …

*'Within days Neil (Harvey) was quoted in the press calling me the worst, most ungracious England captain ever. Who knows, perhaps he was right!'* – Ted Dexter, England cricket captain Ashes series 1962/63

FOUR DAYS BEFORE the start of the First Ashes Test in 1962, on 26 November, English cricket officially ended the distinction between amateurs and professionals – but it seems no-one told 'Lord' Ted Dexter, the England captain.

Lord Ted was no lord at all; he was nicknamed Lord Ted in his school days. It stuck. He was aloof, supremely confident and possessed a strong belief in his abilities as a cricketer and a golfer. He was a young man in a hurry. Educated at Norfolk House, Beaconsfield and Radley College, Dexter strutted his stuff. English satirist, writer and actor Peter Cook was among the young boys at Radley to whom 'a big and strong Dexter inflicted corporal punishment'. In today's vernacular Dexter had 'attitude'.

His captaincy may not have been all that flash, but his batting was often brutally littered with dashing drives, cuts and pulls. Lord Ted hit the ball with astonishing power. Which is odd, because Dexter had been brought into the side as team captain. The gin swillers at Lord's loved his attacking way with the bat and they hoped that he would lead the team with equal dash and flair.

Although a mighty powerful batsman, with all the strokes in the book and a fearless hitter, the Sussex man who always stood tall with the bat in his hand was a very different fellow when wearing the skipper's hat on the field. He wandered about the field as England captain very much with his head in the sand.

Bowlers were treated as second-class citizens by Dexter. The professionals were the ones who traditionally steamed and sweated for England as bowlers, fast or slow. After all, the likes of Harold Larwood and Freddie Trueman both staggered out of the mines at different times in history to grab the chance to play professional cricket. On the field Dexter never stood talking to his bowlers for any length of time. When he wanted a change in attack, say replacing Trueman with Brian Statham, he would typically bark: 'Right Trueman, you are off, out of the attack, be off with you … get down to third man.'

He bewildered Trueman, who summed him up thus: 'Lord Ted had more theories than Charles Darwin.'

Dexter was something else as a captain: aloof to the point of rudeness and not a man to listen to others. The contrast with Richie Benaud could not have been greater.

Australia batted first at the Gabba and scored 404. Brian Booth led the way with a sterling 112. Harvey was bowled by Statham for 39.

England replied with 389, Ted Dexter terrorised the Australian bowlers and fieldsmen with a blazing 70. Batting a second time, Australia amassed 4/362 declared. Bill Lawry hit 98, Bob Simpson, by now Lawry's regular opening partner, scored 71, Norm O'Neill hit a brisk 56 and Harvey cruised to 57. His runs may have eased his nerves, for the previous summer, which was domestic cricket only, had not been a good one, yielding not one century, and just 424 runs at 26.56, with a high of 73.

England needed a near miracle to win the match, but Dexter blasted 99 in less than three hours and while he was at the wicket there was a slim chance. However, Garth McKenzie put paid to that, sending down a searing yorker to send the England captain packing. Match drawn.

England won the Second Test match at the MCG, with Dexter again the fly in the ointment for Benaud's men with a brilliant 93, backed by Colin Cowdrey's 113 for England to score 331 in reply to Australia's 316. Harvey was clean bowled by England medium-fast merchant Len Coldwell for a duck. Australia fared worse in its second innings with a moderate 248. Booth starred again with 103, but he was pretty much a lone star. Bill Lawry got 57. Few others troubled the scorers much. Neil Harvey was run out for 10.

The Third Test at the SCG saw Australia redeem themselves with an eight-wicket victory. England scored 279 in its first innings, Australia replied with 319. Then Davidson (5/25) and McKenzie (3/26) cut their way through Dexter's men like hot knives through butter. The Australian pace pair shot England out for a paltry 104 in its second innings and Benaud's men polished off the necessary runs with little difficulty.

Then on to the Adelaide Oval, which in January is usually baking under a relentless sun. Little wonder the old saying: 'Adelaide 100 in the shade with Bradman 300 in the sun.' Australia was to bat first. Harvey and O'Neill had struggled to score in the series and both were keen to make amends. Neil knew the end was approaching. He knew this would be his final Ashes Test series. He did not want to get dropped for the final Test – and he was well aware that the board and selectors were an unrelenting, unforgiving mob.

It did not start well for Australia: 1/2. Harvey walked to the wicket. He gives a chance; it's missed. Then another wicket. Score: 2/16. Then Harvey gives another chance. Missed again. Jim Swanton, longtime cricket correspondent for London's *Daily Telegraph,* recorded that Harvey was missed no less than four times by the time his score reached 26. Years later, England all-rounder Ray Illingworth would remind Harvey that he was 'dropped twice before he got to double figures – both times off my bowling!' When O'Neill came to the crease the score was 3/101.

Swanton's prose could be a trifle pompous, but he was spot-on when he observed that the field placings of captain Dexter were 'geometrically, arithmetically, psychologically, geographically, and from every other conceivable point of view, often ... completely haywire'.

'Right,' Harvey declared, 'they keep letting me off the hook. Time to get stuck into them.'

By the time he and O'Neill were parted, the tally was 295. O'Neill was gone for 100. Harvey followed soon after, for a majestic 154.

I got in contact with Dexter in November 2020 to rouse some memories from him. He replied:

> *Dear Rowdy, You have come to the wrong chap if you are looking for eulogies. I only saw him (Neil Harvey) bat close to when he was brought back in 1963. He scratched around and then hit one up in the air – which David Sheppard politely dropped. Off the field, the Dexters spent a delightful evening with the Harveys being serenaded by Nat King Cole. Within days Neil was quoted in the press calling me the worst, most ungracious England captain ever. Who knows, perhaps he was right! Since then we have simply swapped the merest courtesies and passed on. Ah! Well. You can't win them all.*
> *Lord Ted*

Much of Dexter's words are way wide of the mark, because Dexter played against Harvey in Australia in 1958/59. They played against one another again in 1961 and, of course, in the five Test matches of 1962/63. Neil's criticism of Dexter's captaincy during the 1962/63 Ashes series obviously coloured Lord Ted's thinking. I pointed this out to Lord Ted. He replied:

*That is typical of an 85-year-old memory – or should I say – lack of it. Ted*

Illingworth reckoned the inner core of 'gentlemen', such as Dexter, Cowdrey, Alan Smith and that old blue-blood of Arundel Castle, the Duke of Norfolk, kept their distance from the professionals.

Harvey recalls leading Australia in the 1961 tour against Lancashire at Old Trafford. 'Their captain Geoff Pullar kindly invited me to see out the match in his room, which was for the Lancashire captain and perhaps a guest for the entire time the match was played.' Harvey asked about his men. 'Where do they fit in?' 'Oh, they are in the other room,' came the answer. 'Don't worry about them.'

'Well, I do worry, Geoff, and if I took up your offer and left them to set up camp in those cramped quarters while I rested in luxury ... why, they'd string me up.'

Harvey politely declined Pullar's offer. A few years later, in 1972, Australian captain Ian Chappell was likewise offered a similar thing: to join Lancashire skipper Jackie Bond in his spacious private dressing-room.

'Gee, thanks Jackie,' Chappelli said. 'This will suit all of us to a tee. Plenty of room here. Much better than those cramped quarters down the hall.'

'Ah, no Ian,' Jackie said, 'the offer is for you and you alone.'

'Sorry, Jackie. Thanks for the offer, but with the 1972 side it is all in or none in. I decline the invitation.'

One of Lord Ted's 'insufferable professionals', Illingworth couldn't believe the temerity of the Dexter camp's amateur brigade when he was unceremoniously ordered by Lord Ted to act as twelfth man because Colin Cowdrey was taking his wife to see the latest film, *Mutiny on the Bounty*.

The Fourth Test had ended in a draw, meaning the Ashes were up for grabs in the Fifth Test.

To add spice to that, the Test would also be a sentimental occasion: both Neil Harvey and Alan Davidson declared it would be their last hurrah on the Test stage. Davidson bowled as he had bowled all summer with accuracy and fire. He took 3/43 in the England first innings off 25.6 overs as England laboured up to 10 hours in scoring 321. He backed it up with 3/80 off 28 overs in the second. Harvey scored 22 and 28 for the match, which fizzled out into an anti-climactic draw.

As if to underline how good a fielder he was, Harvey took six catches in the match, including three on the first day, which equalled the then Test record. Alan Davidson had the pleasure of taking a wicket with his last ball in Test cricket.

And so ended Neil Harvey's Test career. He had played more Tests – 79 – than any other Australian at that time.

He had scored 6149 runs – second at the time only to Bradman, among Australians.

He had scored 21 Test centuries – second at the time only to Bradman, among Australians.

He averaged 48.52 – third at the time only to Bradman, among Australians – and Jack Ryder, who was second on that list.

Harvey would soon happily settle back to family life – the eldest, Robert, was seven years of age; Anne was five and Bruce, three. The Tupperware business was about to get into full swing and the distributorship would provide the Harveys with greater financial security.

Neil Harvey's final Sheffield Shield match would be against South Australia at the SCG. And his innings would be something else.

Nineteen-year-old Ian Chappell was playing for SA in that match. 'Neil batted brilliantly, he scored 231 not out for NSW in his only innings and I told Neil many years later that I chased most of the bastards down the slope towards the Brewongle Stand.

'As a youngster I had watched Neil Harvey's batting at the Adelaide Oval. He was quick on his feet, dancing a long way down the pitch to the spinners. The thing that always stood out to me was the neatness of his stroke-play. He was a compact batsman, who always seemed to have time to play his shots, but it was the neatness – the way everything seemed to be in place stood out.'

SA all-rounder Ken 'KG' Cunningham was fielding at mid-wicket when Neil first came to the middle. 'Neil Hawke was bowling. He delivered one down leg side and I heard a distinct sound of willow on leather. I reckon Harvey edged the ball down leg side and was caught by wicketkeeper Barry Jarman. But no; to our horror the umpire Ted Wykes, said sternly, "NOT OUT." Hawkey went off his tree, but the decision stood and Harvey went on to play a glorious innings. What a player!'

A few years later, on a Saturday morning in the mid-1960s, Neil was watching his son Robert having a hit-up before his turn came to bat. 'Funny thing,' Neil recalled, 'watching Robert hit the ball, I suddenly got the urge to play cricket again.'

It wasn't a return to Test or Shield cricket he yearned for; Neil simply wanted to get into his creams and get out onto the field. He spoke at length with former NSW left-handed batsman Neil

'Harpo' Marks. Marks was a brilliant young left-handed batsman, who had hit sparkling centuries for NSW in a short but glittering career. He had his career cut way too short after it was discovered that he had a serious heart condition. There he was in 1965 speaking with Neil Harvey about a grade-cricket comeback when he said deadpan: 'Of course, Ninna, you will need to work your way up to the firsts. You can start in the thirds.' There was a long pause, then the pair broke out laughing.

Marks stood down as captain for Neil. Soon after the side was playing at Northern Districts' home ground, Waitara Oval. Harpo had heard a rumour that Neil had trouble seeing the numbers on the scoreboard.

'I remember Neil squinting at the bowler as he came in. I never thought of the squint being his way of finding better focus on the ball. We were batting well together; very good for Neil given that this was just his second match of his return to grade cricket in Sydney. After a while we were going along merrily, the scoreboard ticking over nicely, when he wandered down the pitch at the change of an over and said, "Hey, Harpo, what's the score?"

'"Oh, we are 2/100. It is on the scoreboard!"

'"Okay, how many have I made?"'

Harpo looked at Neil quizzically, then said in a ho-hum manner: 'You are 58.'

Marks was and is adamant that Neil Harvey, even by the late 1960s, a few years after his retirement from first-class cricket, was 'so good he could have walked into the Australian Test team of the day'.

'I batted with Neil a few times in first-class cricket, but it wasn't until the years he played with Northern District that I had the chance to see him bat close up. He really had no weaknesses and I doubt that I have ever seen anybody with better footwork.'

*Ian McLachlan*

I remember Neil as a great player, with sparkling footwork, but also I recall that he was a man totally unafraid of saying what he thought. I spent a lot of time at Cambridge University and got some matches playing alongside Ted Dexter. I thought Dexter a terrific player. In the summer of 1962/63 I played for an Australian XI, led by Neil Harvey. Neil knew of my association with Dexter at Cambridge and at training on the morning of the first day's play against England at the MCG, Neil said matter of factly: 'Your mate (Dexter) can't play.' We took the field and Ted Dexter cut loose, smashing all bowlers through the covers with awesome power. As we walked from the ground in the wake of Dexter's blistering 102, Harvey sidled up to me and said, 'your mate *can* play!'

*Ian McLachlan was a hard-hitting batsman for South Australia. He was twelfth man once for Australia. He retired early to manage the family's vast grazing properties in NSW and SA. He was a leading light in South Australian cricket administration and drove the $500 million upgrade of Adelaide Oval. McLachlan was the Defence Minister in the John Howard Liberal Government.*

CHAPTER TWENTY

# ON HIS SELECTION

*'The man at the top (Lawry) had to be accountable. He simply had to go.'* – Neil Harvey

IN 1967 NEIL Harvey was invited onto the Australian Test selection panel. He would sit in judgement of the Australian first-class players alongside Sir Donald Bradman and Jack Ryder – as it happened, the three Australians with the best Test batting averages.

Unlike today, the Test selectors were not handed a fat financial contract. They had to fend for themselves as did the players of the time, the board providing airfares, accommodation and a meagre out-of-pocket expense account.

'The pay wasn't too good,' Neil said. 'Say we were due to watch a Test in Brisbane. The cricket board would organise a return air-ticket for us. We were presented with a daily allowance of $50. For that amount we had to cover our accommodation, food and any other out-of-pocket expenses, including catching a cab. I used to stay at a motel near the Story Bridge and I would save by walking to and from the Gabba.'

The selectors might also have taken advantage of getting to the ground early to partake in tea or coffee and a slice of cake or a biscuit. Lunch and afternoon tea was provided.

The story goes that Neil's time as a selector got off to a bumpy start at the First Test against India in 1967/68 at the very same Gabba. Neil supposedly missed a session, going to the races at the invitation of the Queensland Cricket Association president. Apparently the association then itself complained to the national board. It also tried to get its man, Ken 'Slasher' Mackay, onto the selection panel.

'I cannot remember going to the races during that Test match,' Neil said. 'You know, Bradman said to me when I first joined him and Ryder on the Australian Test selection panel: "Don't think this job is all glamour. There will come a time – plenty of occasions – when you will get sick to death watching these games." And, The Don was right.'

The success of Neil and Iris's Tupperware business certainly helped the family finances. The Harveys were able to fund Robert and Bruce's education at the exclusive boys school, Shore, and Anne attended one of Sydney's best girls' schools, Abbotsleigh, in Sydney's upper North Shore. It was during the same summer that Neil played the last of his matches for Northern District.

That was the year the club won the premiership. Neil wasn't greatly impressed with the side's 'keeper so he told Neil Marks that he intended 'keeping in the final. Harvey had kept wicket for Fitzroy in the junior grades and had stood in for Gil Langley to 'keep in the entire final session of the Fifth Test at The Oval in 1956. Neil Marks reckons Neil's batting in the 1967/68 grand final was something to behold.

'We knocked Sutherland over for about 120 on a wicket that was doing a bit and then lost both our openers for less than 20,'

Marks recalled. 'Suddenly we were in trouble because the wicket was still seaming around. I was batting with Neil and neither of us had scored. Sutherland's captain and Sheffield Shield player Ted Cotton bowled the first ball to Harv: a beautiful outswinger that just missed the outside edge and both bat and stumps. The Sutherland team suddenly realised they could win the match. Next ball they realised they couldn't, when Neil smashed a shot through the covers that Bradman would have envied. Two hours later Harvey was about 130 not out and the game was over. Players like Neil Harvey come along once in a decade; our club was lucky to have him. Even at the sunset of his career, playing at a small suburban ground in the outskirts of a metropolis, he was as good as any player in the world and showed many times why he would be chosen in the greatest Australian team of all time. Neil would be in my team.'

Harvey's time as a selector coincided with upheaval in the game, in particular the gruelling seven-months-long tour of India, then South Africa. As if that were not long enough, the board tried to tack on an extra Test right at the end.

Conditions in India were disgraceful. There was much resentment among the players over playing conditions and the accommodation which, in Sri Lanka and India, was largely infested with cockroaches and mice, even rats as big as cats. Harvey toured Pakistan and India in 1959/60 – he knew all about tough conditions. He, probably alone among the selectors, knew the score. Bradman never toured there. Ryder did tour India in 1935, but he stayed in comfortable surrounds everywhere he went, at maharajahs' palaces and the like.

Lawry's Australians won 3-1 in India, but were taken to the cleaners in South Africa, losing the scheduled four-Test series 4-0. It was a humiliating defeat.

The South Africans wanted to play a fifth match. Australia's board offered to pay the players an extra $300 to play the game. Lawry called a team meeting. He explained the situation and said that the South Africans were so determined to have a fifth Test played that they would offer an extra $200 to make it $500 per man.

However, Lawry also said very firmly that any decision had to be unanimous. 'It is either all in or all out.' There was some procrastination. Some of the Australians said they could do with the extra cash, but the majority refused to play the extra Test. Ian Chappell said: 'This extra $200 the South Africans have offered doesn't mean anything. It has got nothing to do with them. It is all to do with us and the board. If we don't stand up for our rights now, we deserve to be pushed around for the rest of our lives.'

Lawry informed team manager Fred Bennett that the players would not play. Bennett, perhaps fearing his failure to win over the players might jeopardise his future touring manager aspirations, presented the board with a full account. The board saw any sort of rebuke to it as a personal affront to individual board members. Australian society was not then as pathetically soft as it would become, but board members were exceedingly precious for the times.

As for Bill Lawry – his card was marked.

Jack Ryder's final stint as a Test selector was in the Australian summer of 1969/70. Legend has it that Ryder pushed for a slow bowler for his local club, Collingwood, who was yet to gain state selection, to be picked in Lindsay Hassett's Australian touring side for England in 1953. Ryder failed to get his way … on that occasion. However, there was a time just after the war when Ryder got a Collingwood stalwart into the Victoria team. Everard 'Bill' Baker played 216 A grade matches for Collingwood in the seasons 1934/35 to 1955/56. He was an able 'keeper and a good left-handed batsman. But he – as Neil Harvey would attest – wasn't a patch on the Fitzroy batsman-'keeper Bill Jacobs. As it turned out Baker got the state job and Jacobs, who played 266 consecutive matches for Fitzroy, effecting 448 dismissals, never did play for Victoria.

Rivalries and jealousy have been part and parcel of selection since the year dot. In 1957/58 Peter Burge was the third selector on the tour of South Africa, alongside Ian Craig from NSW and Harvey, from Victoria, for precisely that reason. Burge, a Queenslander, was not in the best XI. Cricket writer Gideon Haigh wrote: 'It reflected the Board of Control's paranoia about interstate rivalries, that you could not have two selectors from the same state because they would inevitably conspire – which was a classic transference, they believed the players were as parochial as they were!'

Ryder retired as a Test selector in September 1970, replaced by Harvey's great mate, Sam Loxton. Loxton was meticulous in his preparation. He turned up at Test selection meetings with reams of hand-written sheets for his fellow selectors to read carefully. While Sam copped a little bit of chiding from his mate, the two other selectors were grateful for having accurate statistics on every prospective player in the Sheffield Shield competition.

England toured here in 1970/71, a boisterous tour, with some crowd involvement in Sydney as spectators showed their dislike of England quick John Snow. Lawry's men didn't have the firepower to match England. Graham McKenzie struggled. The selectors – Bradman, Harvey and Loxton – stuck with Victoria's hard-working Alan Connolly and they brought in a tall, thin, gangly Victorian paceman, who bowled off the wrong foot and keep getting Shield wickets like they were going out of fashion: the Coca-Cola loving Alan 'Froggy' Thompson. England had ample batting strength led by Geoff Boycott, who was in the best form of his stellar career, John Edrich and Basil d'Oliveira.

There was some dull cricket. Slow batting meant a dull draw in Brisbane. A slow pitch made for a draw in Perth, the first Test ever in the west. Melbourne was washed out, not a ball bowled, so a Test was added. The Sussex fast bowler John Snow would also prove a thorn in Australia's side.

Brilliant batting by Boycott (77 and 142 not out) ensured England had runs galore in the bank in the Sydney Test. Australia was skittled for 116. Snow bowled magnificently, taking 7/40 off 17.5 overs. Despite Lawry's courageous batting, the Victorian was on thin ice. At no stage did Lawry try and make things happen and that applied to both England innings. The Fifth Test, at the MCG, was another draw. McKenzie looked a shadow of his former self, so too Connolly, who had bowled so well in South Africa.

And so the selectors made two momentous decisions in the next two Tests.

A few days before the Sixth Test at Adelaide Oval, Bradman spoke with Harvey and Loxton. 'Well, fellas. We are bereft of any genuine fast bowlers. Have you blokes seen anyone in your travels capable of bowling with genuine pace?'

Almost immediately Messrs Harvey and Loxton said in unison: 'Yes, we have. A young kid from Western Australia ... Dennis Lillee!'

'Does he know where the ball is going?' probed The Don.

'No. Not at all,' said Sam, 'but the batsman too hasn't a clue where they are going.' The three men decided that Lillee was in the Sixth Test Match. The youngster bowled with genuine pace and got the ball to swing away from the England right-handers. Lillee returned 5/84. Another draw, with more of the most unadventurous captaincy from Lawry. His negativity probably rubbed off on Illingworth, for the England captain failed to force the follow-on, letting Australia off the hook.

And now, the bombshell. With the Seventh Test looming in Sydney, Australia still had a chance of drawing the series.

Bill Lawry was sacked. Sacked from the captaincy. He lost his spot in the team. Out. No Australian Test captain had ever been replaced mid-series in Australia before. He was replaced by fellow left-handed Victorian Ken Eastwood, for his one and only Test – although the story goes that he ended up with two baggy greens, having been given two to try them on for size. Some of the Victorians, especially Keith Stackpole, were shattered. Lawry heard the news via Stackpole, who had received a telephone call from Alan Shiell, the Adelaide cricket writer for *The News*, an afternoon tabloid. He told Stackpole: 'Dramatic turn of events, Stack. Lawry has been sacked as captain and Ian Chappell is the new Test captain.'

All these years later Harvey is unflinching at the decision. 'We had to make a change in the captaincy. Australia was playing very negative cricket and the man at the top (Lawry) had to be accountable. He simply had to go.'

The even greater shock was that Bradman announced he too was stepping down as a selector, straight after the team was announced and before the Test began. He cited health reasons, as he had at the start of the season when he stood down as a South Australian selector.

It was quite remarkable how little has been written about how Sir Donald Bradman might have been involved in having Lawry dropped as captain and replaced by Ian Chappell, with whom he did not enjoy the most convivial of relationships. If Bradman did not go along with the Lawry sacking, how in heaven's name did Messrs Harvey and Loxton bring about what really was a near miracle? Loxton was an obedient disciple of Bradman. Only years later, at the Pennant Hills Golf Club in Sydney, did the truth come out.

It was not long after Ian Chappell had retired from cricket and moved from Adelaide to Sydney.

Harvey had ended his Test selection duties years earlier, in 1979. Harvey had also played a round of golf, but the pair played in different fours. Chappelli's mates had left the bar earlier than usual and there was Harvey standing with his back to a roaring log fire, enjoying a cold beer.

Ian Chappell is not a man to let an opportunity pass by and here was the perfect chance to find out once and for all how it was he was picked as the Test captain way back in 1971.

'I hadn't played with Neil. But there we were, the last two at the bar, when I asked him: "How did I get the captaincy?" Poking himself firmly in the chest, Harvey replied in typically forthright fashion: "Fuckin' me. I got you the captaincy. Fuckin' me!"

'I then asked him how he got the second vote as I was under no illusions that Bradman would have voted for me. He said he talked Loxton around, which surprised me, as the Victorian was a Bradman sycophant. However, Neil had been mates with Loxton from a young age and was able to procure his vote.'

In retrospect, I should have seen that change was afoot. Not long before Lawry was sacked, Neil told me: 'You need more drinkers in the team.' This was a big admission from a guy who was basically a non-drinker for a good part of his playing career. With Lillee, Chappelli and co., he certainly got that!

England won the Seventh Test match and took the series 2-nil. Australia had been totally outplayed, but there were signs of emerging talent soon to blossom in Greg Chappell, Rodney Marsh and Dennis Lillee.

Under the captaincy of Ian Chappell, Australian cricket blossomed. Soon the ultra-conservative Lawry had become a blip in the long and illustrious road of Australian cricket. The Lawry era was full of draws and more defeats than wins.

Chappell's men drew (2-all) a fabulous five-Test Ashes series against Ray Illingworth's 'Dad's Army' in England in 1972, then the side comfortably beat Pakistan at home 3-0 and the West Indies in the Caribbean.

Harvey's selection panel dropped me for the Third Test against Pakistan – when I was bowling at my peak. I took 8/59 in the second innings of the First Test against Pakistan in Adelaide. Getting dropped was my own fault.

I had opted out of the coming Caribbean tour to get a foot in the door in journalism, something I wished to pursue when the cricket was all over. I spoke with Neil Harvey, albeit briefly, at the end of the Second Test Pakistan at the MCG. I have few regrets, but missing the tour to the West Indies is one of them. I should have gone. Watkins took my place in the Third Test in Sydney and he bowled badly. There were times when his deliveries were so wide they barely landed anywhere near the cut portion of the pitch. The umpire was a sympathetic soul, allowing wides to get through to a scrambling, muttering, clearly unhappy wicketkeeper in Rodney Marsh.

Thanks to a magnificent bowling performance by Max Walker (6/15), Australia won the match and took the series 3-0. Funny thing, I know I should have sought Harvey's counsel in advance. He was by far the wisest and best judge of a cricketer among the trio of selectors, the third of whom was now Phil Ridings.

Harvey faced more controversy the next year. In the summer of 1973/74, Chappelli was getting tired of Australia 'not picking its best side', in his opinion. Both Ross Edwards and Ian Redpath had been left out of the team in the three-Test series against New Zealand, which was to be followed by three more Tests in NZ.

Chappelli recalled: 'Before the Third Test in Adelaide and with the touring party to NZ soon to be announced, Keith Stackpole told me that he reckoned he wasn't in the squad. When I asked him why he thought that, he said, "Loxton hasn't looked at me in the eye for a week. I reckon I'm gone."'

Chappelli called a meeting of some six senior players and said if it was Stacky this week it would soon be 'one of us next. I am going to the selectors and I will be telling them if Stacky wasn't in the touring party I wasn't going.'

Those of us at the meeting all agreed for Ian to include our names in the non-touring group.

Chappelli then approached Loxton and 'he reacted in typical fashion: "Ohhhh, we will drop the lot of you."'

Chappell approached Harvey – and told him he made a big mistake in taking the matter to Loxton. Harvey agreed. 'In future if you want to know anything, speak to me,' Harvey told him. Chappelli then asked Harvey if he could guarantee Stackpole was in the touring side and he handed the captain the list. Stackpole was in the party, so too Ian Redpath.

Chappelli always maintained that one of the few weaknesses Harvey had as a Test selector was that he did not rate Ian Redpath as a Test batsman. 'He reckoned Redda too often came down the track to the spinners but then played a defensive shot. He felt that if you came down the track to the spinners it was only to attack them.'

Harvey had the pleasure of seeing his selection decisions bear fruit. Ian Chappell became a great leader. Dennis Lillee became a great fast bowler. When Jeff Thomson joined him for the 1974/75 Ashes, they became a fearsome opening pair, which rolled into the next season, when the Windies toured under Clyde Lloyd and were trounced 5-1 – which set Lloyd on a path to make the Windies great, by going with pace, pace and more pace.

Lillee and Thomson formed one of the most lethal opening attacks in Australia Test history. The pair bowled well enough in tandem in 1974/75 to be ranked alongside Ray Lindwall and Keith Miller of 1948 fame. When they ventured to England in 1975 the wickets were incredibly benign. There was no pace or bounce in the wickets, no life. The Australians suspected that the England administrators were at it again: jiggery-pokery, with pitches to blunt the opposition. Nevertheless, Australia retained the Ashes.

Tony Greig's England team came to Australia for a one-off Test in March 1977, the Centenary Test. Australia won by 45 runs – the exact winning margin of the first Test a century earlier, leading to the great line by Doug Walters: 'You know nothing's changed. England has not improved in 100 years.'

Unbeknown to the Australian establishment, the great event was being secretly undermined by players making all manner of deals and trying to gain the best advantage for themselves. Word had got out and many people knew that the media mogul Kerry Packer was about to launch his World Series Cricket, which would turn the cricket world on its head. Most of Australia's top players signed with Packer – on much better money. While Packer was getting his squads – the Australian, West Indies and World XI – together, the Australian selectors were frantically trying to put a competitive Test side together to face the coming Indian team.

Harvey, now chairman of the Australian Test selectors, was rocked to the core when World Series Cricket fired an arrow deep into the heart of world cricket.

'On the first day of the Centenary Test in Melbourne (March 1977) I had a Test team. A day later all the good players had deserted the ship. I had no players left at all. I hated every minute of WSC and yet now, when I look back, I probably would have been among the players to accept a contract.'

Television would soon bring the players riches beyond their dreams. 'Then, the players got a better deal financially,' Neil said. 'I lived through playing Test cricket and trying to make a living away from cricket. However, this better financial deal has grown into something so ridiculous that it has gotten way out of hand. Today the players are paid far too much. And the IPL is simply ludicrous.'

Bradman was no longer a Test selector, but he still wielded extraordinary power and influence. He took Bob Simpson, the former NSW and Test captain, for a steak and a chat and offered him the Test captaincy for the series against India and beyond.

Once again, I should have got in contact with Neil Harvey. If I had the chance again I would have asked for a meeting with two men – Sir Donald Bradman and Neil Harvey.

Because a few weeks later, Sir Donald rang me at *The News* and offered me a chance to return to the Australian side for the series against India in 1977/78. My last Test had been against the Windies in January 1976.

I was twixt a rock and hard place for I had sought out Ian Chappell for an opportunity of playing WSC. 'I'll have to run it past Kerry,' he said. Unbeknown to me, Kerry Packer was no fan of yours truly. He said something along the lines of 'I'm not giving a contract to that straight breaker'. Finally, I got word that Packer would fly me to Sydney, bat against me for one over. If I got him out twice I was in.

I told Chappelli: 'Tell Packer to go and get f...ed.' I got a contract all the same – without having to bowl to him. But I still wonder if I did the right thing. After all, it is not every day Don Bradman offers you a spot on the Test stage.

The board still had more than their share of members who couldn't even sit on their hands their heads were so embedded in the sand. Packer did not want me. I found myself playing Mickey Mouse games for him in the countryside of Victoria, when I could have been playing Test cricket for Bobby Simpson's Australia team, who played series against India, West Indies, India again and England.

Now, Neil might not recall going to the Queensland races back in 1967, but he does fess up to having a beer at the Adelaide Oval's Chappell Bar in 1979. By that time he had enjoyed a twelve-year stint as an Australian selector. There were times when he felt it was fair and reasonable to slip away and catch up with mates for a jar or two. 'It must have been 1979. I slipped down to the Chappell Bar (back of the then George Giffen Stand) at Adelaide Oval to enjoy a beer with a couple of mates I knew here in Adelaide,' he said. 'Apparently board member Tim Caldwell took objection and his influence was such that I was sacked from the job within a few months. My mate Davo (Alan Davidson) took my place. Seems to me that a bloke in my position as a Test selector should be allowed the odd minute or two to relax and catch up with a mate during the play.'

The Tupperware business had been ticking along nicely. During a routine Tupperware dinner, Neil and Iris met an attractive blond, 43-year-old Barbara McGifford, a divorcee and bank teller. Soon after, Neil and Barbara met by chance in a suburban shopping centre car park. In fact, Barbara had parked her car right beside where Neil was parked. By this stage Neil was 47 – and he and Iris had divorced. He was living alone, renting a house in Mosman. Neil and Barbara hit it off immediately and in 1975 the couple married in a private ceremony in St Ives. They honeymooned in Los Angeles. Neil couldn't resist the urge to buy a Louisville Slugger baseball bat and a baseball glove that, yes, fitted like a glove. Neil and Barbara eventually purchased the property at St Ives. While the Tupperware franchise has a policy that only husband and wife partners run distributorships, the company made an exception and

Neil and Iris continued to work together until Neil remarried in 1975. The distributorship was sold in 1976.

Barbara was a lovely lady, and it was my honour and pleasure to know her. In 2012 Neil, Barbara and I were walking towards the Town Hall clock in Auckland. We had just enjoyed a good steak, washed down by a splendid shiraz, when we noticed something rather weird. The Town Hall clock was acting strangely, the hands of the clock rushing past. It was a scene right out of *Back to the Future*. One of those things that you just never forget.

Barbara's sudden illness and death in 2014 was so sad.

'I see a bit of Neil from time to time,' Chappelli said. 'Apart from needing the aid of a walking stick, he's in pretty good shape. He still has the firm handshake and the bricklayer's forearms. We've had a function each year since Richie Benaud's death to celebrate his life. And at the last Benaud function I asked Neil how he was going. "I am lonely, mate, without Barbara."'

***Ken Eastwood***

Neil (Harvey) was a pretty good selector. He picked me!

*Ken Eastwood hailed from NSW. He opened for Gordon before moving to Melbourne where he played for Footscray and Victoria. Eastwood was picked to play in the Seventh Test against Ray Illingworth's England at the SCG. He replaced Bill Lawry, who was dumped and Ian Chappell was made captain. Harvey was a selector.*

***David 'Evil' Sincock***

I played against Neil a couple of times, even having him stumped in a Sheffield Shield match in the summer of 1961/62. The other occasion I got his wicket was when he holed out in the deep off one of my high full tosses. I retired at age twenty-seven. While you were expected to train and play like a professional, you were paid like a pauper and many young blokes gave up the game very early in their cricket careers. As a young boy I did as most of the boys did in those days. You cut out stories and pasted articles and photographs from the newspapers in your precious scrapbook.

After my cricket career finished, I moved to Sydney and in more recent times I have had the good fortune to get to see Neil Harvey on a regular basis. A few of us – Ian Chappell, Brian

Taber, Neil Marks and company – love to share a meal and a drink and time with Neil. He is a wonderful, generous-hearted man. To give you an idea of Neil's hand-eye co-ordination, I tell you of a day when Neil and I were hitting off on a tee at Pymble Golf Course in Sydney. Neil belted the ball with a two wood and the ball ricocheted off the huge trunk of an ancient gum tree just in front and to the side of the tee. The ball came back at Neil like a rocket and he instinctively hit the ball with the back of his club. It was if he was hooking a fast, lifting ball from England's Frank Tyson at his fastest. The ball careered out of sight. How good was Neil Harvey? Yes … he was that good.

*David Sincock was a big spinning left-arm wrist spinner. Aged sixteen, in his first Sheffield Shield match for SA, Sincock took a sensational 6/51 against the strong NSW batting side on the Adelaide Oval. He played three Test matches and he retired at an age when he could have enjoyed great success at the highest level.*

*Bill Lawry*

Neil was the best all-round fieldsman I have seen in top cricket. He could field anywhere and had a magnificent arm. He consistently threw the stumps down from the extra cover area and few batsmen dared test his arm. Neil's throw was deadly accurate and fast. And when in slips he had sure, safe hands. I admired him as a batsman and a fieldsman. His cricket kit was always immaculate. Neil on the field was always confident, nimble, well-balanced and fleet-footed.

But when he was a Test selector and I was Test captain I didn't like some of the comments he made about certain players, especially Bob Cowper and Ian Redpath. He reckoned Redders should not block a ball when he moved down the track to a spinner. Harv wanted everyone to play like him.

*Bill Lawry captained Australia from 1967/68 until 1970/71 when he was sacked and replaced by Ian Chappell. In sixty-seven Tests Lawry scored 5234 runs at 47.15 with a top score of 210. For years he entertained a generation of cricket fans from the Channel Nine commentary box, known for the phrase 'It's all happening'.*

*Bill Norton*

Neil's daughter and my daughter went to high school together and my first meeting with Neil was a brief one when I collected my daughter from his home after school one day.

Some years later I started playing tennis at his late wife Barbara's sister's court and Barbara played there too of course. Neil played on Sundays and I became quite friendly with him, talking cricket a lot of course. Some time later a friend and I invited Neil to join us at Northbridge Tennis Club on Wednesdays and he played there for some time until a wrist injury forced him to stop. He enjoyed the tennis – and a couple of beers afterwards.

We had several social outings with wives and friends and even met up in London twice, once at Lord's in 2013.

Following Barbara's death in 2014 we enjoyed having Neil for dinner and lunch in our home in Lindfield and that still happens. He has invited me as his guest to various cricket functions such as the Bradman dinner at the SCG, and two trips to Melbourne for Fitzroy-Doncaster dinners. I am very grateful for these opportunities to meet famous cricketers.

I have always found Neil to be honest and straightforward and his opinions about cricket and life in general are much valued.

At ninety-two he is going well, although no doubt due to his wonderful fielding way back he has a few aches and pains in the legs. I regard Neil as one of my best friends and hopefully this will continue for many years.

*Bill Norton is a long-time friend of Neil Harvey. Bill is an active member of the Australian Cricket Society (NSW Branch) and has been a willing volunteer for the branch for many years.*

# AFTERWORD

In the writing of this book every single person I contacted, without exception, was keen to help with their thoughts on Neil as a player and as a man: happy to contribute a word here, a detail there, an anecdote, a memory. That in itself shows the tremendous respect for the man.

Neil Harvey stands solidly on terra firma. He is a warm and generous soul, still with a good head of hair, a clear eye and the confident, firm handshake you would expect from a well-travelled, well-read man. He has won many awards, is a member of the International Cricket Council Hall of Fame, the Australia Cricket Hall of Fame and was named in Cricket Australia's Best Test Team of the 20th Century.

My original idea was a book about the art of playing spin bowling, with the best example of how to do so being Neil himself. As we know now, he used a similar line to those other great players of spin, Victor Trumper and South Africa's Barry Richards: 'You don't have to know which way the ball is turning. Get down the track and hit it on the half volley. That's the way to play 'em. Just get stuck into them.' When you watch today's so-called great players flounder against spin, their bats seemingly tied to their pads as they prod and poke forward in hope, you wonder where all the expertise went. T20 has a lot to answer for: batsmen in T20 either block or slog. There is no subtle working of the ball into the gaps for ones, twos and threes. In fact, the in-out field placements are also the big thing in the Tests. Spinners work to a field that has more holes in it than a Swiss cheese. The Big Bash stuff right in the middle of summer and the school holidays is hurting the Sheffield Shield to such an extent that five years from now the Australian Test side will be languishing at the bottom of the pile. It may not take five years.

From the time he scored 112 in his Ashes debut at Leeds in 1948, Neil Harvey was the darling of the Australian crowds right up to the end, in no short measure because of how he played spin. He played against great spinners. West Indians Sonny Ramadhin, Alf Valentine and Lance Gibbs; South Africans Hugh Tayfield and Tufty Mann; England's Jim Laker, Fred Titmus and David Allen; India's Subhash Gupte and Vinoo Mankad. He had some dramatic battles with Laker and Lock on the spinning wickets prepared from them in England for the 1953 and 1956 Ashes tours. But in Australia he had little trouble with them. Let's not overlook the quicks: Frank Tyson and Wes Hall stand out. 'Tyson and Hall, along with Jeff Thomson at a later time, were as fast as they get,' Neil said.

Harvey lauds the modern players. He rates Shane Warne as the greatest leg-spinner. He greatly admired Sachin Tendulkar and has publicly praised Steve Smith and NZ's Kane Williamson – but he makes no secret that the poor quality of batsmanship against top-class spin bowling irks him. Even India has lost the plot against spin bowling. The pundits keep telling us how good the Indians are against slow bowling, but the pundits are wrong. Even Virat Kohli doesn't play top-quality spin with the assurance he does against the fast men. Players of the ilk of Tendulkar and VVS Laxman must shudder when they witness the current Indian Test batsmen poke and prod, with the occasional wild slog, against spinners of the standard of Moeen Ali and Dom Bess.

That splendid wordsmith Gideon Haigh said Harvey has never had a beef with younger generations. 'He just said what he felt. We used to value that as a society, we've grown a little … brittle.' Indeed. Australia as a society has grown soft. Our top sportsmen have become precious. The merest hint of criticism from one of the game's elders tends to irk even the most thick-skinned of our top cricketers. Neil Harvey's strongly opinionated utterances may well have cost him a lengthy stint as Test captain – not that he would have it any other way.

There is a no-nonsense side to Neil, which does not allow him to abide fools. Indeed, he can be a little blunt. The Neil Harvey idea of being blunt was simply him being straightforward and honest. As he would always say: 'The truth never hurt anybody.'

Some modern cricketers seemingly don't know how to take Harvey. It appears that they think he is something out of the Jurassic Age, a veritable dinosaur. Nothing could be further from the truth.

I thought that perhaps his forebears must have come from Yorkshire, where being blunt is simply being a fair dinkum Yorkie. Freddie Trueman, Sir Geoffrey Boycott, TV host and cricket fan Michael Parkinson – they all share that quality. But no, the Harveys are Cornish ultimately.

Anne Harvey's cousin, Maureen Harvey, has researched the family tree and how the Harveys emigrated from various parts of Cornwall and Wales and settled in the Copper Coast area of South Australia. The Harveys were among thousands of Welsh-based people who descended directly from the Celts. Their habitation of Wales was long established before the Romans invaded, under the command of Julius Caesar, in 55 BC. They were miners.

Mining was in their blood, long before the Romans brought in their legions and teams of engineers to mine all manner of minerals on an industrial scale. By 78 AD, the Romans were mining for gold, copper and lead in a big way. Neil Harvey's forebears can probably be traced back to the many Harveys who migrated from Wales to the fledgling colony of Australia from 1848 to the mid-1850s.

With Neil's strength of opinion came strength of character. We have seen that in these pages: when he insisted to Peter Burge that they could not allow their captain Ian Craig to stand down, even though it would have handed Neil the coveted captaincy; when he threw a deliberate four to get Alan Davidson back into the attack in Manchester, 1961.

There was another time too. In the Second Test against Pakistan at Lahore in 1959/60, the game had come down to a run chase. Neil Harvey and Norm O'Neill were at the crease, and needed runs quickly. The Pakistani fieldsmen were wasting time. Whenever the left-handed and right-handed combination of Harvey and O'Neill took a single, the fielders would change positions very slowly. They were taking up to seven minutes to bowl a single over. Neil saw that the problem was the left-right combination. So he purposely backed away and allowed himself to be bowled, bringing another right-hander, Richie Benaud, to the crease. I cannot think of any Test batsman other than Harvey over the past sixty years who would have sacrificed his wicket so. (Australia got the runs.)

Once asked to name the best five batsmen of his time, Neil couldn't contain his choice to a mere five players. He named his best from England: Len Hutton, Denis Compton and Peter May. The West Indies: Garry Sobers, Everton Weekes, Frank Worrell, Clyde Walcott, Rohan Kanhai. From India he chose Lala Amarnath and Vijay Hazare, who hit those two centuries in the Fourth Test match at Adelaide Oval in the summer of 1947/48. It was Neil's debut Test and he spent much of his time in that game chasing many of Hazare's exquisite cover drives.

The Australians of his time: Don Bradman of course, Lindsay Hassett, Arthur Morris, plus later Ian and Greg Chappell, 'both of whom I watched closely during my long stint as a Test selector'.

Happily, I have got to know Neil Harvey very well. Getting to know Neil was a getting of wisdom period of my life.

We used to meet up with Neil's great mate Alan Davidson and fly to New Zealand, where we'd watch Test matches at Auckland and Wellington.

Robert Neil Harvey, OAM MBE, while always being strong in body and mind and confident in his own ability, has ever been the most self-effacing individual. I have found him to be the most generous-hearted person and a good and loyal friend.

Next time you are at the MCG, make sure when you walk along the avenue of sports stars that you have a good look at the magnificent bronze statue of Neil Harvey in full flight, perfectly executed by sculptor Lis Johnson. It's within a Harvey back cut of the entrance to the MCG, his home ground, the venue of so many of his most glorious innings.

On 8 October 2018 my wife Patsy and I were invited to join Neil, his close relatives and extended family and friends to celebrate his ninetieth birthday aboard a luxury yacht on Sydney Harbour. The Dom Perignon flowed, so too tears of joy. Here was Neil Harvey, the last Invincible, standing tall among his family and friends, having turned the ripe old age of ninety. Neil's children were there – Robert, Anne and Bruce, along with Neil's grandchildren and great grandchildren. The weather was overcast and drizzly, we cruised in a heavy sea – and everyone loved it.

There is one trait that defines him above all: honesty. Neil is as honest as the day.

On that wonderful day in December 1954, when my granddad took me to the SCG to watch my first day of Test cricket, Neil Harvey became my boyhood hero.

Robert Neil Harvey: he was my hero then; he is my hero still.

# ACKNOWLEDGEMENTS

THANK YOU, NEIL, for your patience and the telling of how it was during the early years and throughout your playing career and as a Test selector. The story of your life journey is a story worth telling, and I have thoroughly enjoyed communicating with you on a regular basis and writing it. Pity we couldn't have engaged in face-to-face meetings, but the pandemic put paid to that idea. It had to be regular phone calls. Writing your story has been my privilege. Knowing you as a friend has enriched my life.

My eternal thanks to those former players who played with or against Neil Harvey.

These men, without exception, were eager to speak and/or write of the man. Some of those with whom I chatted about Harvey have long since departed this life, but their words still resonate today.

They include Sir Donald Bradman, Colin McDonald, Barry Jarman, Lindsay Kline, John Reid (NZ), Les Favell, Norm O'Neill, Sam Loxton, Jack Ryder, Neil Hawke, Keith Miller, Johnny Martin, Bill O'Reilly, Ray Robinson, AG 'Johnnie' Moyes, Alan McGilvray, Vic Richardson, Bill Jacobs, Ian Johnson, Ray Lindwall, Ken Mackay, Bruce Dooland, George Tribe, Ian Craig, Pastor Sir Douglas Nicholls, Harold Shillinglaw and Len Fitzgerald.

My thanks to those listed (hope I haven't missed anyone) who contributed with their thoughts on Neil. They include Neil's three children, Robert, Anne and Bruce Harvey, Graham McKenzie, Bill Lawry, David 'Evil' Sincock, Greg Chappell, Ian Chappell, Neil 'Harpo' Marks, Ian Meckiff, Gavin Stevens, Des Hoare, Rod Marsh, John Inverarity, Keith 'Spud' Slater, John 'Pythagoras' Rutherford, Ray Illingworth, 'Lord Ted' Dexter, Laurie 'Doggie' Mayne, Mark Nicholas, Brian Taber, Alan Davidson, David 'Bumble' Lloyd, Rodney Cavalier, Dennis Yagmich, Barry Richards, Sir Geoffrey Boycott, Jack Clarke, Malcolm Linke, Ian 'Banger' Bancroft, Sharnee Rutherford, Jane Allan (nee Rutherford), Ken Cunningham, Martin Rogers, Graeme Pollock, Ken Archer, Grahame 'Tonker' Thomas, Brian Booth, Bill Norton and Thos Hodgson.

Thanks to veteran journalist, broadcaster and author Tim Lane for his memories of Neil Harvey; so too that brilliant wordsmith, Gideon Haigh, for his perceptive insights into the character of Neil Harvey, for whom he has the greatest respect and admiration.

Neil's daughter Anne has been a terrific help in providing gems of information, some photographs and snippets of information which all helped to strengthen the fabric of the tapestry of a cricketing life lived well and to the full. She dug out some good family photographs and Iris's written description of 'fielding' practice in front of the oven when Neil threw the vegetables her way just before she began to cook the Sunday roast.

Special thanks to the great Australian all-rounder Alan Davidson for writing the foreword to this book. Thanks to Bill Norton, long-time friend and driver for Neil and Alan Davidson.

Many thanks to Ronald Cardwell, author and publisher of The Cricket Publishing Company, for his research and obtaining contact details for a number of people and for providing a number of high-quality photographs for inclusion in the book. In addition Malcolm Linke provided some good-quality photographs for possible inclusion in the book. Malcolm also loaned me a number of cricket books for my research. So too did ex ACB chairman Jack Clarke: all invaluable resources for this project.

Adelaide journalist and author Peter Cornwall also provided good background information about two men in Neil Harvey's early Fitzroy days, Harold Shillinglaw and Len Fitzgerald.

Thanks also to Ken Piesse, a prolific writer of sporting books and publisher, who also was generous in his advice, obtaining contact details of various people and in providing high-quality photographs for the book.

My thanks to Hardie Grant's Pam Brewster and her willing team, including designers and senior editor Anna Collett, and to the editor at the coalface, Michael Epis, whose cricket knowledge, keen eye and editing expertise was a great help towards ensuring the manuscript enjoyed a smooth passage to publication.

My thanks to Patsy, my loving wife and first responder to the material I write. Patsy's keen eye, trained from years as a television executive, and sage advice, is ever invaluable to my work. It was some literary journey and I am grateful to all concerned.

*Ashley Mallett*
*Adelaide, 2021*

# BIBLIOGRAPHY

*The Autobiography of a Cricketer*, by Colin Cowdrey, Hodder & Stoughton, London/Sydney, 1976

*Behind the Australian Tests 1956*, by Norman Cutler, Putnam, London, 1956

*Benaud, an Appreciation*, by Brian Matthews, Text Publishing, Melbourne, 2016

*Benaud: On Reflection*, by Richie Benaud, Fontana/Collins, 1985

*A Century of Cricketers*, by AG Moyes, Angus & Robertson, Sydney, London, 1950

*Cricket at the Crossroads*, by Ian Johnson, Cassell & Company, London, 1957

*Eleven, The Greatest Eleven of the 20th Century*, by Ashley Mallett, University of Qld Press, St Lucia, 2001

*From the Boundary*, by Ray Robinson, Collins, London/Sydney, 1950

*Invincible, The Life & Times of Sam Loxton*, by Martin Rogers, Cricket Books, Mt Eliza, 2020

*Keith Miller, The Golden Nugget*, by RS Whitington, Rigby, Adelaide, 1981

*Mr Cricket*, by 'Fergie' WM Ferguson, Nicholas Kaye, London, 1957

*My World of Cricket*, by Neil Harvey, Hodder and Stoughton, London, 1963

*Near Death on the Sub-Continent, The Gavin Stevens Story*, by David Jenkins, The Cricket Publishing Company, 2009

*On Top Down Under*, by Ray Robinson, Cassell, Sydney, 1975

*On Tour with Brian Booth, England 1961*, by Brian Booth and Ronald Cardwell, The Cricket Publishing Company, 2009

*Six Not Out*, by Jack Pollard, Jack Pollard Publishing Company, Wollstonecraft, Sydney, 1964

*Slasher Opens Up*, by Ken Mackay, Pelham Books, London, 1964

*The Slow Men*, by David Frith, Horwitz Grahame in association with Richard Smart Publishing, Sydney, 1984

*The Summer Game*, by Gideon Haigh, ABC Books, 1999

*Swanton in Australia, with MCC 1946–1971*, by EW 'Jim' Swanton, Collins, London, 1975

*Tales for All Seasons*, by Neil Marks, HarperSports, Sydney 1997

*Test Commentary*, by Rex Aston, Stanley Paul, London/Melbourne, 1956

Various editions of *Wisden Cricketers' Almanack*

# INDEX